GROUP LEADERSHIP AND

DEMOCRATIC ACTION···

FRANKLYN S. Saul HAIMAN, Ph.D.

SCHOOL OF SPEECH · NORTHWESTERN UNIVERSITY

HOUGHTON MIFFLIN COMPANY

BOSTON · NEW YORK · CHICAGO · DALLAS · ATLANTA · SAN FRANCISCO

The Riverside Press Cambridge

*I have sworn upon
the altar of God eternal
hostility against every
form of tyranny over
the mind of man.*

THOMAS JEFFERSON

PREFACE

Many books and articles have been written about leaders and leadership. They range from philosophical essays through technical reports of scientific research to historical biographies and "how to do it" manuals. The literature of leadership is spread through every nook and cranny of our libraries. Items may be found in political treatises, sociology books, adult education, psychology, and psychiatry journals, speech texts, church administration pamphlets, and popular magazines.

To our knowledge there has been no attempt to bring together in one place the philosophical-scientific background and the practical techniques of democratic group leadership. This book is such an attempt. In it an effort has been made to strike a healthy balance between theory and practice — a balance which we feel has been lacking in previous works on leadership.

An enterprise of this kind must draw upon many and varied sources — academic disciplines, schools of thought, and "grass-roots" practitioners — from whom our understanding of democratic leadership has derived. The over-all method of organization and classification is, of course, our own. We trust that this particular synthesis does no basic violence to the diverse points of view it attempts to embrace. The writer is resigned, however, to the fact that any such pioneering foray into a field as vastly complicated as this one will not please everybody completely, least of all himself. It can only be hoped that this effort will stimulate further developments and refinements in our understanding of group leadership and democratic action.

A preview of the book's organization may be helpful in orienting the reader to the study ahead of him. Part One, *Approaches to Leadership,* lays the foundation upon which we later build. Chapter 1 defines what we mean by leadership and describes what the social scientists have learned about the ways in which it operates. Chapter 2 considers what the philosophers and theorists have thought about the problem and the kinds of solutions they have proposed. In Chapter 3 the merits and shortcomings of these proposals are examined, and a policy on leadership is suggested. Having arrived at this policy, the next step is to put it into operation. This requires a scientific understanding of group behavior, to which the reader is introduced in Chapter 4.

With the background material completed, Part Two takes up the attitudes and skills of democratic leadership. It looks at the group leader as a person (Chapter 5), and then at his methods of handling: interpersonal relations (Chapter 6), scientific method (Chapter 7), cooperative thinking (Chapter 8), integration (Chapter 9), and majority vote (Chapter 10). Finally, in a brief look at the future, Part Three discusses the methods of training leaders for democracy and the resistances to change which must be overcome.

The writer is greatly indebted to many of his friends and colleagues for their generous help, advice, and encouragement in the preparation of this book. Dr. Dean Barnlund, Miss Louise Goble, Dr. Warren Guthrie, Dr. John Keltner, Dr. Robert Lang, Dean James H. McBurney, Dr. George Perkins, Dr. Clarence Simon, Dr. Naomi Wrage, and Miss Colleen Young are those who have been particularly helpful. A special debt of gratitude is owed to Miss Marian McCulloch, Registrar of the School of Speech, Northwestern University, who devoted many tiresome hours to the task of editing the manuscript.

F. S. H.

Evanston, Illinois

CONTENTS

Part One APPROACHES TO LEADERSHIP

    1. The Dynamics of Leadership   3

    2. Authoritarianism and Democracy   28

    3. Values and Limitations of Democratic Leadership   50

    4. The Dynamics of a Group   75

Part Two ATTITUDES AND SKILLS OF
                 DEMOCRATIC LEADERSHIP

    5. The Group Leader as a Person   113

    6. Leadership in Interpersonal Relations   130

    7. Leadership in Scientific Method   152

    8. Leadership in Cooperative Thinking   166

    9. Resolving Social Conflict: Integration   178

    10. Resolving Social Conflict: Majority Vote   199

Part Three THE FUTURE OF GROUP LEADERSHIP

    11. Training Leaders for Democracy   219

APPENDIX A. *The Barnlund-Haiman Leader Rating Scale*   237

APPENDIX B. *Two Samples of Shared Leadership*   245

APPENDIX C. *Sample Leadership Problems: Case Studies*   285

APPENDIX D. *Bibliography*   293

INDEX   303

Part One

**Approaches to
Leadership**

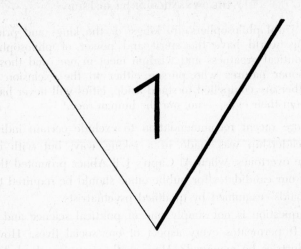

The Dynamics of Leadership

BEFORE THE LAST ECHOES of the thunderous shouting, "Duce, Duce!" and "Seig Heil! Heil Hitler!" have faded altogether from our memories, it is well that we pause to inquire into the nature of man's quest for leadership. As long as men have lived together, whether in primitive families of cave-dwellers or in complex twentieth-century national communities, they have sought and found leaders. Some of their leaders have been good, others bad. Some have led to progress and others to ruin. But, always, there have been leaders.

Recognizing its grave importance to him, man has struggled with this problem of leadership for centuries. He has studied it, he has speculated about it, and he has proposed many solutions. Early in the history of our civilization, Socrates, in Plato's *Republic*, suggested an answer which has continued through the ages to provoke the thoughts of mankind:

Until philosophers are kings, or the kings and princes of this world have the spirit and power of philosophy, and political greatness and wisdom meet in one, and those commoner natures who pursue either to the exclusion of the other are compelled to stand aside, cities will never have rest from their evils, — no, nor the human race.[1]

A more recent recommendation to exclude certain individuals from leadership was made in a joking way, but with distinct Platonic overtones, when Al Capp's L'il Abner promoted the idea that all our candidates for public office should be required to have their "haids" examined by qualified psychiatrists.

The question is not simply one of political science and public office. It permeates every aspect of our social lives. How shall our industries be managed? How shall our unions be led? How shall our schools be operated? How shall our clubs, our lodges, and our professional organizations be influenced and controlled? How shall decisions be made within the family circle? All of these questions involve the problem of leadership, for leadership is present in every social situation.

DEFINITIONS OF LEADERSHIP

We begin our study with the word "leadership" and seek to understand its meaning. In the broadest sense, leadership refers to that process whereby an individual directs, guides, influences, or controls the thoughts, feelings or behavior of other human beings. This influence may be exerted through the medium of his works — his books, his paintings, his inventions — or it may be exerted through personal face-to-face contact. The former type is known as indirect, intellectual, or creative leadership, and includes the scientists, artists, and writers whose significant products and ideas profoundly influence other men.

Direct, face-to-face leadership operates most frequently through the medium of speech, and is the type with which we are concerned in this book.

[1] From the *Republic* of Plato, Book V. Translated by Benjamin Jowett, and reproduced by permission of the Clarendon Press, Oxford.

There are other important distinctions which should be recognized at the outset. The term "leadership" — as well as the terms "guidance," "influence," or "control" — implies a *purpose* on the part of the leader. Leadership is an effort on his part to direct the behavior of others *toward a particular end*. Thus, the act of a bus driver who accidentally breaks his watch, gets off schedule, and thereby causes thirty people to be late for work, though influencing and controlling human behavior, cannot be called leadership. The driver did not intend to control others, nor was the influence aimed in any particular direction. Had he deliberately broken his watch and gotten off schedule *for the purpose of* making his passengers angry with the bus company, that might be considered leadership.

This is not to say that leadership is always a carefully planned and deliberated act. Much of it is quite spontaneous and the leader may not even be consciously aware of his intentions. Nevertheless, whether planned or unplanned, conscious or unconscious, a purpose and a goal are always present.

Returning to our bus episode, let us suppose that instead of making the passengers angry with the bus company as was intended, the driver's behavior makes them angry with him; and one burly passenger puts a fist in his mouth. This is an unanticipated result of the driver's attempted influence. It is certainly not an end he would have wished for. He tried to lead in one direction but his would-be followers moved in another. We must therefore distinguish between leadership and *attempted leadership*. Leadership is an *interaction process*. There can be no leadership without followership. *Attempts* at leadership must be responded to favorably by others before they can be described as *acts* of leadership. The follower must move, to a small degree at least, in the direction indicated by the leader.

Many people tend to add their own subjective connotations to the basic definitions and distinctions given here. Some feel that the word leadership necessarily implies a *subtle method* of control. Hence, they distinguish it from "commanding," which is an overt, unabashed act of forceful control, lacking in tact and subtlety.[2] Writers who feel this way refuse to dignify leaders who operate through force and overt domination with the title of "leader." According to them the typical military officer is not a leader. This is merely a verbal preference which need not detain us long. It is a distinction which adds an evaluative flavoring to the definition and limits the field in a way which the investigator will not find particularly helpful.

Another type of connotation commonly attached to the word is the feeling that leadership implies a firmly dominant kind of influence. Persons who carry this connotation in their minds make a distinction between leadership and "guidance." To them, the moderator of discussion, the democratic teacher, or the personal counsellor is "*only* a guide, and not *really* a leader!" This is the "strong man" concept of leadership. It ignores the fact that even the most easy-going moderator, teacher, or counsellor is in a very real sense influencing and controlling the behavior of others toward some kind of a goal — whether that goal be determined by the leader alone or in collaboration with the followers. We should reject this second type of subjective verbal coloring. Granted that there may be different methods and varying degrees of directiveness involved in any situation, let us recognize that it is all leadership none the less.

LEADERSHIP AND FREEDOM

We are much concerned these days, and rightly so, about the matter of freedom. We hear it said that a crucial issue of our times is to develop an effective "leadership of free people." To write and talk about the leadership of free people is to get perched on two horns of a dilemma. Although the phrase may sound imposing and may stir the sympathy of lovers of democracy, what does it really mean? Can people be both led and free? Is this not a contradiction in terms?

[2] Tead, Ordway, *The Art of Leadership.* New York: Whittlesey House, 1935, pp. 11–14; and Pigors, Paul, *Leadership or Domination.* Boston: Houghton Mifflin, 1935, pp. 95–99.

It depends, of course, on how those terms are defined, and one could define them, if he wished, in such a way as to make them appear not to be in conflict. Let us not avoid the issue by means of diluted definitions. To be free, according to Webster's dictionary, means to be independent, unconstrained, uncontrolled, unrestricted, or "not subject to external power." In short, it means *not to be led.* The issue seems clearly and simply drawn. To be led or not to be led — that would appear to be the question.

It is not. *That* question was answered for us ages ago when civilization began. It was soon learned that a leaderless society is not a society at all, for whenever two or more men form a society and live together there is no such thing as uncontrolled, unrestricted, uninfluenced behavior. There is no such thing as absolute freedom. People inevitably have an effect upon one another. Freedom in any society is relative — a matter of degree. The real issue that confronts us, therefore, is to what extent and in what way human behavior should be influenced by others. It is a question of method and of degree — in brief, *how* shall we be led? The kind of society we have and the kind of lives we live will depend, in a large measure, upon our answers to that question.

We are not ready at this point to answer the question of policy. First we must understand the nature of the problem. We must study the dynamics of leadership — the facts and theories which explain its operations — before we can sensibly discuss our ideas of how it *ought* to be. Actually there are two aspects of the problem. The first concerns the way in which leaders attain their positions. The second concerns the methods of leadership employed once they have "arrived." With help from the psychologists, sociologists, and psychiatrists we shall explore both of these phases.

DOMINANCE AND SUBMISSION

The best available evidence from psychology seems to indicate that dominance and submission are basic facts of most animal existence. Kimball Young points out that:

> Forms as low as lizards develop a hierarchy of dominance and submission in which a stronger and older member comes

7

to control over other members of the species within a certain area.[3]

This author also refers to an arrangement known as the "pecking order" of chickens — a system whereby the most dominant chicken in the yard pecks at all others, the second most dominant pecks all but the first, and so on down the list to the poor, scraggly fowl at the submissive end of the line that gets pecked at by all but pecks no others!

With respect to human beings, Professor Young speaks for most social psychologists when he concludes that patterns of dominance and submission, whether overt or subtle, eventually emerge in all social groups. This does not mean that the pattern is always consciously recognized by the leaders and followers, or officially formalized by an election. Nor does it mean that the relationship is necessarily permanent or that it is institutionalized in the form of a presidency, a chieftainship, or parenthood. More often than not it is a highly fluid pattern which is constantly subject to alterations impelled by changing situations. Thus the leader of a movement for social reform may no longer be a dominating figure when the cause he champions ceases to exist. The leader of a political party may be deposed if his party suffers too many defeats at the polls.

It is interesting to watch the way a group will turn to a particular person for leadership — whether or not he has sought that position and whether or not he is ever formally designated as leader. It is also fascinating to watch the methods of a person who deliberately maneuvers himself into the dominating role. This is called self-constituted leadership, and is made possible only when the members of the group accept the submissive role (assuming that they have the power to do otherwise). But observations such as these do not probe to the core of the problem. They do not face the fundamental issue of dominance: Why does this man move to the top and not another? Is it simply a matter of physical supremacy, as seems to be the case in much of the animal world?

Certainly, to the degree that we are like lower animals (and

[3] Young, Kimball, *Social Psychology*. New York: Appleton-Century-Crofts, Inc., 1944, p. 222.

that varies from time to time and place to place, but is always present to an extent!) physical supremacy is a vitally significant factor. We might go so far as to suggest that it is potentially present in all human situations, and point to the role of the military factor in many governments of the world or to the role of physical size in the adult's relation to the child as evidence of this contention. But to proceed from there to attribute all dominance in human relations to physical supremacy is to ignore the very complexity which makes us humans and grossly to oversimplify the entire matter. As we shall see in a few moments, even the most animal-like human societies are dominated by factors other than physical prowess. Brute force does not even begin to explain the subtleties of leadership in human affairs.

SOURCES OF LEADERSHIP

The question of what gives rise to the leadership of men has been a source of speculation for generations. There is something compelling about the problem which has attracted the time and thought of many philosophers and has inspired extensive research efforts by psychologists and sociologists. Whatever the causes of this interest the effect is clear — a vast body of literature on the subject.

From the time of Plutarch until very recently the investigations and writings on this subject have been largely in one vein. They have been concerned with discovering and listing the traits of character which make men leaders. They have attempted to do this by studying the lives of great men,[4] by observing the behavior of leaders in action,[5] or by experiments to determine the personal qualities that influence human behavior.[6] We shall discuss their findings shortly.

[4] Plutarch, *The Lives of the Noble Grecians and Romans.* Trans. John Dryden, rev. A. H. Clough. New York: Modern Library, 1932. Also Merriam, Charles E., *Four American Party Leaders.* New York: Macmillan, 1926.

[5] Cowley, W. H., "Traits of Face-to-Face Leaders," *Journal of Abnormal and Social Psychology,* XXVI (Oct.–Dec., 1931), pp. 304–13.

[6] Sward, Keith, *An Experimental Study of Leadership.* Ph.D. dissertation, University of Minnesota, 1929; and Haiman, Franklyn S., "An Experimental Study of the Effects of Ethos in Public Speaking," *Speech Monographs,* XVI (Sept., 1949), pp. 190–202.

In the past several years another vein of thinking has emerged. The newer approach revolves around the concept that leadership is specific to differing situations and that the factors which give rise to leadership in one situation may not be the same as those required of the leader in another situation. Leadership is thus the ability to achieve in a specific area that has importance for a given group. It is recognized that various abilities are valued differently by different groups, that leaders embody the ideals of the group in which they operate or the age in which they live, and that leadership is relative and varies according to the nature and functions of the group led.

Ralph M. Stogdill typifies this approach when he summarizes the experimental literature of recent years on the subject of the personal factors associated with leadership, and arrives at these conclusions (among others):

> The qualities, characteristics, and skills required in a leader are determined to a large extent by the demands of the situation in which he is to function as a leader. . . .
> It is primarily by virtue of participating in group activities and demonstrating his capacity for expediting the work of the group that a person becomes endowed with leadership status. . . . The leader is a person who occupies a position of responsibility in coordinating the activities of the members of the group in their task of attaining a common goal. . . . A person does not become a leader by virtue of the possession of some combination of traits, but the pattern of personal characteristics must bear some relevant relationship to the characteristics, activities, and goals of the followers. Thus, leadership must be conceived in terms of the interaction of variables which are in constant flux and change.[7]

By beginning our study of the sources of leadership against the backdrop of both the older and the newer concepts which have been described here we are in a position to avoid two unfortunate extremes. By adhering to the old alone, one is in grave danger of

---

[7] Stogdill, Ralph M., "Personal Factors Associated with Leadership: A Survey of the Literature," *Journal of Psychology*, XXV (January, 1948), pp. 63–64. Reprinted by permission.

breaking completely with reality, of talking in abstract verbal generalizations which have no existence in real life, of compiling long lists of noble virtues which no fallible human being could possibly embody, and of erroneously assuming that all leaders in all situations possess the same qualities. This is a trap into which a good many authors have fallen.[8]

On the other hand, by adhering to the new alone, there is also danger of going to an extreme. There is danger of developing a point of view which holds that since leadership is specific to given situations, there are no universal principles or scientific laws which can be discovered. One can be so enamored of the concept of "interaction of variables" that it leads to the point where we can say nothing at all, in a general way, about leadership.

We take a less extreme stand. We recognize that situational differences are exceedingly important, and that any generalizations which are made about the sources of leadership must be modified according to the social values and functions of the group in which the leader operates. This does not mean, however, that general theories are useless, or that leadership cannot be discussed validly without reference to a particular group. We agree with Stogdill when, having come to the conclusions quoted above, he goes on to say:

> Must it then be assumed that leadership is entirely . . . unpredictable. Not at all. The very studies which provide the strongest arguments for the situational nature of leadership also supply the strongest evidence indicating that leadership patterns as well as non-leadership patterns of behavior are persistently and relatively stable.[9]

In short, those of us who are interested in trying to understand the sources from which leadership springs are quite justified in pointing to certain factors which, in general, seem to account for the phenomenon. At the same time, we must be constantly aware that every group situation is different. Each contains within itself

---

[8] See Casson, Herbert N., *Tips on Leadership.* New York: B. C. Forbes, 1927.

[9] Stogdill, *op. cit.*, p. 65. Reprinted by permission.

a unique complexity of changing forces which can quickly obscure any over-simple explanation of its leadership patterns. With this in mind, let us proceed to a brief examination of the most important facts and theories concerning the general causes of leadership which have emerged from the thousands of studies that have been made.

Personal Characteristics

By far the largest body of material on this subject is based upon the theory that leadership may be accounted for in terms of the personal traits and characteristics of the leader.

One of the most thorough and well-known works in this category was a study of natural leadership in 1313 boys' gangs in Chicago. It was found that gameness, physical prowess, and speed and finality of decision were the personal traits which most tended to determine leadership in the gang situation.[10]

The boys' gang is certainly not typical of most of our social units, either in structure or function, so that we can do little generalizing from the Chicago results. We need to look at other kinds of groups; and in so doing we immediately encounter the popular belief that "intelligence leads and ignorance follows." In truth, there is much scientific evidence to support the doctrine that intelligence is a quality which gives rise to leadership in many areas. This has been found to be particularly true in a group discussion situation.[11]

We could fill several pages with an exposition of all the traits that have been found by investigators to correlate with leadership. Bird summarizes a list of seventy-nine.[12] Stogdill concludes from a survey of fifteen studies that "the average person who occupies a position of leadership exceeds the average member of his group

[10] Thrasher, Frederick, "Leadership in the Gang," Chapter 18 in *The Gang, A Study of 1313 Gangs in Chicago.* Chicago: University of Chicago Press, 1927.

[11] Stogdill, Ralph M., *op. cit.*, pp. 35–71; Sward, Keith, *op. cit.*; and Simpson, Ray, *A Study of Those Who Influence and Those Who are Influenced in Discussion.* New York: Columbia University Teachers College, 1938.

[12] Bird, Charles, *Social Psychology.* New York: Appleton-Century-Crofts, Inc., 1940, p. 379.

in intelligence, scholarship, dependability in exercising responsibilities, activity and social participation and socio-economic status."[13]

Ten of the studies surveyed by Stogdill also support a conclusion that "the average leader exceeds the average member of his group in sociability, initiative, persistence, knowing how to get things done, self confidence, alertness to and insight into situations, cooperativeness, popularity, adaptability, and verbal facility."

A summary of studies concerned with the relationship of physical characteristics to leadership is made by Smith and Krueger:

> Other things being equal, the individual who is above the average in height and weight, and who is attractive in appearance has a better chance of being elected to positions of leadership in the face-to-face types of situations than does the short unattractive individual.[14]

It has recently been suggested that people who do the most talking in group situations are the ones whom the others tend to select as the most liked, wanted and needed members of the group.[15] This hypothesis has been supported by the personal testimony of several college fraternity presidents who seemed to feel that the "secret of their success" lay in the fact that they had always been prominent talkers in chapter meetings. We suspect that there is some truth in this hypothesis, as in the others, and that as a general rule the amount of verbal participation in a group is a contributing factor in determining leadership. We should qualify this generalization carefully, however, for we all know persons of whom it may truly be said that the more they talk the more undesirable they become. Apparently, a great quantity of talk without some degree of quality is not enough to make a leader.

---

[13] Stogdill, *op. cit.*

[14] Smith, Henry L., and L. M. Krueger, *A Brief Summary of Literature on Leadership.* Bulletin of the School of Education, Indiana University, IX (Sept., 1933).

[15] Peterman, Jack, *Verbal Participation, Its Relation to Decision Satisfaction and the Leader Function in Decision-Making Groups.* Paper read at Midwestern Psychology Association meeting, April, 1949, Chicago, Illinois.

This brief condensation of the findings of innumerable research workers should make us sufficiently aware of the possible role of personal characteristics as sources of leadership.

Tradition

Much of the leadership that we find in social units cannot be attributed to any particular characteristics inherent in the leader. As a matter of fact, the leader is often conspicuously devoid of any leadership traits, yet continues to hold his position and exert significant influence on the rest of the members of his group. His leadership can be accounted for only in terms of traditions which are accepted by the followers. One such tradition is the doctrine that makes heredity the major qualification for leadership. Being born of royalty and trained in royal ways — the Divine Right of Kings — is the entree to dominance. In spite of its shortcomings, as demonstrated again and again by weak and even feeble-minded monarchs, this doctrine has been the basis of leadership in kingdoms all over the world. Leadership by inheritance exists and is accepted even to this day, not only in remote and ancient nations, but in many business empires within our own country.

Another widely accepted tradition is that of seniority — seniority in age or seniority in service — the doctrine of leadership by the eldest. It is understandable how this tradition might have come to be accepted. Other things being equal, one might expect the oldest member of any group to be the most experienced and hence the fittest to govern. But other things are rarely equal, and the tradition persists nonetheless. Age, sometimes in combination with heredity and sometimes alone, has been found to be the basis of leadership among most of the primitive societies studied by investigators. The role of tribal chieftain or elder appears to be as ancient as civilization itself, and is certainly the most primitive type of leadership of which we have record. Primitive or not, most of the leadership in the United States Congress is based upon the principle of seniority. Similarly, the leadership in many of our own families is determined in whole or part by the tradition of submission to the oldest member.

Magical Powers

There are two theories concerning the sources of leadership which deserve our attention, not because of their scientific validity (since they are both highly mystical) but because of their widespread currency. The first is known as the theory of cultural determinism. According to this point of view, leaders are created by social situations. If a circumstance develops which requires great leadership, some "knight in shining armor" will rise upon the scene — a magical product of the interplay of social forces. If one man does not come forth to assume the role, another will. The need for a leader will create a leader. It is this school of thought which also argues that if a great responsibility is suddenly placed upon the shoulders of a little-known man, such as occurred in April, 1945, when Franklin D. Roosevelt died and Harry Truman came to office, that man will rise to the occasion.

The theory of cultural determinism receives some telling blows from Thomas Carlyle — a man who, at the time of the French Revolution, was much concerned with leadership. Here is what he had to say.

> This . . . is an age that, as it were, denies the existence of great men. . . . Show our critics a great man, a Luther for example, they begin to what they call "account" for him . . . and bring him out to be a little kind of man. He was the "creature of the Time," they say; the Time called him forth, the Time did everything, he nothing . . . This seems to me but melancholy work. The Time called forth? Alas, we have known times *call* loudly enough for their Great Men; but not find them when they call! He was not there; Providence had not sent him; the Time, *calling* its loudest, had to go down to confusion and wreck because he would not come when called.[16]

Then Carlyle, continuing his attack, proposes an alternative theory. He compares the cultural-situation-in-need-of-leadership of which we have been speaking to

---

[16] Carlyle, Thomas, *On Heroes, Hero-Worship and the Heroic in History*. New York: Crowell, 1840, pp. 20–21.

. . . dry dead fuel waiting for the lightning out of Heaven that shall kindle it. The Great Man, with his free force direct out of God's own hand, is the lightning. . . . All blazes round him now, when he has once struck on it, into fire like his own. The dry, moldering sticks are thought to have called him forth. They did want him greatly; but as to calling him forth — those are critics of small vision, I think, who cry: "See, is it not the sticks that made the fire?" . . . It is the last consummation of unbelief. In all epochs of the world's history, we shall find the Great Man to have been the indispensable savior of his epoch: the lightning, without which the fuel never would have been burnt.[17]

So a second magical theory clearly emerges — a theory which holds that leadership is Providential, that it arises only out of certain men who are natively endowed by their Creator with wisdom, goodness, and valor. Situations-in-need-of-leadership "cry for it in vain." Only God, in his infinite wisdom, can provide us with leaders.

Though most readers would agree that Carlyle goes to extremes, still we must reckon with the basic argument held even today by intelligent men, that leadership is a mystical inborn quality which some persons have and others do not have. Those who have it will inevitably emerge into positions of leadership, and those who do not are predestined to be followers. While it is certainly true, in leadership as in everything else, that some persons have natural abilities and tendencies for it (though not at all mystical) there is sufficient experimental evidence to prove that leadership can also be created, trained and developed in persons of normal intelligence and emotional stability who are willing to make the effort to learn.[18]

Accident

Any observer who has watched the emergence of leadership in a fair sampling of social situations would be a remarkable analyst

17 Carlyle, *ibid.*
18 See Zeleny, L. D., "Experiments in Leadership Training," *Journal of Educational Sociology*, XIV (Jan., 1941), pp. 310–13; Eichler, George A., and Robert R. Merrill, "Can Social Leadership be Improved by Instruction in its

indeed if he claimed to see important explainable forces at work in every case. Let us frankly face the fact that on a multitude of occasions, leadership falls into the laps of those who simply happen to be in the right place at the right time. They do not necessarily have any special characteristics or native endowments, they are not created by an urgent situation, there is no tradition at work — they simply happen, willy-nilly, to get in the way when the roles of leadership are assigned. There is good reason to believe that some of our less eminent American presidents came to office in this way. It also happens frequently among young children in classroom elections where Sally happens to be elected because someone nominates her first. It sometimes happens in adult committee meetings where someone casually says, "Well, Jack, why don't you act as chairman" — and ipso facto, Jack has the job.

Prestige

One of the most distinctive features of leadership activity is the manner in which it increases like a snowball rolling down hill. In attempting to assess the sources of leadership in a given situation we cannot ignore the powerful influence of previous leadership experienced by any members of the group. To have been a leader is to have attained prestige (a position of admiration) in the minds of one's associates. The prestige attained therefrom becomes a part of the individual and plays a significant role in enhancing his leadership possibilities in the future.[19]

We are all familiar with the B.M.O.C. (Big Man on Campus) who piles up one office after another — each one attained largely as the result of the prestige accruing from those gained previously. We are also familiar with the clubwoman who is a member of a dozen organizations and is looked to for leadership in each because

Technique?" *Journal of Educational Sociology*, VII (Dec., 1933), pp. 233–36; Bavelas, Alex, and Kurt Lewin, "Training in Democratic Leadership," *Journal of Abnormal and Social Psychology*, XXXVII (Jan., 1942), pp. 115–19.

19 Studies by Saadi, Mitchell, and Paul Farnsworth, "The Degrees of Acceptability of Dogmatic Statements and Preferences for their Supposed Makers," *Journal of Abnormal and Social Psychology*, XXIX (July-Sept., 1934), pp. 143–50; and Haiman, *op. cit.*, show prestige to be a potent factor in influencing opinion.

of her leadership in the others. Bogardus has discussed this process of what he calls polarization and saturation in a very interesting
chapter in his book on leadership.[20]

Conditioned Needs

Far too many studies of the sources of leadership ignore one of
the most basic psychological factors to be considered — the need,
drive, desire or ambition of the leader to be dominant and the cor-
responding need or desire of the follower to be submissive. For a
thorough analysis we must trace the sources of leadership back to
their foundations in the personality structure of the individuals
concerned. It is obvious that some people are more desirous of
leadership than others, and that this desire is the major factor in
the development of behavior which eventually satisfies that need
for them. But what accounts for these differences in the need for
dominance? Why does one person prefer to lead and another to
follow? As yet we have no completely satisfactory answer for these
questions. We must rely on theory. It will be useful, first, to distinguish between abnormal and normal desires for dominance.

Abnormal desires for leadership have long been recognized. We
are well acquainted with the character whose feeling of insecurity
causes him to want to "hog the show," to "bask in the limelight," to
strive for the "center of attention." Historians have pointed out that
an unusually large percentage of political tyrants (Napoleon and
Mussolini, to mention just two) have been of short physical stature,
and that one of the contributing factors to their drives for power
may well have been the need to compensate for inferiority feelings.
A leader's abnormal desire for dominance may also be the result
of early childhood experiences in which he himself was unusually
dominated, perhaps by a tyrannical father, and as an adult seeks
opportunities to revenge that frustration and satisfy his ego by
dominating others.

Normal needs for dominance are not so readily explained. We
know that some individuals and some societies are more highly

[20] Bogardus, Emory S., *Leaders and Leadership*. New York: Appleton-
Century-Crofts, Inc., 1934, Chapter 21.

motivated to compete for superiority than others. We know that as a general rule, men tend to be more interested and more accepted in dominant roles than women, and as a result are more likely to be selected for leadership in mixed groups. We know that national culture has an influence — that Germans, for example, accept and expect more dominance in the father of a family than do Americans. The authors of *Naval Leadership* develop this point well:

> Take self-assertiveness — the desire to assert oneself, to obtain standing and position, to achieve superiority. In America we are likely to regard this need as a basic component of human nature. . . . But Americans weren't born that way, they learned it. . . . The prestige motive is almost universal. It is probably the most dependable of all the social needs. But there are the Zuni of New Mexico who do not go along with the majority of cultures. The Zuni do not like individual superiority. The best thing they can say about a person is that nobody hears anything about him. If a man wins a race, they will not let him run again. Competition, the thing self-assertiveness thrives on, is practically unknown.
>
> The Arapesh tribe of New Guinea has a similar distaste for competition and superiority. The tribe has leaders, but being a leader is apparently distasteful. The big man retires from office as soon as he can persuade somebody to take over for him.[21]

It would seem that all of the environmental forces which play upon us as we grow up — what our family expects of us and trains us to do, and what society demands of us and conditions us to do — will help determine the degree of our desire for leadership.

The needs for submission, both normal and abnormal, which cause people to accept and enjoy the follower roles are best understood in terms of the parent-child relationship which all of us experience. We are brought into the world as helpless and dependent creatures. The period of time that passes until we are physically and mentally capable of caring for ourselves is longer than that of any other member of the animal kingdom. Little wonder

[21] *Naval Leadership*, U.S. Naval Institute, Annapolis, Md., 1949, p. 41. Reprinted by permission.

that we become so thoroughly imbued with a feeling of submission. We learn to enjoy our dependent role — we like being cared for by our parents. But as we grow we also learn the disadvantages of dependence. We get a taste of freedom and we begin to "feel our oats." Soon we are torn by the great conflict which must eventually come to all of us — whether we are consciously aware of it or not — the conflict between our desire to submit (with all its pleasant security and unpleasant limitations) and the desire to be free (with all its pleasant advantages and unpleasant responsibilities). The way in which we resolve that conflict will, if the psychoanalysts are right, depend upon the way in which our parents have dealt with us. The way in which we resolve that conflict will also determine the degree to which we seek submission in the social groups to which we become attached.

The psychoanalytic approach to submission also helps to clarify the phenomenon of *leader-worship*. The worship of great leaders and the search for super-men to guide our destinies can best be understood as the adult expression of an infantile attitude toward one's parents. When times are difficult and crises occur, we become weighted down and overwhelmed with the responsibilities of maturity and freedom. We yearn again for the days when father or mother would protect us and "make things all right" again. We find in the leader a father figure, and we submit our burdens to him. If we rely on him for support and protection, we must also, in order to feel comfortable, make him out to be a super-man — just as we tended to do with our parents. And the same mixed feelings that parents must come to expect will also plague the leader:

> The ambivalence characteristic of father figures in general is markedly true of leaders. It is astounding to see the savageness with which a previously loved leader may be repudiated and excoriated by the group. Just as the leader may constitute an ideal object for positive emotional feelings, so may he serve as a perfect target for the aggressions of the frustrated, disappointed, disillusioned group. Group members often feel "betrayed" by a leadership that fails, as witness

the violent denunciation of the Nazi leadership after the war
. . . To the extent that the leader assumes responsibility, he
may in event of failure expect blame.[22]

We may conclude, then, that the patterns of dominance and
submission which appear in any group are traceable, in part, to the
psychologically conditioned motivation of its members.

Specific Skills

If the careful observation of group behavior shows nothing else,
it demonstrates quite clearly that as people become more mature,
emotionally and intellectually, they are less influenced in their
leadership choices by the determining factors discussed thus far.
Although we do not yet have experimental evidence to support the
point, one notices, as he watches people grow, that the steady,
thinking individual is not easily swept off his feet by the would-be
leader's physical prowess, verbal facility, or popularity. He is not
unduly impressed by "noble birth" or years of service. He prefers
not to wait for magical powers or accident to provide his group
with leadership. He sees through the glittering halo of prestige and
distrusts the man who is strongly motivated by a lust for power. He
prefers to turn for leadership to individuals who possess specific
skill in the particular jobs that need to be done. As Ordway Tead
so aptly puts it, the type of leadership mature men seek

> may be roughly compared to the role of the professional guide
> in mountain climbing. The guide is not thought of as better
> than or superior to those whom he precedes up the mountain
> side. He is merely regarded — and this is sufficient — as
> superior in his knowledge and skill in reaching the top of a
> particular peak.[23]

It would be naive for us — the present state of social development being what it is — to believe that the possession of specific
skills is a very widely accepted factor in the selection of leaders.

[22] From *Theory and Problems of Social Psychology*, by David Krech and
Richard S. Crutchfield, p. 421. Copyright, 1948. Courtesy of McGraw-Hill
Book Co., Inc., New York.
[23] From *The Art of Leadership* by Ordway Tead, p. 269. Copyright, 1935.
Courtesy of McGraw-Hill Book Co., Inc., New York.

Certainly our civilization is a long way from having achieved a high degree of emotional and intellectual maturity. One need only explore the sources of leadership on any American college campus, whether among students or faculty, to discover that even among our most educated groups the power of prestige, seniority, physical appearance, family "background," accident, and conditioned needs are much to be reckoned with. All that we are suggesting here is that rational men are potentially capable of resisting such forces, and that occasionally we have seen them do so. In such instances, the dominance-submission patterns which are established are determined by the presence or absence of specific leadership skills.

So long as the choice of leaders in our society is determined largely by factors other than skill in leadership there is little we can do to train and prepare for it. Though conceivably one might wait patiently for seniority, or take deliberate steps to enhance his prestige, there is little he can do about his parents or his physique. The advice given in this book for the development of specific leadership abilities assumes that, to an ever increasing extent, leadership patterns will be determined by mature human beings on a thoughtful and deliberate basis.

DETERMINANTS OF LEADERSHIP BEHAVIOR

It was suggested earlier in this chapter that a full understanding of the dynamics of leadership must take into account not only the forces which give rise to leadership, but also the forces which determine a leader's behavior once he has been selected.

There are many different methods of leadership, and they differ from one another principally in the degree of directiveness or amount of control exerted. They range all the way from brute force to gentle guidance. The leader may grab his follower by the scruff of the neck and push or pull him into the desired behavior. He may drive him into it at gun-point. He may give commands which carry behind them the threat of force. He may entreat, he may persuade, he may make suggestions, or he may simply provide conditions which are conducive to stimulating the kind of response which he desires. We shall learn more about the *proper* roles and

22

relationships of these methods later. Our interest at this point is simply to discover the kinds of forces, whether good or bad, that tend to influence a leader's behavior.

These forces may be classified roughly into four groups: (1) the type of job that needs to be done; (2) the leader's personality; (3) the personality of the followers; and (4) the sanctions at the leader's disposal. We shall illustrate the operation of each of these factors.

1. **The type of job that needs to be done.** This matter is made clear by a comparison of two extremely dissimilar situations — a sinking ship and an informal classroom discussion. It should be evident that the demands on the leader in these situations are totally different, and his methods of control will be altered accordingly. It is hardly likely that he will take time for persuasion on the sinking ship or that he will grab a member of the discussion group by the nape of the neck.

2. **The leader's personality.** It is impossible to describe methods of leadership without taking into account the kind of person doing the leading. The two are inseparable — as inseparable as a college professor's teaching methods and his psychological make-up. We cannot study leadership behavior in a vacuum. It can only be understood fully in relation to individual human beings, each of whom is different and each of whom will have a leadership style of his own.

Time magazine not long ago carried a story on Konrad Adenauer, Chancellor of the West German Republic:

> Adenauer, a staunch democrat in politics, is an autocrat of the breakfast and dinner table. His son says: "Father leaves democracy at the door. He rules our family with a strong hand. If a rose tree must be transplanted he decides when and where. If my sister wants to bake a cake, he must say yes or no. This is not unusual in Germany, you know; this is how it should be.[24]

We might well be skeptical and curious about persons like Adenauer who appear to have so neatly compartmentalized their

[24] *Time*, Sept. 5, 1949, p. 25. Courtesy of *Time*. Copyright by Time, Inc., 1949.

lives. We should not be too surprised to find that when a serious showdown comes in public life, the autocrat of the breakfast table may be an autocrat still.

3. **The personality of the followers.** The behavior of any leader, no matter how weak or strong, is inevitably influenced by the reactions of those who follow. The child who is too young to listen to reason has to be dealt with by force. Adults who are thoroughly conditioned to expect superhuman qualities in their leaders will force those leaders to abstain from many human temptations and to hide their human frailties. Followers who are not used to being treated fairly may take advantage of a new leader who gives them a "break," hence compelling him to adopt the tactics of his predecessor. Some people simply will not take orders; others simply will not take a hint!

4. **The sanctions at the leader's disposal.** By sanctions we mean those forces which stand behind the leader and lend external weight to the influence he exerts. They represent the power at his command. Grades are typical of the sanctions at a teacher's disposal. Control over the purse-strings is one of the most common sanctions for leadership in the home. The ability to hire, promote, demote and fire provides the "boss" with important sanctions.

The sanctions a leader has at his disposal do not *necessarily* affect his methods of leadership. A man with great power may use his strength with infinite restraint in accordance with Theodore Roosevelt's dictum to "talk softly and carry a big stick," while the man of few sanctions may bully his way through every effort. Nevertheless, a follower is usually well aware of the real nature of the leader's power, and carefully conducts himself accordingly. Even when the leader wishes it to be otherwise, the follower's consciousness of the unmentioned power in the background will influence their entire relationship.

SUMMARY

Direct leadership is an interaction process in which an individual, usually through the medium of speech, influences the behavior of others toward a particular end. The leader's methods may range from brash command to gentle guidance, but in all cases he limits, to some degree, the freedom of the followers. The term "society" implies the presence of leadership and the absence of absolute freedom.

There are forces at work in every society which determine the way in which leadership arises and which influence the methods employed by leaders. To account for the development of leadership patterns we have looked to the possible roles of personal characteristics, tradition, magical powers, accident, prestige, conditioned needs, and specific skills. We have noted four factors which tend to influence leadership behavior — the type of job that needs to be done, the leader's personality, the personality of the followers, and the sanctions at the leader's disposal.

These are the basic ingredients of our problem. These are the social forces at work. In order to control or change the processes which now account for leadership we must first reach a clear understanding of what it is that we want. Perhaps we can clarify our goals by looking, in the next chapter, at the authoritarian and democratic philosophies of leadership.

EXERCISES

1. Recall any situations during your life in which you have been the leader, and try to account for your reaching that position.
2. Make a survey of the social units of which you are at present a member, all the way from family to nation. Who is the leader of each group and, so far as you can tell, what accounts for the fact that he (or she) is the leader?
3. Give at least one example of leaders you know about who, in your opinion, have come to leadership predominantly because of each of the following:

   a) Personal characteristics
   b) Tradition
   c) Accident
   d) Prestige
   e) Conditioned needs
   f) Specific skills

4. What is the predominant method of leadership used by the head of your family? Can you account for it in terms of the four determining factors discussed in this chapter?
5. The next three or four times that you come together with a small group of people in an informal situation — a social gathering, a luncheon meeting, etc. — watch to see who, if anyone, exerts leadership in the group. For example, does anyone steer the conversation? Who takes the initiative for getting activities under way? For changing the direction of the group's activities? For getting up from the table? For going home? Who got the group together in the first place?

   If, in terms of such an analysis, it appears that one individual in the group is actually the leader, how do you account for it? Is he the oldest? Does he have the most prestige? Does he reveal unusual dominance needs? Is he the most intelligent? What other factors might explain it?
6. Keep a record for two weeks of all the books, newspapers, and magazine articles you read which use the terms "leader" or "leadership." In each instance note the sense in which the

terms are used. At the end of two weeks tally up your records to determine the ways in which they are used most frequently. Do they refer more to direct or indirect leadership? Do they imply leadership by command? By persuasion? By guidance? In what other ways do you find the terms used?

7. Do you believe that most people have a need for leader-worship? Do you think that the great interest Americans have in the lives of England's royal family is an indication of this need? How about the impressive titles (Grand Master, Most Excellent Supreme Potentate) we bestow upon the leaders of our clubs and lodges? Do you feel that General Eisenhower, General Mac-Arthur and the late President Roosevelt have been the objects of leader-worship? How would you explain the fascination that Superman holds for so many comic-book readers?

8. Divide your leadership study group into sub-groups of four or five persons each. Give each group a problem to discuss. Designate no leaders, and do not reveal the purpose of the experiment. Observe who rises to leadership, and how it comes about.

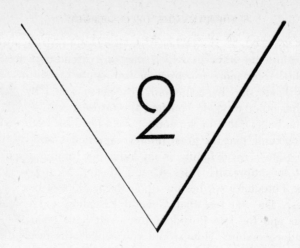

Authoritarianism and Democracy

Find in any country the Ablest Man that exists there;
raise him to the supreme place, and loyally reverence
him: you have a perfect government for that country
. . . what he tells us to do must be precisely the wisest,
fittest, that we could anywhere or anyhow learn; the
thing which it will in all ways behove us, with right
loyal thankfulness, and nothing doubting, to do.[1]

WITH THESE WORDS THOMAS CARLYLE has epitomized the philosophy
of authoritarian leadership in the extreme. Most of us, in twentieth-
century America, will shudder at his ideas, for they sound harsh and
unacceptable to our feelings. We would tend to turn to another
man for a rather different idea:

I know, indeed, that some honest men fear that a republican
government can not be strong; that this government is not

[1] Carlyle, *op. cit.,* pp. 259–60.

strong enough . . . I believe this, on the contrary, the strongest government on earth . . . Sometimes it is said that man cannot be trusted with the government of himself. Can he, then, be trusted with the government of others? Or have we found angels in the form of kings to govern him? Let history answer this question.

Thus spoke Thomas Jefferson on March 4, 1801, in his first inaugural address. Jefferson epitomized the philosophy of democratic leadership. In his view, it was repellent to believe, as Carlyle and many others did, that men should place the determination of their destiny in the hands of a selected few. The chasm between Carlyle and Jefferson cuts wide and deep, and courses across all of the pages of history. At times the gap seems wider than it really is, and it appears that the worlds on either side are in irreconcilable conflict.

It shall be one of the purposes of this book to demonstrate that, in truth, there is a bridge across the canyon — a bridge which has always been there but is usually so enshrouded with fog as to be barely visible. We shall learn that neither the authoritarian or democratic philosophies is sufficient unto itself; that neither is an unmixed blessing or an unmixed evil; that, in fact, neither can survive exclusive of the other. Let us examine these two philosophies carefully. In order to do so we will find it convenient at first to consider each separately — to pretend for the moment that no bridge exists.

THE AUTHORITARIAN TRADITION

Authoritarianism Defined

Authoritarianism is a social process wherein the making of decisions for a social unit is placed in the hands of one man who is presumed to know better than others what the group should believe and do. Having made his decision, the authoritarian leader, or autocrat (as he is sometimes called), directs the behavior of others toward his predetermined ends. His methods of control may be various and sundry. They may even have the appearance of democratic procedures. The crucial factor is that the leader has "authored" the decision and the followers accept it without question. This very clearly implies that the leader is thought of as superior to the followers.

History of Authoritarianism

The authoritarian doctrine has a long and respectable history. Plato is generally regarded as its father and prime spokesman. It was his thesis that in the perfect Republic, political leadership should be entrusted to an especially trained "elite" — the so-called philosopher-kings. These should be men chosen in their youth to receive a special education which would prepare them for the task. Listen to Socrates as he explains this position to Glaucon:

> We must explain . . . whom we mean when we say that philosophers are to rule in the State; then we shall be able to defend ourselves: There will be discovered to be some natures who ought to study philosophy and to be leaders in the State; and others who are not born to be philosophers, and are meant to be followers rather than leaders.[2]

As Plato saw the problem, some men — the philosophers — are by nature capable of contemplating the great, unchanging truths of life, whereas others of less stature are "all abroad among all sorts of aspects of many objects." Just as we would want a sharp sighted watchman rather than a blind one to guard a precious possession, so it is only reasonable, argues Plato, that the philosophers be made guardians of the laws and institutions of the city, since the other citizens "are not much better than blind."

This theme of Plato, that leadership belongs in the hands of a special elite, has recurred throughout history. Alexander Hamilton is often regarded as the exponent of such an "aristocracy of the able" in early America. The doctrine was re-echoed by George W. Curtis in 1882 when he stated that an educated minority is the source of progress in opposing a dictatorship of the majority.[3] It

[2] From the *Republic* of Plato, Book V. Translated by Benjamin Jowett, and reproduced by permission of the Clarendon Press, Oxford.

[3] Curtis, George W., "The Leadership of Educated Men," *Orations and Addresses of George William Curtis.* Ed. Charles Norton. New York: Harpers, 1894, Vol. I, pp. 313 ff.

was re-echoed to this writer in his undergraduate days by his university president who frequently addressed himself to the proposition that "noblesse oblige" in our society means the obligation of educated men to lead the less enlightened masses.

We referred earlier to the doctrines of the Divine Right of Kings and of Leadership by the Eldest which have become traditions throughout so much of the world. These, too, are authoritarian concepts, for they hold that the leader knows what is best and that his rulings should be followed without dispute.

One of the most famous treatises on leadership is Machiavelli's *The Prince*. This manual of advice on how political power is gained and held should be required reading for every would-be dictator. In this particular work, Machiavelli made no attempt to justify or evaluate authoritarianism. He simply assumed that it was a natural state of affairs and proceeded to discuss the ways in which it operates.

Of all the philosophies of leadership based upon the concept of an aristocracy, none is more provocative than the "Great Man" doctrine of Thomas Carlyle. All of history, said Carlyle, is:

> at bottom the history of the Great Men who have worked here. . . . They were the leaders of men, these great ones; the modellers, patterns, and in a wide sense creators, of whatsoever the general mass of men contrive to do or to attain.[4]

Then Carlyle gives us the most frank statement of extreme authoritarianism we can find anywhere:

> Now, sure enough, the cry is everywhere for Liberty and Equality, Independence and so forth; instead of Kings, ballot-boxes and electoral suffrages: it seems made out that any Hero-sovereign, or loyal obedience of men to a man, in things temporal or things spiritual, has passed away forever from the world. I should despair of the world altogether if so. . . . Without sovereigns . . . I see nothing possible but anarchy; the hatefullest of things. . . . All this of Liberty and Equality, Electoral Suffrage, Independence and so forth, we will take, therefore, to be a temporary phenomenon. . . . Though likely

---

[4] Carlyle, *op. cit.*, p. 5.

to last a long time, with sad enough embroilments for us all, we must welcome it, as the penalty of sins that are past, the pledge of inestimable benefits that are coming.[5]

It is indeed strange that Carlyle's views should shock our sensibilities as they do. For in spite of the verbal homage we pay to democratic methods, by actual practice and conditioning we are closer to Carlyle than we know. It is still a minority of families, even in America, where the younger members have liberty, equality, independence and the family equivalent of ballot-boxes — except perhaps on small matters. It would be more accurate to describe the typical youth's relation to his parents as Carlyle's "loyal obedience of men to a man."

It is a rare classroom, even in America, where students have liberty and independence and are equal to the teacher; — and how many have the privilege of deciding the right answers to an examination by taking a vote? It is the rare business establishment where employers share the final decision-making power with employees and where "loyal obedience of men to a man" is not the price of holding one's job. Let us who live in glass houses not be too quick to throw stones at Carlyle — at least until we have looked at the other side of the canyon.

THE DEMOCRATIC TRADITION

Democracy Defined

Democracy is a word which, perhaps more than any other in the languages of the world, means all things to all men. No further proofs of this are necessary other than the fact that the United States and the Soviet Union each calls itself democratic and the other undemocratic, that socialist Britain calls capitalism undemocratic and capitalistic America calls socialism undemocratic, that liberals call Jim Crow and the poll tax undemocratic while Southern Senators shout that proposed civil rights legislation is undemocratic.

For the purposes of our discussion here democracy is understood

[5] *Ibid.*, pp. 165–70.

to be a social process in which the group as a whole is self-governing (not subject to any outside authority) and in which all members of the group are equally represented in the making of collaborative decisions. If irreconcilable differences exist within the group, the decision goes to those who are numerically a majority, and the rest are expected to comply. In order to prevent this aspect of the process from leading to what John Stuart Mill called a "tyranny of the majority," democracy also recognizes that individual freedom must be as great as is consistent with the safety and welfare of the group, and that even a majority has no right to trample on all personal freedom. The democratic leader guides and coordinates the group's decision-making process. He is a discussion leader or chairman of debate whose only predetermined purpose is to preserve and enhance democratic procedures. He determines *how* the members of the group will think and decide, not *what* they will think and decide — and even with respect to the "how" function the group has final authority. He is the group's methodological agent, but only so long as the group finds it convenient and helpful for him to be so. This philosophy very clearly implies that *no* member of the group is superior to the others. One vote is as good as another, because it is believed that every human being has an equal right to make the decisions which affect his life.

To define democracy in this way is to use the term more narrowly than most of us ordinarily do. To use the word more broadly, however, is to dilute its essential meaning. Let us recognize that when people refer to a nation like the United States or Great Britain as a democracy, or when they refer to an organization like a college fraternity as being democratic, they are speaking loosely. Fundamentally those societies may be democratic, inasmuch as *ultimate* authority on all matters rests with the members of the group; but everything that is done within those societies is not done by democratic procedures. When the President of the United States proclaims a national emergency; when a judge decides that a man shall go to jail; when a fraternity president fines a member, appoints a committee head, or buys an ash-tray for the chapter room; when a teacher tells her students to believe that the Declaration of Independence was signed in 1776, these leaders are not operating democratically — nor would many of us maintain that they should. True, they may be operating within a larger democratic framework (which is significantly different from a situation in which their authority might be above and beyond ultimate control by the group) but nevertheless, in their specific functions, they are operating autocratically. They, and they alone, are making the decisions.

History of Democratic Doctrine

Democracy has a history as long and respectable as that of authoritarianism. The Greeks and Romans practiced democracy in the political forum, even at a time when kings and emperors were still the rule of the day. Other seeds of democracy, particularly with regard to the dignity of the individual, were sown by the teachings of Jesus Christ. The writings of innumerable philosophers have contributed something to the tradition. But there are four historic documents which, perhaps more than any others, are worthy of our attention.

The first is John Locke's essay on *Civil Government* wherein the basic idea that final authority rests with a majority of the group is so clearly set forth:

> Men being, as has been said, by nature all free, equal, and independent, no one can be put out of this estate, and subjected to the political power of another, without his own consent, which is done by agreeing with other men to join and unite into a community. . . . When any number of men have so consented to make one community or government, they are thereby presently incorporated, and make one body politic, wherein the majority have a right to act and conclude the rest.[6]

It was John Stuart Mill, in his essay *On Liberty*, who clarified the relationship of individual freedom and social control in a democracy:

[6] Locke, John, *Civil Government*. Ed. Ernest Rhys. Everyman's Library; New York: Dutton, 1924, Chapter 8, Part 95, pp. 164–65.

The object of this essay is to assert one very simple principle, as entitled to govern absolutely the dealings of society with the individual in the way of compulsion and control. . . . That principle is, that the sole end for which mankind are warranted, individually or collectively, in interfering with the liberty of action of any of their number, is self-protection. That the only purpose for which power can be rightfully exercised over any member of a civilized community, against his will, is to prevent harm to others. His own good, either physical or moral, is not a sufficient warrant.[7]

Mill was also much concerned with the apparently valid argument of the authoritarians that since, in fact, some persons are more qualified to make certain judgments than others, it is foolish to sacrifice the value of their experience on the altar of equality. Mill replied:

Nobody denies that people should be so taught and trained in youth as to know and benefit by the ascertained results of human experience. But it is the privilege and proper condition of a human being, arrived at the maturity of his facilities, to use and interpret experience in his own way. It is for him to find out what part of recorded experience is properly applicable to his own circumstances and character.[8]

Our own Declaration of Independence, written by Thomas Jefferson, contains one of the clearest expressions of the democratic philosophy:

We hold these truths to be self-evident, that all men are created equal, that they are endowed by their Creator with certain inalienable Rights, that among these are Life, Liberty and the Pursuit of Happiness — That to secure these rights, Governments are instituted among Men, deriving their just powers from the consent of the governed.

The role of the leader in a democratic society received little direct attention in the historic works we have referred to. It is not surprising that the philosophers of democracy, in their rebellion against the leader-centered concepts of authoritarianism, took a

[7] Mill, John Stuart, *On Liberty and Other Essays.* New York: Book League of America, 1929, p. 13.
[8] *Ibid.,* p. 68.

negative attitude toward leadership and presented little or nothing of a positive philosophy. There is, in the *Discourse upon the Origin and Foundation of the Inequality among Mankind* of Jean Jacques Rousseau, however, a hint of the direction that a positive philosophy of democratic leadership would have to take:

> It is therefore beyond dispute, and indeed the fundamental maxim of all political rights, that people have set up chiefs to protect their liberty, and not to enslave them. "If we have a prince," said Pliny to Trajan, "it is to save ourselves from having a master" . . .
>
> With regard to parental authority . . . it is enough to remark . . . that, by the law of nature, the father is the child's master no longer than his help is necessary; that from that time they are both equal, the son being perfectly independent of the father, and owing him only respect and not obedience. For gratitude is a duty which ought to be paid, but not a right to be exacted.[9]

Rousseau apparently recognized that a democracy, like any other form of society, needs leadership. He also recognized the distinction between an authoritarian leader, whose purpose is to decide matters for other people, and a democratic leader, whose purpose is to provide and protect the conditions in which those people decide things for themselves.

"If we have a prince it is to save ourselves from having a master." This is the essence of democratic leadership. It has been left to men of the twentieth century to expand this embryonic philosophy into a well-formulated doctrine. Because the concepts are so new, and have only begun to permeate our thoughts and feelings, it will be necessary for us to make a rather thorough investigation of these ideas and of the way in which they are emerging.

Modern Developments

In 1924, F. Stuart Chapin stated that the great need of the day

---

[9] Rousseau, Jean Jacques, "From the Social Contract," *The World's Great Thinkers*. New York: Random House, 1947, pp. 279–80. Reprinted by permission.

was the development of "socialized leaders" who would be more interested in helping their groups to achieve common goals for themselves than to build a loyal and faithful following around the leader.[10]

From this beginning in 1924 to the present time large numbers of writers, particularly educators, have devoted themselves to an expansion of Chapin's theme. A significant book written in 1926 by T. V. Smith, then professor of philosophy at the University of Chicago, devoted a chapter to democratic leadership. Professor Smith developed the idea that in our modern, specialized society no man can be omniscient — that in order to become an authority in one area he must choose to be relatively ignorant in other areas. Hence, the necessity becomes apparent for diffusion of leadership responsibilities to many people and the acceptance by every man of the fact that he must be both a leader and a follower.[11]

Henry M. Busch, a professor of social work, wrote in 1934 that the democratic leader — or group builder, as he called him — "attempts to make the group less dependent upon his leadership as it grows in experience." [12]

By 1948, Dean Ernest Melby of the New York University School of Education had called attention to the fact that "In the last three decades a revolutionary change has taken place in our concept of what is meant by the 'expert' in leadership." Formerly it was the one who best knew the answers, but today, "in our best leadership practice the expert is one who knows how to release the creative talents of those with whom he works." [13]

It was this principle of leadership as the release of creativity that motivated Philosopher John Dewey's ideas on progressive education and gave rise to an avalanche of interest in group discussion which has rolled into colleges and universities, business organiza-

[10] Chapin, F. Stuart, "Socialized Leadership," *Journal of Social Forces,* III (November, 1924), pp. 57–60.

[11] Smith, T. V., *The Democratic Way of Life.* Chicago: University of Chicago Press, 1936, Chapter VI.

[12] Busch, Henry M., *Leadership in Group Work.* New York: Association Press, 1934, p. 139.

[13] Melby, Ernest, "Leadership is Release of Creativity," *School Executive,* LXVIII (November, 1948).

tions, social work, and adult forums all over the United States.[14]

The newer concepts of democratic leadership have reached their fullest development since the end of World War II, with the research and training activities in the field of "group dynamics." This movement received its primary impetus from the work and inspiration of the late psychologist, Kurt Lewin. Lewin's colleagues and students have now developed a considerable body of experience and have provided us with new insights into the problems of group leadership. They have established a Research Center for Group Dynamics at the University of Michigan, and a National Training Laboratory in Group Development with summer training programs at Bethel, Maine, and year-round activities under the direction of Leland Bradford in Washington, D.C. Professor Kenneth Benne of the University of Illinois, one of the leaders in this work, gives us the essence of the "dynamics" point of view on leadership:

> It is important to see leadership in terms of functions to be performed in helping groups to grow and operate productively, not in terms of qualities inherent in certain persons.[15]

The "group dynamics" concept provides a methodology for the fulfillment of the basic democratic philosophy that final authority and leadership responsibility rests upon the members of a society. Leadership is not to be thought of as the function of one man — *a* leader — but rather as a series of functions necessary to the productive operation of a group and performable by any member of the group competent to the task. Thus leadership may pass to many individuals at different moments, and the more diffused it becomes the stronger and healthier is the group. The man officially called *leader* performs only those tasks which the group itself is not yet mature enough, intellectually or emotionally, to

[14] For significant publications in this stream of development see: Follett, Mary P., *Creative Experience.* New York: Longmans, Green, 1924; Elliott, Harrison, *The Process of Group Thinking.* New York: Association Press, 1932; Sheffield, Alfred D., *Creative Discussion.* New York: Association Press, 1927; McBurney, James H., and Kenneth Hance, *Principles and Methods of Discussion,* Rev. Ed. New York: Harpers, 1950.

[15] Benne, Kenneth, "Leaders are Made, not Born," *Childhood Education,* XXIV (January, 1948), p. 204.

handle for itself. The leader's goal is to work himself out of a job.

In order to obtain a fuller appreciation and understanding of this modern concept of democratic leadership it will be helpful to examine one of the unique sources from which it has gained strength. Basically, of course, its roots are planted firmly in the democratic political tradition which we have already reviewed. We are quite sure that Rousseau and Jefferson would find themselves at home in this environment. But the methods of group leadership we are now developing have other roots alongside those which are embedded in political philosophy. They are roots which spring from newer soil. They find their origin in the work of Sigmund Freud and follow the paths of the psychiatric tradition which has flowered since his time.

The name of Freud calls up all sorts of connotations in the minds of various persons. To the unregenerate moralist it is a symbol of all that is dirty and evil in the world. To the undiscriminating layman it is a synonym for sex. To the old-fashioned, die-hard psychologist it is a repressed historical fact, the significance of which he has never quite been able to grasp. But to the vast majority of enlightened individuals, regardless of their minor differences of opinion, it is the name of a doctor who fathered an idea that has revolutionized man's insight into man and has opened up a field — known broadly as psychotherapy — which has enabled man to help release his fellow men from the dungeons of emotional ill health.

But what has all this to do with group leadership? The answer is not difficult to discover. You will remember that leadership was defined early in the first chapter as the act of guiding, directing or influencing human beings. Certainly that is what a psychotherapist does. He is, therefore, in a very real sense, a leader. We do not ordinarily think of him as such for two reasons. First his leadership is usually exerted with individuals rather than groups. Second, he deals with "abnormal, emotional" problems rather than "normal, social" problems.

Normal group situations are indeed very different from abnormal individual situations, yet there are significant relationships. Evidence of this is the fact that in recent years many psychiatrists, particularly of the psychoanalytic school, have openly transplanted their philosophy and methods to normal group situations and have taken up a role of group leadership. The outstanding example of this is the work of the Tavistock Clinic in England, headed by Dr. A. T. M. Wilson, who is a medical man and psychoanalyst turned social scientist and group leader. The members of the staff of this clinic offer their services to groups of people, particularly in the area of labor-management relationships, who need guidance in resolving social conflict. These men call themselves industrial consultants, but they point out that actually their role in the social situation is very similar to the psychoanalyst's role with an individual.[16]

Other examples of this same trend, in the United States, include: (1) the work of Dr. Julius Schreiber, another analyst turned social scientist, who organized the National Institute of Social Relations shortly after World War II for the purpose of helping to resolve tensions in areas where serious social conflict existed; (2) the work of J. L. Moreno, a psychiatrist who feels that psychotherapeutic techniques can be used in solving social problems as well as personal problems; and (3) the strong psychiatric orientation of the National Training Laboratory in Group Development in its processes of training for group leadership.

The fact that psychotherapists perform a leadership function with their clients and that many of them have become interested in group leadership indicates that some kind of parallel exists. It does not tell us what the relationship is, nor what the contributions of the psychiatric tradition have been to our ideas on group leadership. Let us turn to those matters now.

Probably the most important single concept that has emerged in the last twenty years from the ever-growing wealth of psychotherapeutic experience is the realization that the most effective way to direct the behavior of human beings is simply to help them direct themselves. Today the competent psychotherapist, whether

[16] Jacques, Elliott, "Interpretive Group Discussion as a Method of Facilitating Social Change," *Human Relations*, I (1947), pp. 433–39.

he be labelled analyst, psychiatrist, or counsellor, recognizes that his job is not to tell the patient what to do but, by skillfully helping him to clarify his own problem, lead him to the point where he is able to discover for himself what to do and how to do it. By the same token, the democratic group leader, instead of doing things for members of his society, is now seen as a person who tries to create conditions under which they are best able to do things for themselves. His job, as Dean Melby pointed out, is to release the creative talents of the followers. In other words, he helps them to analyze their own problems, to work out their own solutions, in line with their own needs and desires. Carl Rogers, one of the outstanding spokesmen of modern psychotherapy, might just as well have been describing democratic group leadership when he said:

> Therapy is not a matter of doing something *to* the individual, or of inducing him to do something about himself. It is instead a matter of freeing him for normal growth and development, of removing obstacles so that he can move forward.[17]

A second fundamental of modern psychotherapy is that the counsellor seeks to create a warm and permissive atmosphere in which the patient feels secure and feels free to reveal his true thoughts and emotions. There is a complete airing of his grievances, his troubles, his pent-up feelings. He brings the skeletons out of the closet and exposes them to the revealing light of day. In a similar way, democratic leadership seeks to develop a warm and permissive atmosphere for the group, where the members of the social unit feel secure and thus free to air their real thoughts and feelings. Successful democratic leadership, according to the newer concepts, establishes a climate wherein honest feelings, whether hostile or friendly, can be accepted and discussed in an objective way. How important this is for the adequate settlement of social problems, and how infrequently it is actually accomplished. How many board of directors' meetings, student-faculty committee meetings, labor-

---

[17] Rogers, Carl, *Counselling and Psychotherapy*. Boston: Houghton Mifflin, 1942, p. 29.

management conferences, or even family dinner-table discussions, all using so-called democratic procedures, really provide a permissive atmosphere in which the participants feel secure enough to express honest emotions?

A third basic premise of current psychotherapy [18] that gives support and elaboration to the concept of democratic group leadership is its respect for the right of the individual — given the facts and freed from disruptive emotional pressures — to make his own decisions and choices. As Rogers puts it:

> Non-directive counselling is based on the assumption that the client has the right to select his own life goals, even though these may be at variance with the goals that the counsellor might choose for him. . . . The non-directive viewpoint places a high value on the right of every individual to be psychologically independent and to maintain his psychological integrity. The directive viewpoint places a high value upon social conformity and the right of the more able to direct the less able. *These viewpoints have a significant relationship to social and political philosophy as well as to techniques of therapy.* [Italics mine.] [19]

It would appear from this brief survey that the democratic group leader and the psychotherapist are twin fighters in a common cause — each gaining support and insight from the other.

THE BRIDGES BETWEEN

We have examined the authoritarian and democratic traditions, and their implications, as though they were mutually exclusive concepts. For expository convenience we have thought of them, temporarily, as opposing philosophies, distinctly different from each other. It is now time that we bring them into perspective, and stop thinking of them as isolated worlds across a chasm. Let us take a look at the bridges which connect them.

The relationships about which we are concerned are frequently

[18] Perhaps not accepted by all psychotherapists, but apparently by a majority of them. See Waelder, Robert, "Areas of Agreement in Psychotherapy," *American Journal of Orthopsychiatry*, X (October, 1941), p. 708.

[19] Rogers, *op. cit.*, pp. 126–27.

represented diagrammatically — usually by a straight line or continuum. One of the most common of these illustrations is the continuum from anarchy to totalitarianism pictured below.

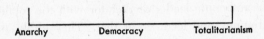

The idea is simple. This diagram is intended to convey the notion that the difference between anarchy and totalitarianism is *simply one of degree* — that these two forms of living represent opposite ends or poles of the *same* continuum. The continuum represents the amount of individual freedom which members of a society possess. Freedom is a variable — that is, it can exist in varying amounts or degrees. In some countries, like the United States, the amount of freedom of choice possessed by individuals is large. In other places, like present-day Russia, it is reputed to be small. The end poles or extremes of this particular continuum are absolute freedom (no social control over men's lives), which is called anarchy, and absolute bondage (social control over the *totality* of men's lives), which is called totalitarianism. According to this way of looking at it, democracy is thought of as a midway point on the continuum. In an anarchy every man makes all his own decisions and does exactly as he pleases. There is no leadership, for each man is his own leader and goes his own way. Under totalitarianism, the individual has no freedom of choice and submits all his behavior to the decisions of society. Democracy is thought of as a kind of compromise between the two extremes, wherein some freedoms are given up by members of the group and others are retained. Thus, in the United States, we give up our freedom to drive on the left-hand side of the street, we give up our freedom to pay wages that are less than the minimum required by law, but we retain our freedom to travel where and when we please, and we retain, almost intact, the freedom to say what we are thinking (except when hysteria leads intolerant men to attempt the suppression of that which they disapprove).

Thus far, the relationship of anarchy to totalitarianism, with democracy in between, should be quite clear. Confusion arises if we try, as many writers do, to locate autocracy on this line. (Autocracy is synonymous with authoritarianism — a society in which one man makes and enforces social decisions.) These writers simply identify the autocratic leader or dictator with the totalitarian end of the continuum, and let it go at that. They glibly assume that authoritarianism and totalitarianism are the same thing. By so doing, they introduce a new and complicating factor into the picture. The term autocracy, or authoritarianism, when used to describe a particular society tells us *how* the social decisions are made in that society — namely *by* one person *for* other people. It has nothing to do with *how many* decisions are social ones (and thus made by him) and how many matters are retained by the individuals as questions of personal decision.

What we need for autocracy is a second continuum — one which represents the extent to which the members of a group participate in the making of those decisions which come within the province of social control. The end poles of this continuum are autocracy,

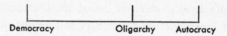

Democracy   Oligarchy   Autocracy

where social decisions are made by one person, and democracy, where all the people have an equal voice in the making of these decisions. An oligarchy is a social unit in which social control is in the hands of a few people.

It is only coincidental that totalitarian societies are usually autocratic and that autocracies tend to be totalitarian. It is conceivable that a society might exist in which very little freedom would be surrendered by the individuals to group control, and yet that freedom which was given up would be surrendered to one man — an autocrat — for decision, rather than to the group as a whole. Such, in fact, is the case in many Latin American countries. Or, all freedom of action might be surrendered by the individuals, and yet surrendered to a decision-making body in which everyone is equally represented. That is what John Stuart Mill called the tyranny of the majority. In either case, the result is a curious combination of autocratic or totalitarian with democratic philosophies.

It may help us in keeping these variables clear if we remember that the term "democracy" is popularly used to refer to two different things. It refers not only to a society in which group decisions are made by all the people, but also to a society in which there are a large number of personal decisions beyond the control of the group. Confusion arises simply because of the failure to realize the different senses in which the term is being used at a given time. If one is comparing the relatively uncontrolled economy of the United States with the more planned economy of Great Britain, and maintains that the former is more "democratic" than the latter, he is speaking in terms of our first continuum — in terms of the degree of personal freedom which has been surrendered by the individual to group determination. If, however, one is comparing the parliamentary government of Great Britain with the congressional system in the United States, and maintains that the former is more "democratic" than the latter, he is speaking in terms of our second continuum — in terms of the extent to which the people have a say in the making of social decisions.

It would no doubt help us avoid confusion if everyone would use the term "democracy" in only one sense — preferably in the sense referred to on our second continuum which, in consideration of the term's roots,[20] is literally the most correct. The first continuum, as we have said, deals with the question of individual freedom and liberty versus social control and conformity. One can reasonably argue that democracy, in its most correct sense, has nothing to do with this question. There can be democracy with much individual liberty and there can be democracy with little individual liberty — the only requirement of democracy being that authority rests with the members of the group.

Desirable as this distinction may be for the purposes of semantic clarity, the fact remains that the vast majority of people still use, and will continue to use, the term democracy in more than one way. Our wisest course is simply to accept that fact and, whenever

[20] From the Greek: *Demos* the people + *kratein* to rule; *kratos* authority.

45

the word is used, attempt to discover the sense in which it is intended.

There is another type of relationship that bridges the gap between the authoritarian and democratic traditions. It is possible to have these two philosophies of leadership combined in the same person. Leaders can be democratically selected, but after their selection *rule* absolutely. Such is the case, to a degree, of the Roman Catholic Pope, who is elected by a democratic vote of the College of Cardinals. Conversely, leaders can be undemocratically selected, yet lead democratically. Such is the case of the average committee chairman in our social and professional organizations. His appointment and tenure as chairman are usually dependent on the president of the organization, and hence beyond the jurisdiction of the committee members. Yet within the committee he may operate in accordance with democratic processes. So long as either the leader's operating methods or his selection are not democratic he cannot be considered a completely democratic leader. In so far as his methods are not democratic, the group members are not represented in the making of decisions. So long as his selection is beyond the control of the group there is no assurance that, although his methods are democratic today, they may not become autocratic tomorrow.

To refine this point further, we might suggest that even *within* the processes by which a leader is selected or *within* the processes by which he operates there may well be combinations of authoritarian and democratic procedures. The two philosophies, as we have said before, are by no means mutually exclusive. Frequently they shade into one another almost imperceptibly. At one moment the leader may say to his group, "Shall we vote on this matter now?" and two minutes later he may say to them, "We've had enough discussion. Let's vote! All in favor of the motion say 'aye.'"

SUMMARY

Our purpose in this chapter has been to review, clarify and show the relationships between the two major philosophies of leadership that have currency in the world — authoritarianism and democracy. It now appears that the essential difference between the two is a difference in attitude toward the rights and capabilities of human beings. Authoritarianism is based upon the assumption that the leader knows better than others what should be done and should direct the behavior of the group accordingly. Democracy is based upon the assumption that the group has the right and the capacity to make its own decisions and that the leader's function is to help it to do so in the best way possible. To state the difference in this way is to state the extremes. We have recognized that in practice the two philosophies may shade by degrees into one another and that rarely does either exist in pure form. It is not an either-or proposition. The real question, which we have not yet answered but shall proceed to forthwith, is: Toward which end of the continuum do we wish to be moving?

EXERCISES

1. "If all things whatsoever that we look upon are emblems to us of the highest God, I add that moreso than any of them is man such an emblem. . . . We are the miracle of miracles. . . . And now if worship even of a star had some meaning in it, how much more might that of a Hero! Worship of a hero is transcendent admiration of a Great Man. . . . No nobler feeling than this of admiration of one higher than himself dwells in the breast of man. . . . Religion I find stand [sic] upon it. . . . Hero-worship, heartfelt, prostrate admiration, submission, burning, boundless for a noblest godlike form of Man — is not that the germ of Christianity itself?" — CARLYLE

   Do you agree with this point of view? Defend your position.

2. Make a list of the social units of which you are a member, and name the leader or leaders in each of those groups. What philosophy of leadership do you think that each of them most nearly represents most of the time?

3. One of the assumptions of democracy is that all persons are entitled to equal respect as human beings. How can leadership be reconciled with this assumption? When all is said and done, aren't leadership and autocracy actually synonymous? Discuss.

4. Consider three social units of which you are a member — your family, your fraternity, and your school, for example. Make a comparison of these three social groups with regard to:

   a) The amount of freedom of choice which is given up by yourself to the group for decision.

   b) The number of people who have a say in the making of group decisions.

5. "Leadership, as we use the term, is a broader and deeper and finer thing than supervision. It is the ability to stimulate, guide and 'show the way,' so that people are caused to do those things the leader wishes them to do — willingly, intelligently, skillfully." [21] — GEORGE D. HALSEY

   Do you agree with this point of view? Defend your position.

[21] Halsey, George D., *How to Be a Leader*, p. x. New York: Harpers, 1938. Reprinted by permission.

6. What basis is there for assuming, as the democratic leader and psychotherapist do, that it is not desirable to impose their own values on the followers or clients? Discuss.

7. In his book, *Functions of the Executive*,[22] Chester Barnard takes the position that, even under an autocratic leader, ultimate authority inevitably rests with the members of the group. He notes that orders are repeatedly disobeyed in all sorts of organizations, and reminds his readers that the Ten Commandments and many provisions of the United States Constitution are constantly being violated. He states: "Which specific laws will be obeyed or disobeyed by the individual citizen are decided by him under the specific conditions pertinent."

After suggesting that even under the threat of force an individual can choose to die rather than submit, Barnard concludes that "the decision as to whether an order has authority or not lies with the person to whom it is addressed, and does not reside in 'persons of authority' or those who issue the orders."

If Barnard's point of view is valid it would appear that one of the major distinctions made in this chapter between authoritarian and democratic leadership is fallacious. Discuss.

8. " . . . the greatest of all democracies is an Army. Discipline and morale influence the inarticulate vote that is instantly taken by masses of men when the order comes to move forward . . . but the army does not move forward until the motion has 'carried.' " [23]

Do you agree with this argument? Discuss.

[22] Barnard, Chester, *Functions of the Executive*. Cambridge: Harvard University Press, 1948.

[23] Harbord, Major General James G., *The American Army in France*. Boston: Little, Brown, 1936.

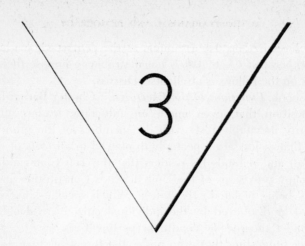

Values and Limitations of Democratic Leadership

MOST READERS OF THIS BOOK will be people to whom the democratic philosophy of leadership would hardly seem to need justification; it is taken for granted. The symbols and shibboleths of democracy are poured into us from the time we are old enough to go to school. They are mouthed on the floors of Congress and loudly proclaimed from public platforms, *but* by men whose behavior often belies their very words. Terms like "freedom," "equality," and "consent of the governed" are so abused and misused that they frequently become hollow shells devoid of meaning. The result is that many of us believe in democracy, *feel* that it is good, but do not know why and hence do not always practice what we preach. When we are challenged to defend democracy's value, or protect it from antagonistic philosophies, we are at a loss to explain ourselves. Particularly is this true when it is pointed out to us that modern science has disproved many of the assumptions on which democracy was built, such as John Locke's belief that man is *by nature* free, equal, and independent.

Does this mean that democratic leadership cannot be rationally justified? We think not. On the contrary it is our contention that modern science, though it may have cast doubt upon John Locke, has in general reinforced the validity of democratic leadership. We believe it clearly apparent that unless men develop more democracy and less authoritarianism in present-day societies they are headed for stagnation and ultimate destruction. Here are the reasons why.

VALUES OF DEMOCRATIC LEADERSHIP

1. The only circumstances people fully understand are those they have themselves experienced. The only ideas they fully grasp are those in whose formulation they have participated. It is an old truism that a man is not really the master of an idea until he is able to express it himself. It has been demonstrated by experimental studies that college students retain more knowledge from discussions in which they have participated than from lectures (authoritarianism) to which they have been exposed.[1] Many of us have seen for ourselves how much more readily our prejudices against minority groups are overcome — or reinforced — by favorable — or unfavorable — personal contacts with members of those groups than by all the movies, books, posters, and sermons to which we are exposed. Those of us who have studied geometry or algebra know how much more adept we become at using mathematical formulae which we have derived for ourselves than those which are handed to us by the teacher. Progressive education is built upon the idea that the student must participate actively in the learning process if he is to profit from it. He must think problems through for himself, and not rely upon the authority of his instructors. "Only so much do I know as I have lived," said Ralph Waldo Emerson in *The American Scholar*. By the same principle, members of

[1] Rickard, Paul, "An Experimental Study of the Effectiveness of Group Discussion in the Teaching of Factual Content," Ph.D. Dissertation, Northwestern University, 1946.

a social unit must have a share in the making of group decisions if they are actually to understand the full meaning and implications of those decisions.

2. **Decisions which are a synthesis of a group's own efforts elicit more solid and enduring support than the edict of one man.** Just as children obey the rules of their parents more faithfully if they understand the reasons for those rules, so it is found that adults who have participated in the making of social decisions, and hence understand the reasons for those decisions (Principle 1), will support the group's actions more willingly and for a longer period of time. This principle was predicted by Thomas Jefferson in his First Inaugural Address when he said:

> I believe it [democratic government] the only one where every man, at the call of the law, would fly to the standard of the law, and would meet invasions of the public order as his own personal concern.

Woodrow Wilson attempted by himself to sell the League of Nations to the United States and failed. Franklin D. Roosevelt enlisted "bipartisan support" in behalf of his foreign policy, and America became the staunchest supporter of the United Nations. It is impossible to know how much of Roosevelt's success was due to his respect for the principle we are now discussing and how much of it was due to the change in world conditions which made Americans less isolationistic than in Wilson's time, but no doubt some credit is owed to the former factor.

One of the most convincing pieces of evidence in support of the superior effectiveness of group decisions over edicts from above was an experiment conducted during World War II in connection with the government's campaign to increase the food-saving habits of American housewives. The traditional approach to this problem had been to make persuasive appeals to housewives urging them to save more food and suggesting ways of doing so. Lectures, posters, and films were some of the media of communication usually employed.

A controlled experiment was set up in which the traditional

method was compared to a newer method in which groups of housewives were called together to discuss the problem and arrive at their own decisions on how best to save more food. It was found that the women who were in the groups which made the decisions themselves increased their food-saving habits significantly more than the women who were simply exposed to persuasive appeals by the government and its representatives.[2]

To be sure, there are hundreds of historical examples which demonstrate that the overwhelming support of people can be won by effective propaganda. Certainly Adolf Hitler, the Japanese warlords, and the rulers of present-day Russia have received fanatical support from millions of people who have had no part in the formulation of the policies they adhere to. But like all things which are not rooted in solid understanding, this kind of support tends to come and go with the shifting winds. An excellent case in point is the manner in which the youth of Eastern Germany who ten years ago were fervently heiling Hitler and parading under the banner of National Socialism are today marching for the Soviet Union and just as fervently paying homage to the masters of the Kremlin.

3. Democratic leadership enables a society to draw upon all of the human resources that are available to it. Although we do not unqualifiedly endorse the old saying that "two heads are better than one" (since it depends on what heads you're talking about) it is certainly true that, in general, a society will be richer for having fertilized all its acres and having drawn sustenance from them all than if it relies for its strength on only one source. T. V. Smith makes a significant distinction between authoritarianism and democracy when he points out that the autocratic leader is "strong in proportion to the ignorance of his followers," whereas the democratic leader is "strong in proportion to the intelligence of the followers."[3]

4. Democratic leadership creates strong, responsible, self-reliant

[2] Lewin, Kurt, "Forces Behind Food Habits and Methods of Change," National Research Council Bulletin No. 108 (Oct., 1943), pp. 60–63.

[3] Smith, T. V., *op. cit.*, p. 186.

individuals who cannot so easily be pushed around by the first tyrant that comes along. This point is self-explanatory. Democracy, like tyranny and smoking cigarettes, is habit-forming.

5. **Democratic leadership builds a group which will not fall apart if something happens to the leader.** It is clear that when a group becomes overdependent upon authoritative leadership, its members get out of practice in taking care of themselves. Their potential leadership "muscles" grow weak and flabby, and if anything happens to "der Führer" they are unprepared to shift for themselves. Cases have been cited during the last world war in which German or Japanese troops disintegrated when leadership was destroyed, whereas American troops in similar circumstances were more likely to carry out the group's responsibilities.

6. **Democratic leadership makes for higher morale in a society than does autocratic leadership.** If we are to be objective, we should recognize that this point is only an hypothesis, not a proven principle. There are several experiments which lend it support. One of the most well-known of these is described by Lewin. It involved a comparison of two recreational groups of children at the Iowa Child Welfare Research Station — one led autocratically and the other democratically. The study found that morale was higher and the children happier in the democratic group.[4]

Professor Kimball Young points out the possible flaw in such experiments when he objects that since the members of all the groups involved had grown up in a predominantly democratic culture they would naturally feel happier in such an environment. Would the same conclusions hold true if the experimental subjects had been Germans or Japanese? [5]

In other words, it may be that high morale and happiness are simply a result of having one's expectations fulfilled — the assumption here being that people are the happiest in those conditions which most approximate what they have become accustomed to. There is already some evidence from the field of group dynamics

---

[4] Lewin, Kurt, "Experiments in Social Space," *Resolving Social Conflict.* New York: Harpers, 1948.

[5] Young, *op. cit.,* pp. 240 ff.

that democratic leadership can frustrate and make an autocratically-oriented group unhappy as readily as autocracy can demoralize a democratically-oriented group.

One might speculate that morale in a democratically-oriented group is made of sterner stuff than morale in an autocracy. But we must be cautious of wishful thinking on that score. A great deal more experimentation still needs to be done before any valid conclusions can be reached.

7. **Those who disagree with group decisions are free to express their discontent, even though they may have to abide by the decision.** At first glance, this would not seem to be a very significant value. As Henry D. Thoreau so aptly put it:

> How can a man be satisfied to entertain an opinion merely, and enjoy *it*? Is there any enjoyment in it, if his opinion is that he is aggrieved? [6]

The answer intended by Thoreau's rhetorical question is obviously, "No!" Unfortunately for Thoreau's argument, the scientifically accurate answer is, "Yes!" Any modern psychologist would agree that, even if you do not have the slightest chance of persuading anyone else to change, there is still inherent value in expressing your grievances, in "blowing off steam," in "letting the other guy know how you feel," and thus giving *yourself* an emotional catharsis.

8. **There is no particular virtue in social unity unless it has been achieved through diversity and is constantly subject to the ever-changing pressures of individual differences.** Without doubt the greatest single value in democratic leadership is that it not only *allows* for differences of opinion, but it is *at all times open to the possibility of change* as a result of these expressions of difference. This principle is expressed in a motto which all of us carry around on every piece of money in our pockets, but which few of us fully appreciate — E *pluribus unum* — "Out of many, one." The real significance of this motto lies in the fact that variety is not only the spice of life — it is the source of all human progress. Many a dic-

[6] Thoreau, Henry D., "Civil Disobedience," *The Writings of Henry D. Thoreau*, Riverside Edition. Boston: Houghton Mifflin, 1898, Vol. X, p. 144.

tator, from Caesar to Hitler, has sought and achieved the "great goal" of absolute conformance and unity, only to discover that it is a hollow triumph. A society which tolerates no diversity, which insists that everyone be stamped from the same mold, is bound to be static. How can any changes take place if the group is unanimously content with the *status quo* and the leader guarantees that no one will challenge it? How can progress be made if no one holds an opinion which is contrary to the prevailing customs, laws, and mores? The more a society succeeds in eliminating its so-called foreign elements and in silencing the voices of dissent, the more it tends to stagnate and eventually rot away.

There is danger that we in the United States are beginning to ignore the principle of *E pluribus unum*. We are developing a stereotyped concept of what constitutes a "good American." We are intolerant of those who do not fit into our pattern and we apply all sorts of subtle social pressures to cause them to conform. This tendency is a second-rate imitation of the Soviet technique for "disciplining" those who deviate from the party line. We must reverse the trend before it becomes a national mania. More leadership of the democratic type, providing hearty encouragement for the democratic processes of discussion and debate, is at least a partial answer to this challenge.

There are understandable reasons why this pressure for conformity exists. A group or society can be so torn by differences and dissension as to become paralyzed and immobile. In order to take any action a group must *agree*, at least for the time being, on one policy. The problem is to strike a proper balance between unity and diversity. The sub-title of Bertrand Russell's recent book, *Authority and the Individual*, states the question most succinctly:

> How can we combine the degree of individual initiative necessary for progress with the degree of social cohesion necessary for survival?

It is interesting to note that pressures for conformity exist with respect to personal behavior as well as social action. Most of us agree that an individual whose behavior deviates widely from the norm is a case for a mental institution. But here too we must strike a balance between conformity and deviation. We can go too far in pressurizing people to become "normal" and "adjusted" to their society. That this is apparent to some writers is evidenced by the title of a recent book, *Be Glad You're Neurotic.*[7]

9. **The method of making social decisions is as important as the decisions themselves, inasmuch as means are inseparable from ends.** The democratic leader does not believe, as the autocrat usually does, that a "good end" justifies any means of achieving it. Rather, he believes with Ralph Waldo Emerson that "The ends pre-exist in the means." That is to say, society's achievements are themselves influenced by the methods of their attainment. A "good" society cannot be attained by "evil" methods any more than real love or friendship can be bought. We often hear it said that since the autocratic leader can get things done more efficiently we ought to let him handle the situation. We hear it said that the expert knows what is best, so why not let him make the decisions. We hear all sorts of non-democratic political systems, particularly Communism, defended on the grounds that they simply seek a better life for all the people — and that such unpleasant things as one-party elections, secret police, and violence are necessary evils which must be accepted for the sake of accomplishing the "greater good."

Those who understand the philosophy of democracy believe that means and ends are inseparable. They believe that our methods of making decisions are as valuable as the decisions themselves because they are, in reality, an integral part of the decisions. Democracy is open-minded about everything but open-mindedness, and on that it insists absolutely. It cannot tolerate the abandonment of democratic methods, for it is the methods that are the heart of democracy and democracy does not believe in committing suicide.

LIMITATIONS OF DEMOCRATIC LEADERSHIP

We believe that the case presented here for democratic leadership (which is, by implication, a case against authoritarianism) is a powerful one. It is our belief that it thoroughly justifies democratic

[7] Bisch, Louis E., *Be Glad You're Neurotic.* New York: McGraw-Hill, 1946.

methods wherever they can reasonably be applied, and we suspect that this includes millions of situations where democratic leadership is not now practiced. It is our hope that through an explanation of democratic techniques, as provided in this book, and through training in their use this growth may take place.

Let us not, however, allow our enthusiasm to blind us to the limitations of democracy. This is a common tendency with people who think they have discovered a cure-all for the world's problems. They fail, or refuse, to recognize the possible shortcomings of their philosophy. Perhaps this is because there are so many other people who would regard any admission of weaknesses as a sign of total inadequacy. It is all part of our cultural conditioning which causes us to see things in terms of black and white, and which leads us to seek a perfection and a finality which simply do not exist anywhere in the real world. For these reasons, and because we are so firmly convinced of the essential validity of the democratic concept of leadership, we hesitate to discuss its limitations. Nevertheless, we are compelled to do so by our equally firm conviction that, in the long run, a theory will be stronger rather than weaker, by virtue of the recognition of its imperfections.

In an earlier chapter, it was stated that neither the authoritarian or democratic philosophies is sufficient unto itself — that neither is an unmixed blessing or an unmixed evil. We also learned that the two philosophies are not isolated opposites, but that there are connecting bridges across which one concept shades by degrees into the other. As we move now to explore the limitations of purely democratic leadership, we shall find that the gaps which are left can and should be filled by various degrees and types of authoritarian leadership. As we take up each limitation, we shall point out the types of leadership it requires.

The Fact of Inequality

Democracy, it will be remembered, is based upon the assumption that no member of the group is superior to the others. One vote is as good as another because it is believed that all men are created equal and that each human being has an equal right to make the decisions which affect his life. To recognize that, in fact, men are not equal in education, intelligence, or maturity is not necessarily to deny that each man is the best guardian of his own interests. It is simply to recognize that although men may be equal in rights, they are not equal in ability nor in the physical and mental contribution which they are able to make to the group. To say that every individual, from the moron to the genius, is valued and respected as a human being, does not require that we place an equal value upon the contributions made by each. Yet democracy, *carried to its extreme,* would do just that. It would imply that the competent should share leadership equally with the incompetent. It would insist that the views of the student are as valid as the views of the teacher, and that the judgment of experts is no better than the judgment of the common man.

To admit the superior judgment of the teacher or expert is to admit that authoritarianism has a legitimate role in our lives, and unless we are fools this is precisely what we will do. We do not have the time in one life-span to experience everything for ourselves, to create everything for ourselves, or to struggle through all of life's problems without benefit of what other men have learned before us. The one fact which makes mankind capable of a degree of progress unknown to lower animals is that he can record his experiences and pass them on to others who can take up where he left off without retracing his steps. To do this is to accept what he tells us — to accept it on his *authority.* Of course, this can be carried too far. Wise parents recognize that although they should help their children to avoid foolish mistakes, some lessons are best learned or only learned by personal experience.

Much of the conflict over so-called progressive education centers around this point. There is little doubt that the progressive educators are right when they insist that traditional education is far more authoritarian than it should be — that only through more participation by the student and less by the teacher will anything enduring be learned. However, there is also little doubt that democracy in education, carried to an extreme, would soon reduce us to a nation of eagerly participating nincompoops. To place as high a value on mediocrity as on talent is to discourage the genius and make a fetish of equality.

If in any social unit differences of ability are extreme, attempts to operate democratically are likely to degenerate into a sham and mockery of democratic processes. The uneducated and unintelligent will be manipulated, under a cloak of seemingly democratic procedures, by clever leaders who seek to control the situation. Far better in these circumstances that we should openly recognize and admit the need for an authoritarian instructor-type of leadership — the expert, the trainer, the teacher, the counsellor, the coach, the doctor, the lawyer.

Democratic leadership assumes intellectual and emotional maturity on the part of the members of the group. There is no real democracy, nor can there be democratic leadership, when there are members of the group who cannot read or write, who cannot think for themselves, or who, having thought, cannot give adequate expression to their ideas. Either those who are capable must take over the reins of oligarchic leadership, or the society will die of inertia and stupidity.

The Abstract Nature of Social Policies

Decisions which are made by the democratic processes of discussion, debate, and vote-taking are *verbal* agreements (policies, laws, etc.) arrived at by people *talking* together. This is the only way we have ever discovered for putting the democratic philosophy into practice. But anyone who understands the basic principles of semantics knows that there is a tremendous gap between the "world of words" and the "world of actions." We may agree verbally to an abstract idea that disabled war veterans should be provided with free homes by the government, but along comes concrete case number one — G.I. Joe who lost his little finger opening a keg of beer at Fort Sheridan, Illinois on V-J day. Is he a disabled veteran? And, what is a home? Is it a four-room cottage in the city or an eight-room house in the suburbs? Obviously all these specific questions cannot be anticipated and settled by those who draw up the nation's policies.

Even in a small lodge or fraternity the policies which are agreed upon verbally in democratic meetings under democratic leadership do not automatically provide an answer to every specific question which arises. It may be agreed that twenty-five dollars should be spent for stationery, but the group as a whole will not be convened at the corner bookstore to select a particular brand of paper. It may also be agreed that excessive drunkenness will not be tolerated at the organization's parties — but you can be certain that a meeting of the lodge will not be called halfway through a barn dance to determine whether Brother Jackson is so inebriated as to warrant being sent home. Decisions such as these must be left to the society's *executive* and *judicial* leaders. These are persons who have the *authority,* in specific cases, to apply and interpret the general policies which have been determined by the group. An organization which attempts to discuss, debate and settle democratically every move that it makes will soon die of sheer exhaustion. Clearly then, democratic leadership should not be expected to function at every level of human behavior. Judicial leaders are those to whom we delegate authority for deciding how our general policies apply to concrete cases. Executive leaders are those to whom we delegate authority for carrying out the specific aspects of our policies. In either instance, the leaders operate in an authoritarian manner, even though their authority may have been derived in a democratic way, and may be subject to democratic review.

The Tyranny of Indecision

Dictators and majorities are not the only tyrants to which a society may succumb. If it attempts to carry democratic methods to an extreme, it may become victimized by the tyranny of indecision. To debate an issue fully and fairly and arrive at a democratic decision by majority vote is a time-consuming process. One needs only to observe the pace at which legislation grinds through Congress for verification of this point. This is nothing, however, compared to the time consumed in informal discussion where there are no time limitations on the right to speak, and where decisions by unanimous consent rather than majority vote are sought. The leader who operates in these situations may sometimes find his organization seriously threatened by the tyranny of indecision. Action must be taken immediately, but the group members cannot or will not make up their minds as to what they want to do. In the true open-minded spirit of democracy the members of the group want to talk about the problem some more, or wait until more of the facts are available. Commendable as this attitude may be, if the building is on fire we cannot devote too much time to a discussion of how best to put the fire out. The leader may have to short-circuit the democratic process in order to take swift and arbitrary action. Thus he begins to bark orders and becomes an authoritarian of the *executive* type.

The inability of group members to make up their minds on an issue or to feel a need for action also makes necessary another type of semi-authoritarian leader, the *advocate*. This is the type of leader who, having come to a decision on a problem, thinks it would be well for others to feel the same way, and so sets out to persuade them to his point of view. If, in order to gain acceptance of his views, it becomes necessary to short-circuit rational processes and stimulate the emotions, most advocate leaders will not shrink from so doing. They will defend their methods, as does the authoritarian, on the grounds that the end justifies the means. In moments of crisis, this may well be so. Persuasion may be the only way to secure action, and action may be essential.

Individualism — The Unwillingness to Conform

It may seem strange to the reader to find individualism listed as a limitation of democracy. Ordinarily we think of democracy and individualism not only as being compatible but as being practically the same. We hear the democratic way of life praised by Fourth of July orators *because* of the individualism it champions.

While it is true enough that democracy permits far more individualism than does a totalitarian society, we must face the fact that democracy is still a form of social organization, and that all social organizations — regardless of their structure — inevitably impose limits on the individual and require some degree of social conformance. If an individual is to work or live with other people he sooner or later has to submerge some of his personal interests and desires to the interests and needs of the group. In the last analysis, individual decision and social decision, individual action and social action, are opposed to one another. Thus it is that democracy may block individuality and, by the same token, that individualism or unwillingness to conform may block democratic action. Any type of leadership, whether democratic or not, will eventually be faced with the problem of an individual who refuses to conform to social decisions. This is a particularly severe trial for democratic leadership, since pure democracy assumes the willingness of group members to abide by the group's decisions and to conform to them voluntarily. This assumption is not always warranted. The most obvious exception is a criminal, who must be brought into line by authority and force exercised through executive and judicial leaders.

The criminal, however, is not the only one, nor the most important one, to concern us here. What about the individual who feels that certain areas of his life over which the group claims jurisdiction are too sacred to be submitted to the control of others? What if his differences or dissents from the group are too great to be compromised or integrated? What of the Henry D. Thoreaus who say:

> I think that we should be men first and subjects afterward.
> It is not desirable to cultivate a respect for the law, so much
> as for the right. The only obligation which I have a right to
> assume is to do at any time what I think right. . . . A wise man
> will not leave the right to the mercy of chance, nor wish it to
> prevail through the power of the majority. There is but little
> virtue in the action of masses of men. . . . Unjust laws exist:
> shall we be content to obey them, or shall we endeavor to
> amend them, and obey them until we have succeeded, or shall
> we transgress them at once? Men generally, under such a
> government as this, think that they ought to wait until they
> have persuaded the majority to alter them. . . . If the injustice
> is of such a nature that it requires you to be the agent of
> injustice to another, then, I say, break the law. . . . The
> authority of government . . . can have no pure right over my
> person and my property but what I concede to it. . . .[8]

[8] Thoreau, *op. cit.*, pp. 134–46.

In the face of such an attitude as this, democratic leadership is impossible. Either the dissenter must be permitted to go his own way or an authoritarian leader must force him to conform. The latter course of action should be undertaken only after careful consideration — even if the leader's authority is derived from a majority of the group. As Bertrand Russell warns:

> Those who believe that the voice of the people is the voice of God may infer that any unusual opinion or peculiar taste is almost a form of impiety, and is to be viewed as a culpable rebellion against the legitimate authority of the herd. This will only be avoided if liberty is as much valued as democracy, and it is realized that a society in which each is the slave of all is only a little better than one in which each is the slave of a despot. There is equality where all are slaves, as well as where all are free. This shows that equality, by itself, is not enough to make a good society.[9]

In assessing the inadequacies of democratic leadership, therefore, we must recognize that there are people who, habitually or with respect to only certain issues, have a greater interest in maintaining their own point of view than in preserving the existence of the group. Such is sometimes the case in labor-management disputes where the company would just as soon go out of business as to operate under conditions it does not like. It is also true of families who would rather move than adjust their differences with the neighbors. Social units such as these cannot be held together democratically. They must break up or be held together by force.

Chester Barnard has suggested that unless certain conditions are met in a society, the problem of non-conformity will be so great that democratic procedures are impossible. The conditions Barnard sets out are: first, that the members of the group not be too divergent in basic attitudes; second, that certain fundamental rights (such as religious beliefs) be excepted from social control; and

---

[9] Reprinted from *Authority and the Individual*, pp. 48–49, by permission of Simon and Schuster, Publishers. Copyright, 1949, by Bertrand Russell. Permission for rights outside of the U.S.A. granted by George Allen & Unwin Ltd., London.

third, that the desire to maintain the social unit at any cost of personal interest be held by every member of the group.[10]

The Obstacle of Numbers

In discussing limitation number two, it was pointed out that truly democratic decisions can be arrived at only by people *talking together*. Our emphasis in point two was on the word "talking," and on the limitations imposed by the verbal, hence abstract, nature of social policies. Our concern here is with the word "together." Democratic leadership, in its purest form, is only applicable in *face-to-face* situations where all members of the group are able to participate and express themselves fully. Almost all of the values of democratic leadership set forth in this chapter assume a universally participating group, and cannot be achieved in any other way.

But there is a physical limit to the number of people who can work together conveniently at one time. Two thousand people meeting together in convention at the Chicago Stadium cannot possibly operate with the degree of democracy available in a hotel room to a discussion group of ten. The citizenry of many American cities cannot meet together at all because no gathering place is large enough to hold them. Even if there were such a place, the personal contacts could hardly be described as face-to-face.

The obstacle of numbers can be overcome only by compromising with democracy. We have done this in the United States, England and other "democracies" through the representative system, wherein a *spokesman-leader* is designated to represent the interests of a small group in an assembly of delegates from other small groups. This assembly, or legislature, may itself operate democratically *so far as the delegates are concerned*, but it can hardly be said that the common citizen has as much voice in his government as has the Congressman who represents him — and also represents 300,000 others. The representative system would be more democratic than it usually is if the representative actually came from face-to-face groups in the first place. Even that, however, would not solve the

[10] Barnard, Chester, *Dilemmas of Leadership in the Democratic Process*. Princeton: Princeton University Press, 1939.

problem, for if the leader were completely bound by his group's decisions (like the Russian delegates to the U.N.) he could not operate open-mindedly in the larger assembly. If he was not so bound, his own opinions and reactions would become more important than those of any member of his group. This is an irreconcilable dilemma. It would seem that the advocates of decentralization and of the "back to small communities" movement in our country are correct in their assumption that such a program is necessary if we wish to achieve a greater degree of democracy than we now have.

These are the limitations of democratic leadership. We do not hide them nor apologize for them. We simply recognize them as inevitable barriers — as boundaries beyond which the democratic philosophy of leadership is inapplicable and is, in fact, dangerous. This does not lessen our faith in its validity within the areas where it is appropriate, nor does it lessen our enthusiasm for extending and promoting its use.

TYPES OF LEADERSHIP

Through our discussion of the limitations inherent in democratic leadership, we have come to realize the necessary role of various kinds of authoritarianism. It will be helpful at this point to review all of the types of leadership that have been discussed and to perceive them in relationship to one another. We now have five categories, ranging from complete authoritarianism to complete democracy.

The Executive

The function of the executive-leader, or administrator, is to translate verbal policies into action. He directs and supervises the behavior of a society of subordinates. He makes specific decisions and orders their execution. He is purely and simply an autocrat. Books may be written, and there are dozens of them,[11] concerning

[11] See Whitehead, T. N., *Leadership in a Free Society*, Cambridge: Harvard University Press, 1936, and Hannaford, Earle S., *Conference Leadership in Business and Industry*, New York: McGraw-Hill, 1945, for two of the better ones.

ways and means of making administrative leadership palatable to the led — like asking an employee, "Don't you think it would be a good idea to do so-and-so?" rather than telling him to do it outright. But making it pleasant and clothing it in the garments of democracy — like holding a conference to get an idea across — does not make it democratic. Decisions are made above and carried out below, and when they are not the process can no longer be described as an executive function.

Executive or administrative leadership is a commonplace and a necessity in many areas of society. The leadership in our military establishments is almost entirely of the executive type. Likewise, in the administrative branches of our federal, state, and local governments executive functions are required. Schools and colleges of public administration like the Maxwell School of Public Administration at Syracuse University have been set up to train men specifically for these tasks. The bulk of our business and industrial structure depends upon administrative leadership, and we have schools of business administration, like that at Harvard University, as well as training courses for foremen to prepare leaders for jobs in this area. Educational, charitable, and other public service institutions often call upon experts for administrative leadership within the organization. For example, a man trained in medical administration will be summoned as director of a hospital, or a man trained in academic leadership (or even military!) will be made president of a university. Since the executive leader, commanding officer, or "group compellor" (as he has been called) has extensive functions which require specialized training, and which constitute an entire field of study in themselves, we will no longer focus our attention upon him here.[12]

The Judge

The leader as judge, or arbitrator, is an ancient and respected character. References to this function in the Bible are legion; as a matter of fact, in Biblical times most tribal leaders were called

[12] An excellent book in this field which we recommend to the reader is Chester I. Barnard's *The Functions of the Executive.* Cambridge: Harvard University Press, 1948.

Judges. In modern society, judicial responsibilities, at least officially, rest in the hands of an especially qualified and designated group of leaders, known collectively as the courts (or, in another area, the corps of baseball umpires). But nearly every person in a position of leadership in any social unit, large or small, is called upon at one time or another to function as a judge. Mother or Father has to settle the quarrel between Johnny and Jimmy by telling one to play with the red car and the other the green car. The office manager has to arbitrate a conflict between Ethel and Mildred as to who is going to take care of the files between G and P. The leader as judge is an autocrat. For regardless of whether his power has been conferred upon him by the parties to the conflict — as in the case of the voluntary arbitration of labor disputes — or by an outside authority, his decision is absolute. The only appeal available is to another judge — another autocrat.

The Advocate

The leader as advocate, "partisan," propagandist, charismatic spokesman, or "mobilizer of public opinion," is an extremely important agent in any society. He may operate as the advocate of an idea within a social unit or he may represent that unit as "group exponent" and spokesman before the rest of the world. The advocate is the kind of leader who often inspires men and around whom legends grow. Frequently he is a colorful person and almost always a master of the spoken word. Often he is a social pioneer, fighting for causes that are new and changes that people feel must come. If he is alone in his advocacy and far ahead of the crowd, he tends to become the incarnate symbol of the idea for which he stands. Such leaders were Moses, Jesus, Mohammed, Martin Luther, John Wesley, and Mohandas Gandhi. Such also were Lincoln, Lenin, Winston Churchill, and Franklin D. Roosevelt. Such leaders today, on a lesser scale, are men like Robert A. Taft, Norman Thomas, Walter Reuther, and John L. Lewis — all men closely associated with a cause. But advocate-leaders are not found in national life alone. The little man who stands up in the city council and demands, on behalf of the Negro population, that public housing be non-discriminatory is functioning as an advocate. The college boy who leads a rally in praise of the prowess of the football team is an advocate-leader. The preacher who exhorts his congregation to love its neighbors, the "Grand Dragon" of a lynch mob, and the salesman who advocates "Ipana for the smile of beauty," are all advocate-leaders. Each of these people has a belief that he feels others should share, and he deliberately sets out to persuade them to accept it. To that extent all advocates are authoritarian. But beyond that point the similarity among advocates ends, for there are some who will stop at no means to achieve their goals, whereas others have sufficient respect for human dignity to refuse to employ such persuasive techniques as manipulation of facts and exploitation of emotions even though they know that those techniques may work.

It seems to us that this distinction among advocates parallels some of the differences between the authoritarian and democratic viewpoints which have been stated earlier. Since the autocratically-inclined advocate is convinced that his program is good for the followers and must be accepted by them, he will not very likely hesitate to use whatever means of persuasion are available for the accomplishment of his ends. The democratically-oriented advocate may be just as firmly convinced of his own views as the autocrat, but he recognizes the right of each man to make his own choices. He will try to convince others that he is right, but he is more likely than the autocrat to do so with methods that are compatible with preserving the integrity of the individual to whom his persuasion is directed. To him the means are as valuable as the ends. He will hesitate knowingly to distort facts or to exploit the fears, loves, and hatreds of his followers in the manner that a lynch-mob leader does not hesitate to do.

Although he is of immeasurable importance in any democratic society, we do not discuss the advocate-leader any further in this text. There are many excellent books on the subject, and we refer the reader to these.[13]

[13] Aristotle, *The Rhetoric*. Trans. Lane Cooper. New York: Appleton-Century-Crofts, Inc., 1932; Whately, Richard, *The Elements of Rhetoric*. London:

The Expert

The leader as expert, instructor or information-giver, is in a special position in relation to the social unit with which he works. He is presumably more learned than the members of the group. His leadership rests upon that assumption and that assumption alone. He retains, or should retain, leadership only by virtue of that fact, and only in those areas where it is a fact. Included in this category are the teachers, social group workers, lecturers, doctors, lawyers and others whose positions of influence are attained and maintained because they have knowledge to give to others.

Much has been written in the last few years, particularly for teachers and for group leaders in social work, about making their leadership democratic. It is for the most part excellent material, and many of the ideas expressed in this book are based upon it. Teachers and social workers can and should use democratic procedures wherever appropriate and possible. There is a factor, however, which makes it impossible for the expert, *as such,* to be democratic, and which even makes it difficult for him to shift from the instructor to discussion leader role. It lies in the very relationship that makes one an instructor-leader — namely, the fact that he has more knowledge than the members of the group and that his essential function is to enlighten the group. His very reason for existence is that "he knows and they don't know," — in short, that he is an authority. This, then, cannot possibly be a unit which is self-governing, in which all the members of the group are equally represented in the making of decisions.

As one writer points out, no man or woman can be truly democratic as a leader who is not completely convinced that his group, as a whole, is wiser than he.[14] To buttress the point further another

B. Fellowes, 1841; Phillips, Arthur E., *Effective Speaking.* Chicago: Newton Co., 1908; Hollingworth, H. L., *The Psychology of the Audience.* New York: American Book Co., 1935; Sarett, Lew, and W. T. Foster, *Basic Principles of Speech.* Boston: Houghton Mifflin, 1946.

[14] Cooper, Alfred M., *How to Conduct Conferences.* New York: McGraw-Hill, 1942, Chapter 1.

man, widely experienced in observing face-to-face leadership in action is quoted as saying that:

> Those who have had the hardest time to become good discussion leaders were those who have the cards stacked against them by their previous training — ex-teachers and ex-ministers.

He goes on to say of *other* people that:

> Society has never provided them with tidy, waiting audiences all lined up in neat rows . . . Teachers and ministers, on the other hand, have been trained to meet audiences that come together at stated times and places for the precise purpose of listening.[15]

Let us, then, applaud and encourage all efforts of the instructor-leader to operate democratically. But let us also remember that his function as teacher is basically not a democratic process, and that authoritarian techniques will be required.[16]

The Discussion Leader

The individual who completely fulfills the criteria of democratic leadership is the person who assumes the role of discussion leader. When the executive turns to democratic methods, he is no longer an executive but a discussion leader. When the teacher turns to democratic methods, he is no longer an expert but a leader of discussion. Free discussion is the only process we know in which "the group as a whole is self-governing and in which all members of the group are equally represented in the making of decisions." It is through discussion that a leader can release the creative talents of the members of a group, help them to solve their own problems, and reach their own decisions. It is through discussion that the nine values of democratic leadership presented in this chapter may be attained.

V   V   V

[15] Overstreet, Harry A., and Bonaro W. Overstreet, *Leaders for Adult Education.* New York: American Association for Adult Education, 1941, p. 72. Reprinted by permission.

[16] We recommend for those readers especially interested in instructor-leadership Jacques Barzun's *Teacher in America.* Boston: Little, Brown, 1944.

It should now be apparent why authoritarianism and democracy are both necessary in any society. It should be obvious that a leader, whether he be called by the title of president, chairman, director, dean, or supervisor may at various times be called upon to fulfill any of the five leadership roles described above. They are not self-sufficient categories. They supplement each other. When we, in this book, focus our attention on the discussion leader, it is not because we feel that the others are unnecessary, but rather because we have so much more to learn about this type of leadership. It is in the area of democratic group leadership that we are the most deficient. It is here, if democracy is to meet the challenges of the twentieth century, that we need the greatest increase in skill.

SUMMARY

We have identified nine values of democratic leadership: (1) people fully understand only those ideas they have helped to formulate; (2) group decisions receive more support than autocratic edicts; (3) democratic leadership draws upon all available human resources; (4) it creates self-reliant individuals; (5) it builds a self-sustaining group; (6) it may lead to higher morale; (7) it provides an emotional catharsis for dissenters; (8) it allows for differences, hence progress; and (9) it has inherent value as a method.

We have also discussed five categories of limitations on democratic leadership: (1) the fact of inequality; (2) the abstract nature of social policies; (3) the tyranny of indecision; (4) individualism — the unwillingness to conform; and (5) the obstacle of numbers. These limitations have led us to recognize the need in any society for a combination of five types of leadership: (1) the executive; (2) the judge; (3) the advocate; (4) the expert; and (5) the discussion leader.

Inasmuch as our society is most deficient in the skills of democratic leadership, and since that is the direction in which we hope to move, it is necessary that we proceed as rapidly as we can to acquire the understandings and techniques that will help to make group leadership and democratic action effective.

EXERCISES

1. The President of the United States is usually referred to as the nation's chief executive. Is that term accurate as a description of his function in our society?
2. Does the King of England fit into any of the five categories outlined here? If so, which one? If not, is he then not a leader?
3. Organize a small group discussion with yourself as the leader. Without telling the members of the group what you are doing, try out three styles of leadership — autocratic, democratic, and laissez-faire (doing nothing) — each for about fifteen minutes. Note the reactions of the group.
4. It is widely advocated in educational circles these days that the discussion process be used more extensively in the classroom, and that the instructor become more of a discussion leader. Discuss the advantages and disadvantages of this proposal.
5. Do you agree with Chester Barnard's idea referred to in this chapter, that a society cannot function democratically if the members of the group have exceedingly divergent attitudes? Isn't a democracy supposed to be a place where people can hold different views? Discuss.
6. You are the president of an organization. An election for a new treasurer is coming up. You feel very strongly and sincerely that Member X is most deserving of the position. He is a capable, hard worker and has the best interests of the group at heart. None of the other likely candidates can compare with him. X is a very frank and honest person — much less diplomatic than you are. As a result he has antagonized many members of the group who do not respond favorably to such straightforward behavior. You know that by using your personal influence, doing some politicking in the right places, you can swing the election in favor of X. You also know that if you do not engage in any manipulations X will lose the election. You are troubled by the question: Does the end justify the means in this case? What should you do? Discuss.
7. "That a wise social policy will establish areas of privacy for individuals . . . within the society is undoubtedly true. . . . But

the determination of the proper boundaries of these areas must, in an interdependent society, be based on a collective judgment." [17]

This statement appears to be in direct conflict with the viewpoint of Thoreau which was referred to in this chapter. With which of these approaches do you agree? Discuss.

[17] Benne, Kenneth D., "Democratic Ethics in Social Engineering," *Progressive Education*, XXVI (May, 1949), 204–07.

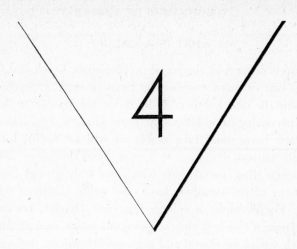

The Dynamics of a Group

BEFORE A DEMOCRATIC LEADER CAN BEGIN to operate effectively, he must understand his group. He must understand the dynamic forces at work within its structure. Intuition and old-fashioned common sense are helpful, and often amazingly discerning, but not always enough to provide him with the kind of knowledge he should have. The dynamics of any group are highly complex, and require scientific study to be fully comprehended. Those social scientists who are today exploring the field of group dynamics are pioneers in a relatively undeveloped area. Nevertheless, many worth-while insights have already been achieved which it will profit the would-be leader to understand.[1]

---

[1] This chapter is not intended as an extensive survey of theories and findings in the fields of group dynamics or social psychology. For more thorough analyses the reader is referred to: Allport, Floyd H., *Social Psychology*. Boston: Houghton Mifflin, 1924; Bales, Robert F., *Interaction Process Analysis*. Cambridge: Addison-Wesley Press, 1950; Benne, Kenneth, and

WHAT IS A GROUP?

A group is defined by the social psychologists, Krech and Crutch-field, as "two or more people who bear an explicit psychological relationship to one another." [2] In order for people to have an explicit psychological relationship some kind of interaction on a face-to-face basis must take place. It will be useful for us to accept this narrow definition of a group, and thus draw a distinction between those social units which are truly groups and those where many of the members have only indirect contact with one another. For example, a college fraternity chapter, an air force combat crew, a baseball club, a girl scout troop, or a construction crew each would be considered a group. However, the American Federation of Labor, the citizenry of Texas, the employees of General Electric, or the student body of Northwestern University would be considered societies or organizations but not groups. Small groups have many features in common with broader social organizations, but there are also significant differences. We are concerned, in the remainder of this book, primarily with small groups — in the narrow sense. We are interested in larger societies only in so far as they are similar to groups.

There is another distinction that should be made. A collection of human beings who are *physically together* in the same place at the same time do not necessarily constitute a group. The definition requires that there be a psychological relationship — interaction — of some sort. This distinction might be illustrated in any college class that is conducted by the discussion method. Before class begins on the first day of the fall term there is simply a collection

Bozidar Muntyan, *Human Relations in Curriculum Change.* Illinois Secondary School Curriculum Program Bulletin No. 7, June, 1949; Krech, David, and Richard S. Crutchfield, *Theory and Problems of Social Psychology.* New York: McGraw-Hill, 1948; Sherif, Muzafer, and Hadley Cantril, *The Psychology of Ego-Involvements.* New York: Wiley, 1947; Newcomb, Theodore, Eugene Hartley, *et al., Readings in Social Psychology.* New York: Holt, 1947; Thelen, Herbert, "Educational Dynamics: Theory and Research," *Journal of Social Issues,* VI (1950), No. 2; and Wilson, Gertrude, and Gladys Ryland, *Social Group Work Practice.* Boston: Houghton Mifflin, 1949.

[2] Krech and Crutchfield, *op. cit.,* p. 18.

of twenty human beings in a room. A few know each other; most do not. One individual has his mind on fraternity rushing, another has his mind on an attractive brunette in the third row, and another is, psychologically, still on summer vacation. The professor enters the room and begins to speak. All the students are now responding in some way to the same stimulus. Psychological interaction has begun and the class has started to become a group. After a few discussions, each student will begin to have feelings about the others — positive, negative or indifferent. Leadership patterns and sub-groupings will begin to emerge. Eventually members of the class will use the term "we" to refer to themselves. What was formerly a mere collection of human beings has now become a group. It is difficult to draw a clean line which indicates exactly where a collection of individuals leaves off and a group begins. "Groupness," like almost everything else in the world, is a matter of degree.

Perhaps the reader will find the following definition helpful in summing up the limits within which we propose to work in dealing with the problems of group leadership.

> A small group is defined as any number of persons engaged in interaction with each other in a single face-to-face meeting or series of such meetings, in which each member receives some impression or perception of each other member distinct enough so that he can, either at the time or in later questioning, give some reaction to each of the others as an individual person, even though it be only to recall that the other was present.[3]

Inasmuch as speech is the basic medium through which interaction takes place, it might further be pointed out that we will be concerned primarily with "talking" groups.

WHY DO GROUPS EXIST?

There is one basic reason why groups exist. It is because each and every member believes that he can fulfill some need or needs

[3] From Bales, Robert F., *Interaction Process Analysis* by permission of Addison-Wesley Press, Inc., publishers. Copyright, 1950, P. 33.

in collaboration with other people that he cannot fulfill by himself. It follows, then, that a member will remain in a group only so long as he believes it more advantageous for him to stay in than to leave. The boy or girl who joins a college fraternity or sorority, or who participates in extracurricular activities, does so because he derives some kind of satisfaction from them. He remains an active member only so long as his needs continue to be fulfilled. The same is true of Kiwanis, Rotary, Lions, and the P.T.A. This principle applies not only in voluntary groups, but *to some extent* in nonvoluntary groups as well. Take the military service as an example. The individual whose needs to be out of the group are stronger than his needs to be in may become a conscientious objector, may go A.W.O.L., may get himself captured by the enemy, or, if his psychic needs are powerful enough, may even acquire a neurosis or psychosomatic illness which gains him a medical discharge. The belief, sometimes attributed to dictators, that the individual exists for the state rather than the state for the individual, may be an interesting verbalization but in fact is relatively meaningless. Even the most ruthless tyrants have known that they could survive on a permanent basis only so long as their followers were kept fairly well satisfied.

Most psychologists and sociologists have now abandoned the old concept of a "group-mind." When we consider group behavior we must always remember that the phenomena we are discussing have had their origin in individuals and will have their ultimate effect upon individuals.[4] This does not mean that interaction among individuals is unimportant or that the leader need not study group phenomena. On the contrary, he must study them and learn them

[4] For a full, competent, and interesting treatment of this theme see Allport, Floyd H., *Institutional Behavior*. Chapel Hill: University of North Carolina Press, 1933. Allport's view is also well summed up in another place (*Social Psychology*. Boston: Houghton Mifflin, 1924, p. 4), as follows: "There is no psychology of groups which is not essentially and entirely a psychology of individuals. Social psychology must not be placed in contradistinction to the psychology of the individual; *it is a part of the psychology of the individual*, whose behavior it studies in relation to that sector of his environment comprised by his fellows. His biological needs are the ends toward which his social behavior is a developed means. Within his organism are provided all the mechanisms by which social behavior is explained."

well. But he must at the same time guard against the temptation to think of his group as a living, breathing organism with a heart and soul of its own. One often hears people talk about the "spirit of a group" as though it were something different from the spirit of the individuals who make up the group. Although it is true that individuals may behave quite differently under group conditions — such as those of a lynch mob — than they would singly, nonetheless it is still the individual who is doing the behaving. Bertrand Russell does a good job of pointing up the "group-mind" fallacy:

> When it is said that a nation is an organism, an analogy is being used which may be dangerous if its limitations are not recognized. Men . . . are organisms in a strict sense: whatever good or evil befalls a man befalls *him* as a single person, not this or that part of him. If I have a toothache or pain in my toe, it is *I* that have the pain, and it would not exist if no nerves connected the part concerned with my brain. But when a farmer in Herefordshire is caught in a blizzard, it is not the government in London that feels cold. That is why the individual man is the bearer of good and evil, and not any collection of men. To believe that there can be good or evil in a collection of human beings, over and above the good or evil in the various individuals, is an error.[5]

TYPES OF GROUPS

We have said that groups exist for the sole purpose of fulfilling the needs of the persons who compose them. Generally speaking, individuals join "talking groups" to satisfy two kinds of needs — the need to learn from others and the need to act with others.

The need to learn from others, to share with them our ideas and feelings, to achieve a better understanding of the people and the world about us — this need provides the motivation for what we call *learning groups*. The need to cooperate with others in making decisions and in planning work which we are incapable of handling alone provides the motivation for what we call *action groups*.

[5] Reprinted from *Authority and the Individual*, pp. 73–74, by permission of Simon and Schuster, Publishers. Copyright, 1949, by Bertrand Russell. Permission for rights outside of the U.S.A. granted by George Allen & Unwin Ltd.. London.

These two types of motivation are very different. As a result, the goal of a pure learning group is not the same as that of a pure action group. The purpose of a learning group is *individual growth* — an enlargement of the insights and abilities of group members. The aim of an action group is *group productivity* — getting group decisions made efficiently and taking effective united action.

Let us not oversimplify this distinction. Rarely, except in academic circles, do we find *pure* learning groups. And rarely, except in emergency situations, do we find groups dedicated solely to action with no concern for individual learning and growth. Even the most production-minded factory, or better yet, the most action-oriented college football team recognizes the need to provide for its future by giving the scrubs a chance to gain experience. Only in crucial circumstances do most groups devote themselves exclusively to productivity and forget entirely about the need to train and develop the abilities and insights of individual members.

The majority of talking groups with which we have everyday contact are, to one degree or another, concerned with both learning and action. Some, like production staff meetings, fall nearer to the action end of the line. Others, like a meeting of the local P.T.A., are closer to the learning pole of the continuum. Furthermore, the same group may, at different times, be at different points along the line. A diagram may help to clarify these relationships.

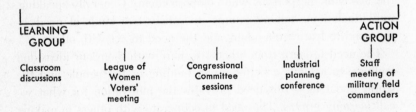

LEARNING GROUP				ACTION GROUP
Classroom discussions	League of Women Voters' meeting	Congressional Committee sessions	Industrial planning conference	Staff meeting of military field commanders

It is important that the group leader have a clear picture, at any given moment, of the relative strength of the learning and action needs of his group. As we shall see later, this consideration will often be *the* determining factor in his choice of leadership techniques.

THE INDIVIDUAL IN THE GROUP

The first question the leader should attempt to answer with respect to the individuals in his group is: Why are they here? What do they expect from their membership in this group? No one can solve this problem for him in a textbook, because it is specific to the individuals with whom he deals. We can only suggest a few generalizations.

As was said earlier, the individual is in the group because he seeks to satisfy some specific needs, and he feels that being a part of this group may help him fulfill those needs. Once he is in the group he may discover that the needs which brought him there are not satisfied, but that other unexpected advantages are gained which warrant his continuance in the unit. For instance, a worker may take a job because he thinks the prospects of regular wage increases are good. He later discovers that this was a false hope, but finds the working conditions so pleasant that he stays on. Often a group will induce new needs in its members. Students often sign up for a course in which they are not particularly interested, because they need the credit-hours, and it is the only class that fits into their time schedules. Early in such a course something may be said which stimulates their interest. They become involved in a discussion on the point. This leads to further interests. Two weeks later they are among the most eager members of the class.

In discussing the needs which bring an individual to a group and keep him there it is sometimes helpful to distinguish between those needs which are related to the avowed purposes of the group and those which are accessories or by-products. Adult education provides an interesting example. The avowed purpose of adult education groups is learning — a broadening of the individual's knowledge — and it is for that purpose that most people participate. Some of the most important results of adult education meetings, however, are by-products. Take the case of Participant A, a woman who works on an assembly line all day and looks after an ailing mother every evening. She is a rather shy person who, in her everyday life, is completely anonymous — no one pays any attention to her. One night a week she gets a chance to be with other people and derives tremendous satisfaction from that social opportunity alone, regardless of what she learns. She has an opportunity to be somebody in the group because she knows a little more about the subject than some of the others. For this individual, the by-products of group membership are more important than the central objective of the meetings.

The reader can surely name many other examples of accessory needs: the college girl who goes to school not to get an education but a husband; the man who joins a lodge or fraternity not because he is interested in the purposes of the organization but so that he can wear its insignia and show the world that he too "belongs"; the woman who works on a charity drive not because she is interested in the charity but because her friends will disapprove if she does not. Certainly these motives will influence an individual's behavior in the group, and for that reason an understanding of these needs is necessary for effective group leadership.

Involvement and Identification

The individuals in any group vary in the degree to which they are really a part of the organization and committed to achievement of the group's goals. Some are on the fringes — they are peripherally involved. Some devote the major part of their lives and thoughts to the group — they are centrally involved. The others range in between. Why are some members more involved than others? The answer is to be found again in terms of the individual's need-satisfaction. The centrally involved individuals are the ones who find satisfaction for a wide range of their needs in this group. The president of a club not only gets the benefits which go to all members of the organization, but in addition he acquires prestige, a feeling of importance, opportunities to represent the group on the outside, a certain amount of influence, a strong feeling of belongingness, etc. Is it any wonder, then, that he will be more interested and more active than the blacksheep of the outfit who is cordially disliked and much abused by all, whose opinion is not respected, and who is made to feel inferior whenever he tries to participate?

The degree to which an individual becomes involved in the activities of a group is directly proportional to the amount of "psychic income" he receives from that group.

Also correlated with these same variables is the degree to which the individual identifies himself with the group and is loyal to it. Is he proud of his organization? Does he like to let others know that he is in this group? Does he have a strong "we" feeling? Is he personally concerned about the group's success and failure? If the answer to these questions is in the affirmative, that individual is one who is centrally involved, strongly identified, and receiving a great deal of psychic income. If the answer is negative, we are dealing with a person who is peripherally involved, weakly identified, and whose psychic pay check is small.

Social Behavior

It is not possible for any leader to know too much about the psychology of personal adjustment — about what makes people behave as they do in their face-to-face contacts with other human beings. In order to be prepared to exercise effective group leadership, a man must have insight into the personality structure of those he would lead. He must understand some of the most important causes of their behavior, and must be able to predict, by some means better than guesswork, how they are likely to respond to various kinds of social stimuli.

For many years psychologists have argued the question as to whether human behavior is traceable primarily to hereditary "instincts" or to environmental conditioning. Although the problem is by no means completely settled, it is not the controversial issue that it once was. It is now agreed almost universally that while a person's heredity places certain physical and glandular limitations upon his personality structure, his environmental and cultural conditioning profoundly influences and alters his total being, particularly during the formative years of early childhood. It is also agreed that conditioning plays a smaller role with regard to physique and intelligence than it does with regard to the emotional factors in personality — namely an individual's loves, hates, and fears. Though many psychologists suspect that even these three universal emotions are, at root, native human responses, they all agree that the multitude of sizes and shapes that they assume in adult life, in the form of attitudes and behavior toward other people, are completely learned or conditioned reactions. Thus, if we wish to understand the social attitudes and behavior of people, we must know something of their environmental and cultural background.

What is it that causes Jim to shrink away from other people, seemingly afraid to participate in the group's deliberations? Why is Mary so sugary-sweet, never daring to disagree with anyone and shedding love and affection all over the place as a collie sheds his hair on a hot summer's day? Why does Jack flush with anger every time someone so much as doubts a single word he says? Why does Harry behave as though he believes everything that he says to be straight from the lips of God? Why must Sarah constantly chatter, whether she has something to say or not? Why does Andrew insist on talking like a Phi Beta Kappa when everyone knows that he hasn't the slightest idea of what he is talking about? Why does Jeanette act so aloof and superior, as though the group's activities were beneath her dignity?

These are real people, people whom each one of you knows, people like those with whom you associate in your various social activities, people you have to deal with in trying to establish healthy interpersonal relationships in the groups which you may lead. How can you possibly do this wisely and skillfully unless you have some understanding of what makes them "tick"? Let us briefly examine a few of the most universal kinds of behavior patterns found in social situations and analyze their causes. This should serve at least to start us in the direction of insight and understanding.[6]

1. **Compensation.** We should be familiar, first, with the patterns

[6] Those readers who wish to pursue the problems of social behavior to a deeper level of understanding are encouraged to study such standard textbooks in the field as: Shaffer, Laurance, *Psychology of Adjustment*. Boston: Houghton Mifflin, 1936; and Cameron, Norman, *The Psychology of Behavior Disorders*. Boston: Houghton Mifflin, 1947.

known as compensation and overcompensation. Every human being possesses a great variety of motives or desires. These range all
the way from basic physiological needs for food, water, and sex to
complex psychological cravings for mastery, security, and social
approval. When a person is inferior or is denied adequate satisfaction in any of these important areas — whether he be starved
for food or starved for love — he attempts to compensate for that
shortcoming and strives for superiority in other ways. Thus, we
have the familiar pattern of the cripple who seeks to become a
great artist, the man of short physical stature who carries a chip
on his shoulder, the frustrated schoolteacher who is short-tempered
with her students, and economically insecure persons who compensate by asserting their superiority over members of various
minority groups, or who, upon accumulating some small wealth,
flaunt it in the faces of others. When Andrew, whom we spoke of
earlier, talks like a Phi Beta Kappa, or when Sarah chatters, they
are perhaps compensating in these ways for deep-seated insecurity
feelings of which even they may not be aware.

Many of the troublesome "individual roles" described by observers as being common in discussion groups may be attributed to
overcompensation. For instance, the recognition-seeker, the dominator, and the playboy.

> The recognition-seeker works in various ways to call atten-
> tion to himself, whether through boasting, reporting on per-
> sonal achievements, acting in unusual ways, struggling to
> prevent his being placed in an inferior position. . . .
> The dominator tries to assert authority or superiority in
> manipulating the group or certain members of the group.
> This domination may take the form of flattery, of asserting a
> superior status or right to attention, giving directions author-
> itatively, interrupting the contributions of others. . . .
> The playboy makes a display of his lack of involvement in
> the group's processes. This may take the form of cynicism,
> nonchalance, horseplay and other more or less studied forms
> of "out of field" behavior.[7]

[7] Benne, Kenneth D., and Paul Sheats, "Functional Roles of Group Members," *Journal of Social Issues,* IV (Spring, 1948), pp. 45–46. Reprinted by
permission of Society for Psychological Study of Social Issues.

Overcompensation may also help to explain the cases of Mr. Blue-Nose and Mr. Suspicious.

> Mr. Blue-Nose. His sensibilities are easily shocked. He is straight-laced and conventional. He has an amazing nose for moral issues and moral implications, and an amazing lack of warmth and magnanimity. His chilling influence is felt whenever the discussion is earthy, gustful, and vigorous. . . .
>
> Mr. Suspicious. He finds it difficult to believe that anyone can be frank and honest. He suspects hidden motives and selfish purposes. He sees sinister designs where none exist. . . . As a result he is a cynical, unhappy person and a troublemaker.[8]

2. Aggressive Behavior. Another familiar pattern, which considerably overlaps the first, is that known as aggressive behavior. It takes the form of an attack, either physical or verbal (the latter being much more common), upon other individuals. Psychologists have discovered that aggression of this kind is the result of frustration, and have evolved what is known as the "frustration-aggression" formula. The point is simply this — that whenever a person is blocked in his efforts to reach a desired goal, an exceedingly common reaction is to become angry. This is true particularly when he cannot overcome that which blocks him, in which case his anger may easily be vent upon some innocent bystander. When we once understand that aggression in various forms — malicious gossip, angry outbursts, cutting insinuations, habitual negativism (being against anything and everything the group wants to do) — is the result of frustration, we are in a much better position to know how to deal with it.

3. Withdrawing Behavior. People do not always react aggressively when they are deprived and frustrated. Sometimes they withdraw and henceforward try to avoid all persons and situations which might lead to similar discomfort. This may explain in part the behavior of many people whose participation in group behavior is so reluctant or nonexistent as to cause the leader grave concern. Basically, their behavior is rooted in fear — fear of being stepped

---

[8] McBurney, James H., and Kenneth G. Hance, *Discussion in Human Affairs*. New York: Harpers, 1950, pp. 263–65. Reprinted by permission.

on, fear of being mocked, fear of being hurt in one way or another. Although such persons may cause less actual trouble for a group than other types, no group can reach its maximum effectiveness so long as any member is withholding his share of creative talent.

4. Rationalization. One of the most frequent types of adjustment made by human beings in defense of faltering egos is that known as rationalization. This is a process by which an individual gives a "socially acceptable" reason for his behavior or his attitudes in order to keep himself and others from acknowledging the real reasons, which he regards as inferior or blameworthy. Most of the time it is not a conscious type of camouflage but a kind of self-deception as well as an attempt at deception of others. An illustration will clarify the concept.

> Mr. X harbors a deep resentment against Jews. The real reason for this prejudice is that, at one time he had his heart set on a job to which a member of that minority group was appointed. Mr. X is an intelligent man and recognizes two hard facts: (1) that the other man was more deserving of the job than he, and (2) that the other man is only one Jew, not all Jews. However, the jealousy and frustration of X is so great that emotionally he is unable to admit these facts to himself. He has worked out a rationalization for his prejudice toward Jewish people — one which is more "socially acceptable" than his jealousy. He claims that the "reason" for his prejudice is that the Jewish faith denies the divinity of Christ, and that his religious convictions on the subject are so strong that he cannot help resenting this point of view.

Here is but one example of rationalization. It will be encountered again and again in all sorts of social situations and must be understood if it is to be dealt with sensibly.

Values and Sentiments

Not only should the leader understand the specific adjustive techniques of people in his group, such as those we have discussed, but he must know something of the permanent and enduring sentiments or values to which each member of his group adheres. Jack is an extremely patriotic man, with a deep and somewhat sentimental attachment to his country. Why is this so? Is it because he came to America in his youth as a refugee from European persecution and has a deep appreciation of the good life he has been able to attain here? Or is it because he can trace his ancestry back to the Mayflower and prides himself on a "100%" American lineage? It may be exceedingly important to the effective handling of this man's human relations for the leader to know the answers to these questions.

Or here is Frank involved in a heated discussion with some of his associates over the problem of what can be done about the housing situation for Negroes in Chicago. The group, composed entirely of upper-middle-class white people (including Frank), does not know that Frank grew up in a slum district immediately adjacent to the "black belt." They cannot understand nor appreciate his attitude toward the subject until this information is made known. Then it becomes clear why he resents the group's theorizing and takes a hard-bitten, highly realistic view of the problem. Only then is the air cleared of the tension which had marked all of Frank's previous contributions.

It should be emphasized that the patterns of social behavior and the sentiments we have been discussing in this chapter are not limited to trouble-makers and psychiatric cases. All of us, at one time or another, to some degree, engage in compensation, aggression, withdrawal, and rationalization. Each of us has sentiments and values to which he is attached. The man who would be an effective leader can, by careful observation of the behavior of the people with whom he associates and by constant alertness to every clue in their past histories which might lead to better understanding of that behavior, develop an acute sensitivity with respect to human relations.

INTERACTION IN THE GROUP

At the outset of this chapter we emphasized the point that one cannot understand the dynamics of a small group without understanding the psychology of individuals. For in the last analysis, all group behavior is the behavior of individuals in a group — acting differently, to be sure, in one situation than they might in another, but acting under their "own steam" none the less. We have therefore begun our treatment of group dynamics with a discussion of individual motives and behavior patterns. But we cannot stop there. If we are to work successfully with groups of people we must understand not only the individuals as such, but also the ways in which they affect each other. This leads us to a study of the complex but intensely interesting problems of social interaction.

As we approach the problems of interaction within a group, we will find it helpful to divide our attention between two levels of activity. First is the level of ideas — the area in which members attempt to communicate with one another for the purpose of solving the problems with which the group has been organized to deal. Second is the social-emotional level — the area in which members attempt to feel each other out for the purpose of establishing the kind of interpersonal relationship which makes them comfortable and happy. Though we may not always be aware of it, both kinds of activity go on in every group. Various experts use different labels in distinguishing the two areas. The first level is sometimes referred to as the *task area*;[9] and when group activity is focused there the members are said to be "content-oriented" or "problem-oriented." The second level is called the *social-emotional area.* While engaged in these activities the members are "process-oriented" or "ego-oriented."

Another way of making the same distinction is to say that at every meeting of a group there is not only a regular agenda (items of business to be discussed in handling group tasks) but also a "hidden agenda," consisting of difficulties in personal relationships which must be worked out before the members are free to cooperate effectively with one another. From the point of view of a typical member the "hidden agenda" might look something like this: "I don't like the way the leader is running this show. What, if anything, am I going to do about it? How am I going to respond to him?" "What kind of role in this group do the other members expect me to play? Am I expected to be seen and not heard? Am I

9 Bales, *op. cit.*

being looked to as an expert?" "I don't like the role in which they seem to have cast me in this group. What, if anything, am I going to do about it?" [10] "I'm disturbed by the way in which some of the other members of this group operate. Joe talks too much. I wish he'd shut up." "I'm not really interested in this problem they're discussing. But I guess I better go along with the group and pretend that I am." "If I said what I really felt about this thing, Mr. Black would hit the ceiling. I can't afford to antagonize him. Maybe I'd better just keep quiet." "This group wastes so much valuable time. How can people be so stupid? I'm beginning to think these democratic procedures are a lot of nonsense. What we need is somebody to take hold of things here and get some action!"

It is becoming increasingly obvious to students of group dynamics that the presence under the surface of a long list of hidden agenda items such as those just indicated blocks effective cooperation and makes it impossible for the group to solve its content problems in an intelligent way. Undercover struggles for security, recognition, status, power, and satisfactory group procedures make a mockery of contributions which pretend to deal with the group's avowed agenda but are subtly designed, either consciously or unconsciously, to reorganize the group's interpersonal structure in directions that will be more satisfying for the participant.

Jennings and Thelen [11] have both given considerable thought to this matter of the relationship between what they call *socio-group* and *psyche-group* activities. Socio-groups are those where attention is devoted to the solving of external, objective problems. Psyche-groups are informal gatherings where individuals can express their personal feelings and "blow off steam." If a group is too large, too heterogeneous, too formal, or too lacking in freedom and intimacy for social-emotional problems to be dealt with at its reg-

[10] For an interesting treatment of the development of social roles see Cameron, Norman, *The Psychology of Behavior Disorders.* Boston: Houghton Mifflin, 1947, Chapter 4, "Language, Thought and Role-Taking in Behavior Disorders."

[11] Jennings, Helen Hall, *Leadership and Isolation.* New York: Longmans, Green, 1943; Thelen, Herbert, "Educational Dynamics: Theory and Research," *Journal of Social Issues,* VI (1950), pp. 19–21.

ular meetings, we inevitably find smaller psyche-groups forming in the halls, over cups of coffee, in cars on the way home, or elsewhere, to air grievances and share feelings related to the hidden agenda.

It would be a far healthier group if at least some of these problems could be aired, *and then solved*, by all the members acting together. Most learning and action groups we have observed not only avoid such problems, but group members and leaders are not even conscious of their existence.

It is, of course, possible for a group to become overly pre-occupied with procedural-emotional difficulties — to the point where its objective tasks are neglected and its members become morbid in pursuit of their own tails. Effective group interaction requires the achievement of a proper balance between the fulfillment of socio-needs and psyche-needs, between content and process, between problem and ego-orientation. Before we move to Part Two of this book, which will be concerned with specific techniques for handling both content and process interaction, we shall first need to sketch in a few of the major dimensions of group behavior which must be dealt with on each level.

Content Interaction

The difficulties which arise when a group of individuals attempts to solve an objective problem together may be classified into several categories or dimensions. At this point we shall simply indicate the general nature of these categories, and will discuss them more fully in Part Two when we come to suggest techniques for dealing with them.

1. Flexibility. One of the first considerations that requires the attention of a leader is the degree of flexibility concerning group problems that exists among the members. By flexibility we mean the degree to which each member is uncommitted to fixed beliefs or attitudes. The person who comes to a group with flexible attitudes and an open mind will behave in a cooperative fashion. The individual who has a set attitude and a mind closed to the possibilities of change will behave in a competitive fashion. The average mem-

ber is not usually at either extreme of the cooperation-competition continuum. He will be more competitive than cooperative to the extent that he is not a free agent, but is bound by the dogmas of church or state or by previous commitments to outside groups. Likewise, if he has a special interest to defend or a great personal stake in the matters being dealt with by the group he will be less flexible than otherwise. Labor-management negotiations tend to be strongly competitive because of the special interests involved. It is much simpler for a college student to discuss the problems of labor and management in a cooperative spirit because he has less to gain or lose by the outcome.

Rarely, if ever, is any member of a group either completely competitive or completely cooperative. To be absolutely cooperative at all times would require that the individual have no fixed values and no special interests which might clash with the interests of others. This is hardly possible, let alone desirable. To be competitive at all times would require that the individual have absolutely no values in common with the others. If a person felt that this were true he would not remain in the group or bother discussing problems with the others. Though verbally he may seem to be completely uncooperative, the mere fact of his continued participation and presence belies the superficial appearances. The time to be convinced of his complete inflexibility is when he walks out of the meeting. The one exception to all of this is the person who remains in a group for the sole purpose of attempting to destroy it.

2. Communication. Another array of problems in the area of content interaction arises out of the difficulties people have in making themselves understood to one another. Language, our principal vehicle of communication, is an imperfect instrument. In some instances we cannot find any words to adequately communicate our ideas and feelings. But even when we find the right word, it may have different meanings to other people. We have already seen an example of that in an earlier chapter when we talked about "democracy." Words may also carry emotional connotations which vary from one individual to another. To mention the name Frank-

lin D. Roosevelt to some persons is akin to speaking of the devil himself and elicits all kinds of negative reactions, while to others the name inspires surges of good feeling. As a result of these differences, and of the ensuing inability of people to make each other understand how they think and feel, we often find group interaction breaking down. Group leaders will therefore find it worth their while to acquire an understanding of the nature and causes of semantic difficulties.[12]

3. Logic. Not every member of a group is capable of a high degree of clarity and system in thinking through a problem. Some individuals, as a result of native intelligence and training, are keenly analytical and can systematically move through a difficult problem with little wasted energy. Others, either because of insufficient native endowment, or lack of practice in the use of analytical tools,[13] tend to be fuzzy in their logic and susceptible to endless forays into irrelevant areas. The witless introduction of tangents and *non sequiturs* (ideas that do not follow logically from previous comments) may cause great confusion and frustration for the group and lead to a breakdown of rational interaction.

4. The confusion of disagreement with personal hostility. Any careful observer of human relations will notice the tendency that people have to become emotionally involved and personally identified with the ideas and points of view which they contribute to a group. As a result, when some other participant questions the validity of that contribution, this is regarded by the first person not only as a rational doubt about the value of his idea but as a personal attack upon himself. Feeling this way, he is likely to respond in an emotional manner and further intensify the atmosphere of personal strain which has already begun to develop. It becomes a vicious circle and before long what started out as a reasonable difference of opinion has boiled over into a strong per-

[12] For this purpose we recommend to the reader: Lee, Irving J., *Language Habits in Human Affairs.* New York: Harpers, 1941; Chase, Stuart, *The Tyranny of Words.* New York: Harcourt, Brace, 1938; and Johnson, Wendell, *People in Quandaries.* New York: Harpers, 1946.

[13] See Bellin, Seymour, and Frank Riessman, "Education, Culture, and the Anarchic Worker," *Journal of Social Issues,* V (1949), pp. 24–32, for an interesting analysis of this matter.

sonal antagonism. This is known as extrinsic conflict, in contrast to intrinsic conflict, which is confined to the merit of the ideas themselves.[14]

We have all known friends, parents, teachers, or employers who, to one degree or another, seem unable to cope in a rational way with someone who differs with them. They confuse disagreement with personal disrespect, and respond as though their egos were under fire. Perhaps they are not always this way. Perhaps most of the time they are quite reasonable. But when you begin to tread on what they regard as a sacred preserve, when you move into those "forbidden areas" where they fancy themselves to be the final authority, any attempt on your part, no matter how tactful, to present a different point of view is met with totally irrational, highly emotional, personal antagonism. This is a problem that is encountered every day in our interpersonal relationships. Let us not deceive ourselves into believing that it is always the other fellow who behaves that way — never ourselves!

We cannot go into a detailed analysis here of the causes of the type of behavior we have just described.[15] We should like to suggest, however, that it may well be deeply rooted in our childhood conditioning, wherein parents cause confusion in their children by withholding love, and the security it represents, as a weapon for the punishment of specific behavior. Thus they produce human beings who are in turn incapable of responding intelligently to specific disagreements without the accompaniment of an overall emotional hostility characteristic of one who fears for his personal security.[16] If it is true that fear and insecurity lie at the bottom of

[14] This distinction is made by McBurney and Hance, op. cit.

[15] The whole problem of the identification of persons with ideas, and the causes and effects thereof, is being studied intensively by a group of social psychologists, principally at the University of Kansas. See: Heider, Fritz, "Social Perception and Phenomenal Causality," Psychological Review, LI (1944), pp. 358–74; Heider, Fritz, "Attitudes and Cognitive Organization," Journal of Psychology, XXI (1946), pp. 107–12; and Horwitz, M. W., J. Lyons, and H. V. Perlmutter, "Induction of Forces in Discussion Groups," to be published in Human Relations.

[16] See Newcomb, Theodore M., "Autistic Hostility and Social Reality," Human Relations, I (1947), pp. 69–86, for a further development of this concept.

extrinsic conflict, then the leader who understands this will be in a better position to handle the difficulties when they arise.

5. The inhibition of emotional responses. Just as the members of some groups tend to become emotionally overwrought at the slightest provocation, so there are other groups that operate in an atmosphere of unnatural "sweetness and light." The members are so afraid of becoming emotionally involved in conflict that they run away from every aspect of the problem which promises to lower the barriers and reveal in stark, naked reality the differences of opinion that exist. This phenomenon can probably be traced to the same cause as is responsible for overabundance of emotional involvement — only this time working in reverse. Because the individuals recognize that disagreement might lead to unpleasant personal hostility they prefer to say, "Oh No! Let's not go into that." [17]

Perhaps it was incorrect to have discussed "the confusion of disagreement with personal hostility" and "the inhibition of emotional responses" under the heading of content interaction. In reality, they are categories which straddle the border-line between the task area and the land of interpersonal relations, all of which goes to prove that neat boundaries drawn artificially in order to clarify and explain an idea get us into trouble if we are not prepared to abandon them after they have served their purpose. Let us therefore abandon this one and proceed to a discussion of other social-emotional problems.

Interpersonal Relations

We have already seen the importance of a group's "hidden agenda." The job for the group leader is to find out as much as he can about how the members of his group feel toward one another and about the ways in which changes in those feelings are induced. If possible he should attempt to discover the centers of greatest influence in the organization, the kinds of cliques and subgroups that exist, and the patterns of friendship and hostility. A

[17] See Rosenberg, Morris, "The Social Roots of Formalism," *Journal of Social Issues*, V (1949), pp. 14–23, for a further elaboration of this theme.

relatively new science, called sociometry, is developing which helps us to understand these matters.[18] Workers in this field have devised interesting sociometric methods to determine and portray the complex network of interrelationships that exist. The principal device used is the sociogram, a graphic charting of the relationships within a group based upon questions that are asked by secret ballot of members of that group about each other. For example, each member may be asked to indicate the one person in the group with whom he prefers to work. On the basis of the answers to this question a chart is drawn (see illustration) which shows in graphic form the choices that have been made, the persons around whom the centers of gravity in the group seem to revolve, and the persons who tend to be socially isolated.

A variety of questions can be asked of group members and the answers charted on sociograms. Members can be asked to indicate the persons with whom they would most like to discuss personal problems. They can be asked to indicate their choices for a leader, thus revealing the patterns of dominance. By studies of this type, in which the acceptances and rejections of people are uncovered,

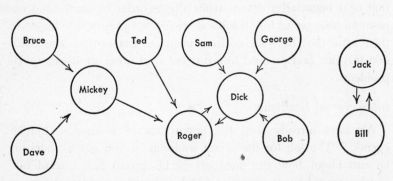

This chart indicates that Jack and Bill like to work with one another but are completely isolated from the rest of the group. Roger and Dick appear to be the most influential and, together, would be a team which would have the respect of almost the entire group.

[18] J. S. Moreno, publisher of the journal called *Sociometry*, has been a leader in this field.

a great deal can be learned, by one glance at a sociogram, about the kind of interpersonal structure that exists in a group.

Another type of chart which we have found useful is not based upon a balloting of the people involved, but upon diagrams drawn by an observer. One of the most helpful techniques for understanding interpersonal relations is to plot the path of conversation — to follow the verbal ball as it is tossed from one person to another. Are there some people to whom the ball is tossed more frequently than others? Do members of the group talk directly to each other or always to the same people? Who do people look at when they speak?

One of the best clues to a leader-dominated discussion is a diagram of conversation that looks like this:

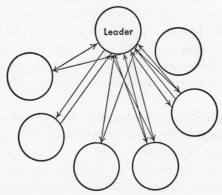

This chart reveals that members of the group consistently talked to the leader rather than to each other, and that the leader apparently entered the conversation after every contribution.

Another useful device for ascertaining group feeling is the "post-meeting reaction sheet." Immediately after a meeting, each group member is asked to fill out a questionnaire (preferably without putting his name on it) which seeks to determine his degree of satisfaction with the meeting, his degree of satisfaction with the leadership, and other matters of a procedural nature which may be pertinent to that particular group.

In using diagrams or ballots of any kind we must remember that they represent the situation only as of a given time. Interpersonal patterns are constantly subject to the possibility of change as the result of changing situations or of things that are said and done by the members. A sociogram or a tally of satisfaction which is made one day may look completely different from one made a week later. It is just as important to understand the forces which cause changes in interpersonal patterns as it is to understand the patterns themselves. We will not try here to examine all the dynamic forces and group phenomena which affect interpersonal relations. We shall only suggest a few of the most common.

1. **Changes in the Group Function.** Let us look at the case of Jack, who is president of his college social fraternity. A sociogram based upon ballots written after a chapter meeting places Jack in a central position with many lines of influence and goodwill leading to him. The same group of men also participate as a team in intramural football. Jack is a poor football player. He would not be flattered by a sociogram based upon lines of influence and goodwill on the athletic field. This is a simple illustration of the way in which the different functions of a group affect interpersonal patterns.

2. **Changes in Group Membership.** To add one new member to a group may complicate the inner networks of the unit far beyond what one would reasonably expect. To draw upon personal experience, we can cite the case of ten G.I.'s who had lived together in a small quonset hut on an airfield in England for over a year. They had spent many a cold winter night huddled around a grossly inadequate pot-bellied stove discussing various aspects of their unhappy lot — most frequently the officers under whom they worked. (Obviously a psyche group!) Six of them had a college education, and the other four were of college calibre. They all held technical and responsible jobs in a bomb group headquarters — as important (they thought) as enlisted men could be. There was a strong "we" feeling and the hut was their sacred retreat. One evening they returned "home" to find that a new man had been moved in by the sergeant-major. He was a squadron cook, had little education, and spoke with a foreign accent. Some were nicer to the

new man than others. All were affected. As the cook became part of the group, old patterns and networks were broken and new ones were formed. Shortly thereafter another man moved in. The behavior of the group, its habits and its patterns, were soon markedly different than they had ever been before. There were never again any round-the-stove discussions, and friendships became confined to small cliques.

Not all groups, of course, would behave as this one did, in response to the introduction of new members. Some groups are more permeable (less exclusive) than others. The reactions to the entrance of a new member (or, for that matter, to the departure of an old one) will depend on a variety of factors — the degree of intimacy among the members, the degree of cohesiveness (we-feeling) in the group, the amount of homogeneity (sameness of age, background, values, etc.) that exists, as well as the personality of the individual entering or leaving the group. It is safe to assume that the entrance or departure of an exceedingly dominant person will have a more profound effect upon the interpersonal patterns than the comings and goings of quiet and retiring members.

3. **Development and Change in Group Standards.** When a number of individuals join together in a talking group for the first time the primary item of business on the hidden agenda is a process by which each member feels out the situation in order to determine what kind of an interpersonal structure can be developed, and what roles each member will play in that structure. Just as a dog, coming into a strange room, sniffs around to orient himself to the situation, so a human being, in a new group setting, needs to test out his relationships with others — to "try them on for fit." Needless to say, most of this takes place quite unconsciously, with some members establishing themselves in dominant positions and some settling back into submissive roles; some reacting positively to leads that are suggested; some agreeing and some disagreeing with one another; some beginning to feel friendly and some hostile to each other. It is not long before these interpersonal patterns have begun to solidify and the group has arrived, perhaps quite unconsciously, at an established method of working together.

It is characteristic of the individual's need for security and self-preservation that he seeks to know what kinds of situations he is getting himself into. The only way he can do this is to be able to predict the behavior of others with whom he associates. It is therefore to his advantage to aid in the establishment of a stable interpersonal structure — even if it be a bad one — so that he will at least know what to expect of others and what others expect of him. Once established, this structure tends to be resistant to further change, for each change carries with it uncertainty and is a possible threat to the individual's status in the group.

The method by which these established patterns are protected is known commonly as social pressure. Social pressure is a subtle process in which the members of a group "put the screws on" a deviant individual to force him into line with group standards that have been developed. This may be done in the most "refined" and "dignified" yet devastating ways. Social pressure is the psychological equivalent of a steamroller. It may be applied against an individual whose opinions do not agree with those of the rest of the group. It may be used to give support and reinforcement to prejudices that are shared by all the members. It may be used to guarantee that nobody deviates from the "party line." It may even be used to push an "undesirable" member into psychological isolation and perhaps eventually force him out of the group.

An example of one manifestation of social pressure is provided by Kurt Lewin in his report of the experiment by Lippitt at the Iowa Child Welfare Research Station. This was the experiment in which comparisons were made between autocratic and democratic groups.

> Of particular interest was the transfer of one of the children from the autocratic to the democratic group, and of another from the democratic to the autocratic one. Before the transfer the difference between the two children was the same as between the two groups they belonged to, namely, the autocratic child was more dominating and less friendly and objective than the democratic one. However, after the transfer the behavior changed so that the previously autocratic child now became the less dominating and more friendly and objective

child. In other words, the behavior of the children mirrored very quickly the atmosphere of the group in which they moved.[19]

It should not be inferred from all this that the establishment of group standards and the use of social pressure to enforce them is an evil phenomenon. Like all types of power, it may be used for good or ill. It is absolutely essential to productive group action that certain standards or ways of working together be set up which are understood and adhered to by all. It may be as simple a matter as agreeing not to speak without recognition from the chairman, or as subtle a principle as agreeing that any member who attempts to impose his will upon the group by force will be socially quarantined.

It is not necessary that group standards be verbalized or written into a constitution in order to be effective. Verbalization may be helpful in order to insure that everyone understands what is expected of him; but we have seen many verbalized group standards "go by the boards" because group members never really understood or accepted them. One example of this was a group that agreed verbally at its first meeting to operate according to majority rule, but made few decisions thereafter without first obtaining unanimous consent. By the same token, we have seen other group standards (such as the discouragement of profane language) which have never been verbalized but which have been enforced with consummate effectiveness.

Social pressure, as we have implied, operates most frequently to resist rather than provoke changes in the role structure of a group. Once a standard has been established and accepted, particularly in a formal or rigid group, it is not easily changed. If and when change is attempted it can only be made effective by the operation of social support in its behalf. Though difficult, it is not at all impossible for such changes to take place. In fact, every new act or contribution of any member is potentially capable of inciting a group response which alters the entire structure. If enough individ-

---

[19] Lewin, Kurt, "Experiments in Social Space," *Resolving Social Conflict.* New York: Harpers, 1948, p. 80. Reprinted by permission.

uals in the group are dissatisfied with prevailing patterns, an apparently insignificant act may be enough to set the wheels of social pressure in motion and bring about basic alterations in the group's interpersonal patterns.

One instance of this that we recall occurred in a group of twenty-seven people whose pattern of participation was highly unbalanced. Four or five individuals dominated the conversation every time the group met. Finally one submissive group member became bold enough to suggest that the group was serving the needs of just a few dominant individuals and that the rest were being taken for a ride. This set off a chain reaction of events which eventually caused the membership to accept a new (and unverbalized) group standard which created and enforced a more balanced pattern of participation. It is by virtue of such processes of change that group growth is made possible.

GROUP GROWTH AND MATURITY

One of the hypotheses suggested by research workers in the field of group dynamics is that group interaction can go through a process of growth and maturation similar to that of individuals. In infancy, the group, like a newborn baby, is awkward and unco-ordinated in its behavior. It is also highly dependent upon the leader. As it grows to adolescence its members struggle with the same conflicts of dependence versus independence that the teen-ager goes through. They begin to learn how to do things for themselves and to operate in an efficient manner. The group does not yet know how to handle its emotional crises. Eventually, under the proper conditions, that problem too can be faced and solved in a constructive way, and the group can achieve a state of maturity analogous to that of intelligent and happy adulthood.

If we are going to talk about groups growing to maturity it will be necessary for us to define what we mean by mature group inter-action. When can a group be said to have reached optimum conditions of interaction? What are the signs or symptoms of group maturity?

It is as difficult to answer these questions with any degree of certainty as it would be to define maturity in an individual. What we say is likely to be both incomplete and controversial. Recognizing those limitations we would suggest the following criteria. A mature group is one which:

1. Has a clear understanding of its purposes or goals.
2. Makes progress toward its goals with a maximum of efficiency and a minimum of wasted effort.
3. Is able to look ahead and plan ahead.
4. Has achieved a high degree of effective inter-communication.
5. Is able to initiate and carry on effective, logical problem-solving.
6. Has achieved an appropriate balance between *established* ways of working together and *readiness to change* its procedural patterns.
7. Is objective about its own functioning; can face its procedural-emotional problems and intelligently make whatever modifications are called for.
8. Strikes an appropriate balance between group productivity (socio-group functions) and the satisfaction of ego needs (psyche-group functions).
9. Provides for the diffusion and sharing of leadership responsibilities.
10. Achieves an appropriate balance between content and process orientation.
11. Has a high degree of cohesiveness or solidarity but not to the point of exclusiveness or the point of stifling individuality.
12. Makes intelligent use of the differing abilities of its members.
13. Faces reality, and works on the basis of fact rather than fantasy.
14. Provides an atmosphere of psychological freedom for the expression of all feelings and points of view.
15. Is not over-dominated by its leader or by any of its members.
16. Has achieved a healthy balance between cooperative and competitive behavior on the part of its members.
17. Strikes an appropriate balance between emotionality and rationality.

18. Can readily change and adapt itself to the needs of differing situations.
19. Recognizes that means are inseparable from ends.
20. Recognizes the values and limitations of democratic procedures.

SUMMARY

We are concerned in this book primarily with small, face-to-face talking groups. All such groups exist for the purpose of fulfilling the needs of their members, and usually have as their major goals individual learning and/or group decision-making. An individual may join a group for a variety of motives, and becomes involved in its activities to the extent that he finds satisfaction for his personal needs. His behavior in the group may at times cause difficulties for the other members and the leader, particularly when he engages in overcompensation, aggressive or withdrawing behavior, and rationalization. His attitudes toward group problems will be influenced by his environmental background, which has built up within him a set of values and sentiments.

Interaction among individuals in a group takes place on two levels — the content level and the area of interpersonal relations. Unresolved interpersonal difficulties tend to block effective group action, and unless they are faced and handled in group meetings will lead to the formation of smaller psyche groups on the outside.

Some of the problems which groups encounter on the level of content interaction are difficulties in: (1) flexibility, (2) communication, (3) logic, (4) the confusion of disagreement with personal hostility, and (5) the inhibition of emotional responses.

On the interpersonal level, sociometric methods can be helpful in diagnosing the feeling patterns of a situation. The patterns are always subject to alteration induced by: (1) changes in group function, (2) changes in group membership, and (3) development and change in group standards. Group standards are at the same time both a necessary element of productive functioning and a strong source of resistance to change. Nevertheless, every new contribution by a group member carries with it the potentiality for change, and thus group growth is made possible.

Groups which have grown to maturity tend to possess a number of characteristics which we have enumerated and which closely resemble the characteristics of a mature, adult human being.

EXERCISES

1. Visit a class in group discussion and draw a sociogram, making guesses, on the basis of your observations of the discussion, as to the pattern of personal preferences within that group. At the conclusion of the discussion collect personal preference ballots from the members of the group and draw another sociogram based upon those ballots. Compare the two sociograms and analyze your errors.

2. Visit a group discussion in your community and make an analysis of the group phenomena you observe there — such as, the confusion of disagreement with personal hostility and the inhibition of emotional responses.

3. Most groups tend to place a high premium on conformity and to discourage all radically divergent behavior. What factors might be operating to cause such a tendency? Discuss this problem in a group.

4. Develop a questionnaire and take a survey of one of the social units of which you are a member to determine the primary and accessory needs which brought people to the group.

5. Prepare some post-meeting reaction sheets for the next group meeting that you attend. At the end of the session ask each member to fill one out. Report your results back to the group at its following meeting and encourage them to discuss the significance and causes of your findings.

6. Visit a group discussion as an observer and:

   a) Attempt to classify each contribution that is made according to whether it appears to fall primarily in the content area or the social-emotional area.

   b) Make a list of the problems which appear to you as items on the group's "hidden agenda."

   c) Rate the group on the following scales:

FLEXIBILITY OF MEMBERS

Highly cooperative   Highly competitive

COMMUNICATION CLARITY

Little misunderstanding   Much misunderstanding

LOGIC

Highly systematic   Highly unsystematic

CONFUSION OF DISAGREEMENT WITH PERSONAL HOSTILITY

Much confusion of
disagreement with
personal hostility   Little confusion of
disagreement with
personal hostility

EMOTIONAL INVOLVEMENT IN DISCUSSION

High degree of
emotional involvement   Low degree of
emotional involvement

COHESIVENESS

High degree of
We-feeling   Low degree of
We-feeling

LEADER–DOMINATION

High degree of
Leader-domination   Low degree of
Leader-domination

PARTICIPATION SPREAD

Much spread   Little spread

RIGIDITY OF GROUP STANDARDS

Highly rigid   Highly fluid

d) Using the twenty criteria suggested in this chapter, rate the group on the following scale:

Very mature   Very immature

Part Two

Attitudes and Skills of
Democratic Leadership

Introduction

THE PROBLEMS which have been dealt with in Part One were designed to lay a foundation for group leadership. We have studied the psychology of leadership and the factors at work in group situations for the purpose of broadening our understanding of these processes and increasing our sensitivity to them. We have also studied the interrelationship of various concepts and types of leadership, for the purpose of arriving at a sound philosophy concerning the role of leadership in a democratic society. Without such a philosophy to underpin our efforts, specific techniques and skills of group leadership are meaningless and purposeless.

Through the approaches to leadership presented here, we have arrived at a position which clearly implies that the healthiest kind of leadership for a democracy is that which is diffused throughout the group. Since final authority and responsibility rests with the members of the group, it is desirable that they themselves utilize as much of it as possible, delegating to designated leaders only that degree of authority and responsibility which they themselves are really incapable of handling. This means that the leadership skills we are about to discuss in Part Two are *not* the exclusive concern of the one man in every group *called* "the leader." They are simply functions that need to be performed in any democratically operated group, and whoever can do them most conveniently and effectively should be turned to for leadership at that point.

Every member of a democratic group should share leadership to the utmost of his ability. Leadership should constantly pass around from one to another. Hence the man who is nominally *the* leader needs to fulfill only those responsibilities which the group itself, because of inability or inconvenience, cannot perform. The more

111

mature the group, the less the man designated as leader will have to do. The greater the number of people in any group who possess the attitudes and skills to be discussed in Part Two, the less will there be need for superhuman leaders who possess them all. One of the most discouraging features of most books which describe the skills desired in a group leader is the impossibility of any single person being that able. The reader of such books can only conclude that a leader must be a genius and saint, and that he is neither. Thus, we caution the reader, as he moves into Part Two of this book, not to be discouraged by the rigid requirements of effective leadership set out here. Though we may speak in terms of *the* leader, this is only for grammatical convenience. Anyone, at a given moment, may be the leader. Only if the one man *called* leader is an autocrat who cannot tolerate growth on the part of his followers will all the responsibilities discussed in Part Two rest on his shoulders. The excellence of democracy lies in the fact that it is realistic — it recognizes human frailties and does not rely on nonexistent supermen to make it work.

We deal, in Part Two, primarily with the leadership of discussion — which is but one aspect of group leadership. There are three reasons for doing this:

1. Discussion leadership is the most purely democratic type of leadership that exists, and discussion is the only completely democratic method we know for the conduct of human affairs.

2. The need for improvement in the methods of the democratic type of leader is one of the most urgent requirements of our society.

3. The attitudes, principles and skills dealt with in a study of discussion leadership have application far beyond the discussion group. We recommend to the reader that he keep alert to these ramifications and that he read this, not as a study of discussion leadership alone, but as a study of *leadership principles* which are valid in many kinds of group situations.

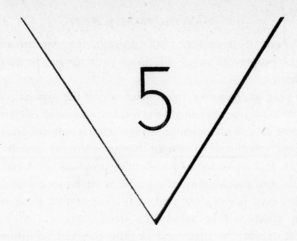

The Group Leader as a Person

WHAT KIND OF person is the democratic leader? What does it take to stimulate and guide effective group discussion? How must one feel about other people in order to want them to grow up emotionally and intellectually, to be willing that they take over some of the leadership themselves? What attitudes must one have if he is to release the creative talents of a group?

A WELL-ADJUSTED PERSONALITY

Let us first look at the leader's mental and emotional health. It has long been debated in many circles whether or not effective leaders are persons with well-adjusted personalities. There are some who maintain, with strong evidence to support their view, that the most effective executive and advocate leaders are those who are *not* personally well-adjusted, whose desires for dominance are, for one reason or another, abnormal, whose aggressiveness and dynamic force may be attributed to personal instability, and who frequently end their careers with ulcers or nervous breakdowns. We do not propose to argue the issue with respect to executives and advocates.

We do propose, however, that in the case of the group discussion leader a well-adjusted personality is a *sine qua non* of effectiveness. We suggest that a democratic leader who is not relatively free from excess emotionalism cannot be an adequate group guide. We submit that in order to handle the problems of social interaction in a constructive way, the leader must be secure and confident in his own personality, and to the extent that he is not, his leadership ability will be reduced in effectiveness.

Lack of stability, security and healthy personal adjustment are the very forces which give rise to excessive desires for dominance and thus make it difficult for the leader to encourage a free atmosphere or allow others to behave independently. It is a well-known fact in psychology that parents who are overdominant or overprotective of their children are themselves maladjusted individuals. They resist the growth of their children to an independent status because they are too insecure to face the fact that the offspring can get along without their services.

You have probably been in situations where the group spirit has completely disintegrated because of a leader who insisted on doing everything himself. His over-ambitiousness, his desire for dominance and his craving for recognition made it impossible for him to delegate authority or to admit to himself that he was *not* indispensable and that others in the group were capable of assuming responsibility. The truly effective group builder must be free of these compulsions. He must be able to "enrich a social environment without overshadowing others." He must be willing to be a follower some of the time. Only then will leadership be passed around. Only when the leader is himself mentally and emotionally mature will his group be able to grow to maturity.

A BASIC RESPECT AND CONCERN FOR OTHER HUMAN BEINGS

This brings us to a second quality of effective group leadership. We will call it, broadly, a basic respect and concern for other human beings. It involves an attitude of understanding other people, of being interested in them, of enjoying their company, and of respecting them as individuals. As we explore this quality, and others to follow, we will become aware that they are all closely interrelated. The relationship between this second quality, for example, and the first, is clarified by Baxter and Cassidy when they comment that a person must believe in himself if he is to be capable of believing in others. "The insecure and deprived personality has not the basic requisites for full and free belief in others and for identification with their problems and needs."[1] Psychologists have discovered again and again that people who are too "wrapped up" in their own problems are simply incapable of being much concerned with the problems of others. In such cases leadership ability is most assuredly reduced.

There are three aspects of this matter of respect and concern for others that merit special attention. The first is referred to by some authors as *social sensitivity*. By social sensitivity is meant a person's capacity to feel out the concerns which are of greatest importance to the members of his group and to gain insight into their needs and desires. That people who possess this quality to an unusual degree tend to be leaders is the major conclusion reached by Helen Hall Jennings in her summary of the experimental literature on leadership.

> They (leaders) apparently earn the choice status of most wanted participants because they act in behalf of others with a sensitivity of response which does not characterize the average individual in a community . . . Analysis of behavior shows they are individuals who see beyond the circumference of their own personal needs into the wider range of needs of their fellow citizens. By their conduct they go further than the majority of the population in relating themselves to others and in translating the needs of others into effective outlets.[2]

[1] Baxter, Bernice, and Rosalind Cassidy, *Group Experience — The Democratic Way.* New York: Harpers, 1943, p. 3.
[2] Jennings, Helen Hall, "Leadership — A Dynamic Redefinition," *Journal of Educational Sociology,* XVII (March, 1944), p. 431. Reprinted by permission.

Closely akin to what we have called social sensitivity is a second aspect of the attitude of respect and concern for others. Not only must the leader be capable of understanding others and feeling them out, but he must also enjoy doing it. He must like to deal with people. This characteristic is often referred to as *extroversion*. The extrovert has an "out-going" personality in contrast to the introvert, whose interests are focused inward and who would prefer to read a good book on a subject rather than to participate in a discussion about it. But, you may say, "I like to do both." In fact, research indicates that the vast majority of the population possesses both extrovertive and introvertive tendencies. People do vary, however, in the degree to which they possess one or the other. Studies of leadership have made it quite clear that there is a correlation between group leadership and extrovertive tendencies. This is no more than we would expect. Granted that a highly introverted person might provide great indirect, intellectual leadership in a society, it is hardly to be expected that he would be an outstanding discussion leader.

The third and most important aspect of the attitude we are discussing is a *belief in the value of the individual* — an honest respect for other human beings and for the points of view they represent. One must do more than pay lip-service to this attitude. As the Overstreets point out, "Many persons theoretically respect others. But not everyone who declares that Man is a rational animal treats living men as rational." [3] These authors illustrate the point with the story of a minister who complained that when he led discussions he somehow could not keep from talking too much. "Someone always says something that goes so much against the grain that I can't help trying to set him right or at least trying to keep others from being misled by what he says," stated the preacher.[4]

There follows an enlightening and provocative analysis of this case:

> What is wrong in such a case? Is it simply that he is a man of strong convictions? That cannot be the answer. The best

[3] Overstreet and Overstreet, *Leaders for Adult Education*. New York: American Association for Adult Education, 1941, p. 64.

[4] *Ibid.*, p. 65.

chairmen in the field are men of strong convictions. . . . He had convictions, but an honest conviction about the worth of discussion was not among them. Discussion was for him a method of letting people believe they were saying something important. Nothing in his comments suggest that he himself had ever expected to capture some new idea from the group. He was letting people, as it were, play at thinking for themselves because it was a wholesome kind of play for them to engage in. But it must not be allowed to go too far. If really stupid things were said, or really dangerous things, then he must step in and remonstrate, "Now children, this won't do." [5]

The authors then draw a significant "moral" from the story.

To pretend to believe in free discussion and yet, in practice, to try cautiously to keep it going in the "right" direction is to commit a crime against the human spirit. Such pretense is far worse than open opposition to free speech. The latter can be recognized for what it is. But the former creates an atmosphere of tension and timidity, or of hearty and unconvincing goodfellowship, that takes all the bite out of discussion and makes people turn from it in bored disgust.[6]

A sincere belief in the dignity of the individual, as we see it, is practically synonymous with an intelligent belief in the value of free discussion. To affirm one of these beliefs is to affirm the other. To deny one is to deny the other. And we cannot stress too strongly the central importance of both in the personality structure of the democratic group leader. The reader who does not adhere to these values might just as well stop studying this book right now. No bag of tricks can help him. The skills and techniques of democratic leadership that he may acquire will not fool many people for long. Sooner or later he will be "caught with his attitudes showing."

Without intending to minimize the necessity for developing the skills we shall be discussing in the following chapters, we do want to make absolutely clear at this point our firm conviction that the leader's attitude toward people is infinitely more important than a carload of techniques. We recall one instance in particular (and

---

[5] *Ibid.*, pp. 65–66. Reprinted by permission.
[6] *Ibid.*, p. 66. Reprinted by permission.

the reader can surely recall others) of a young man whose overt activity *appeared* quite autocratic. He bullied, he barked and in general behaved in extremely tactless ways. Yet everyone who knew him also knew that under the surface lay a deep and abiding respect for other people. As a result, his behavior was accepted playfully by others — much as one reacts to a frisky young pup — and he served as an effective and stimulating discussion leader with a group of people who knew and understood him.

SENSITIVITY TO THE BASIC TRENDS AND MOODS OF THE GROUP

As well as being sensitive to other individuals, those who are effective group leaders — and this is apparently true of all types of leadership — tend to possess still a third quality, very closely related to the second. We shall call it a sensitivity to the basic trends and moods of the group as a whole. Perhaps it is what Plato had in mind when he contrasted leaders with those who "are all abroad among all sorts of aspects of many objects." We are sure it was what Charles Merriam was referring to in his study of the lives of Lincoln, Theodore Roosevelt, Woodrow Wilson, and William Jennings Bryan when he summarized the leadership qualities common to them all and concluded that "all were highly sensitive to the strength and direction of significant social and political tendencies, and seldom mistook the eddy for the main current." [7]

This is the quality which people have in mind when they talk about the politician "keeping his ear to the ground." It is what Coyle means when she speaks of "the ability to see what is at stake in broader and deeper terms." [8] This quality is not necessarily the same as intelligence and not necessarily the same as the ability to understand people as individuals. It is rather the ability to capture the total feeling of a group, to sense its underlying currents of thought, and to perceive it all in relationship to a bigger and

[7] Merriam, Charles E., *Four American Party Leaders*. New York: Macmillan, 1926, p. 98.

[8] Coyle, Grace, *Group Experience and Democratic Values*. New York: Woman's Press, 1947, p. 26.

broader stream of events. It is an ability aptly illustrated in the following passage from Robert Sherwood's *Roosevelt and Hopkins*:

> One time Churchill, Roosevelt and Hopkins were having lunch together in the Oval Study in the White House. They were thrashing out in advance major problems which were coming up for discussion at a full dress conference to be held later that afternoon. As usual, both Roosevelt and Churchill were wandering far afield. (Churchill might have been re-fighting the Battle of Blenheim and Roosevelt recalling the tactics employed by John Paul Jones when the Bonhomme Richard defeated the *Serapis*.) It was for Hopkins to bring these soaring imaginations down to earth, to contemplation of the topic immediately at hand.
>
> When he did so, with his usual brusqueness, Churchill turned on him and said:
>
> "Harry! When this war is over His Majesty's Government is going to reward you by conferring upon you a noble title."
>
> Hopkins remarked sourly that membership in the House of Lords was one reward that he did not covet. But Churchill went right ahead:
>
> "We have already selected the title. You are to be named 'Lord Root of the Matter'." [9]

KNOWLEDGE

Throughout this book we have repeatedly referred to the idea that in a democratic society leadership is passed around, that ideally a person should be a leader in some areas and a follower in others. If this is a valid concept, then it implies that leadership ability is not a permanent, basic part of one's personality structure, that it comes and goes, that it is present in some situations and not in others, or that at least it varies in degree from one situation to another. This is clearly the case with respect to our fourth quality of leadership, namely knowledge.

There can be little doubt that knowledge is an important factor in group leadership. We can no more imagine an effective President of the United States being ignorant of the nation's political,

[9] Sherwood, Robert, *Roosevelt and Hopkins*. New York: Harpers, 1948. Reprinted by permission.

economic and social problems than we can a boy who knows little or nothing about football being a good captain of his football team. Leaders can possess all of the other personal attitudes and skills of leadership, but if they lack a working knowledge in the area where they are expected to lead, their prospects of success are not bright. Experimental support for this assertion is provided by Simpson, who found among college students, a significant correlation between scholastic standing and the influence they exerted in group discussion.[10]

This is not to say that leaders know or need to know more about the total problem dealt with than the rest of the members of the group. If this were the case they would and should become instructors rather than discussion leaders. However, *other things being equal,* we are likely to find that in any group the one who will be leader in fact, if not in name, is the one who knows the most about the particular task in which the group is engaged at the moment.

The limitation of this principle lies in the fact that other things are rarely equal. Other qualities of leadership, such as those we have already discussed and more we are about to discuss, may enter the picture and relegate the factor of knowledge to a secondary position. For instance, the member of a college social committee who knows more about "throwing a dance" than anyone else in the group may take a back seat to another member of the committee who knows a little about it (though not as much as the first man), but who also possesses other important qualities of effective group leadership which the first man lacks. We must always bear in mind this constant interplay of factors when we talk about knowledge, or anything else, as an attribute of leadership. We must also remember that every individual will have his own peculiar combination of traits and characteristics, strong in some suits and weak in others, but adding up to a total effect which makes him capable of leadership in a given situation.

[10] Simpson, Ray H., *A Study of Those Who Influence and Those Who Are Influenced in Discussion.* New York: Columbia University Teachers' College, 1938.

FACILITY IN VERBALIZING THE IDEAS OF A GROUP

A quality of effective group leadership which is often overlooked but which is of undeniable importance is facility in verbalizing the ideas of the group.[11] This involves a speaking ability which makes it possible for the leader to give effective oral expression to the desires, thoughts and feelings of the members of his group. He need not be a Demosthenes nor a William Jennings Bryan. He need not have the style of a Churchill or the persuasive ability of a Roosevelt. But he does need to be able to put into words clearly and simply, at appropriate times, the ideas and sentiments which his group is trying to formulate. Whether it be in the form of a simple summary of that which a committee has discussed for half an hour or in the form of a Gettysburg Address giving dramatic voice to the aspirations of an entire people, the function is similar.

RESTRAINT

One of the most interesting and widely discussed problems of group leadership concerns the possible conflict of the "leader as leader" with the "leader as human being." It is frequently suggested that a leader must inhibit some of his personal wishes, feelings, and opinions. He must restrain his own desires for self-expression because failing to do so might stifle or suppress members of the group. He must hold his own opinions under control because their expression might jeopardize his position as a fair, impartial leader who is concerned only with the good of the group as a whole. He must live a "model" life.

Many experts in the field of discussion leadership insist that an effective leader must never cease being objective, that he must never take sides in the group's conflicts.

> Toward the ideas presented in discussion the leader's attitude should be one of strict impartiality. He cannot afford to compromise his position as moderator by becoming a party to the argument. Usually he should even avoid revealing what his own opinion is on the question under discussion. . . .

[11] Simpson, *op. cit.*, p. 85, found a significant correlation between scores on the Scholastic Aptitude Test of Verbal Ability and influence in discussion.

Whether the moderator approves of the conclusion is immaterial.[12]

Another author has suggested that the difference between a "public" man (leader) and a "private" man (group member) is that the former "has control of his individual impulses, a checking of them against the good of all." [13]

This same point of view, or at least a similar one, we feel, underlies the old advice to leaders that "familiarity breeds contempt" — an adage surely believed in and practiced today by vast numbers of people in positions of leadership. (Witness the sharp distinction between officers and enlisted men in the military services.) Again, the principle involved is that if the leader allows the group members to regard him as a human being with feelings, opinions, and shortcomings, his effectiveness as leader is reduced. As Bogardus puts it:

> A thinking man who keeps his thoughts to himself baffles and attracts attention. . . . The holding of associates at a distance, by persons of ability, may be a leadership trait, for it arouses interest and may create respect. . . . To the extent that a person is inscrutable, he seems to possess something that others do not have and hence becomes an object of their attention and their followership.[14]

If all of these suggestions be valid, then group leadership is indeed a difficult assignment, for there is no human being without interests and emotional conditioning of his own and consequently without a certain amount of partiality which may at times run counter to the feelings of the group as a whole. To expect a leader to submerge those interests, or at least to suppress the open expression of them, is to expect of him an ability which some people are incapable of achieving and which others achieve only as the result of a long, hard struggle with themselves.

For these reasons, plus others which we will state, we do not

[12] Utterback, William, *Group Thinking and Conference Leadership*. New York: Rinehart, 1950, p. 59. Reprinted by permission.

[13] Coyle, *op. cit.*, p. 26.

[14] Bogardus, E. S., *Leaders and Leadership*. New York: Appleton-Century-Crofts, Inc., 1934, pp. 165–70. Reprinted by permission.

completely endorse the suggestions reported above with respect to the leader's inhibition of personal wishes, opinions, and behavior. We feel that they reflect too much of the superhuman concept of leadership. It is not only their difficulty of attainment which disturbs us. We are not convinced of their desirability.

In the first place, advising a leader to remain a person apart from "ordinary human beings" assumes that there is something nonleaderlike about honest behavior. It assumes that the leader must deceive his followers into thinking he is something that he is not. It assumes that this is the only way he can maintain their respect. It all seems reminiscent of Machiavelli's famous advice for a prince on "Whether it is better to be loved than feared," when he says:

> It is much safer to be feared than loved, when, of the two, either must be dispensed with. Because this is to be asserted in general of men, that they are ungrateful, fickle, false, cowards, covetous, and as long as you succeed they are yours entirely . . . but, when [need] approaches, they turn against you.[15]

These assertions about the nature of mankind may be quite correct in many situations and consequently justify aloofness and restraint on the leader's part. We suggest, however, that maintaining these assumptions to be universally and inevitably true is to deny the very foundations upon which democratic leadership is built. It is our belief that truly mature individuals, in a democratic group, cannot and need not be deceived. On the contrary, they can accept leaders who are also human beings. They will, in fact, prefer them.

There is a second reason why we question the restraint of personal feelings by group leaders. As Professor Coyle points out, the leader has great "assets which should not be sterilized by putting their possessor in a position where he cannot exercise them." [16] Presumably a group leader is one of the most valuable members of a group. How foolish to make him an idea-eunuch, and deprive the group of his intellectual and emotional virility!

[15] Machiavelli, *The Prince*. Ed. Ernest Rhys, trans., W. K. Marriott. Chapter 17, p. 134. Everyman's Library; New York: Dutton, 1908.
[16] Coyle, *op. cit.*, p. 27.

It is interesting to note that even the rigid rules of parliamentary law take cognizance of this paradox by permitting the chairman to turn his gavel over to someone else and step down from his chair in order to express his personal views. This is certainly a neat way of evading the real issue and making an artificial split between "the leader as leader" and "the leader as human being." It preserves the technical niceties of the doctrine of impartial leadership, but at the same time admits its practical limitations. And, after all, who is really deceived by this game of musical chairs? Granted, lip-service is thereby paid to the notion that the leader can and should be "above" the conflict. But the psychological effects of his remarks are virtually the same whether he is in the chair or out of it. Whether or not the members are unduly influenced by his prestige will be determined by their maturity and not by the physical location of the leader.

Yet, having said all this, we recognize the real dangers and limitations of uninhibited leadership. It is undoubtedly true that many people are so indoctrinated with the "infallible man" concept of leadership that to treat them with honesty and familiarity *would* breed their contempt, lose their respect, and cause them to turn to another leader who would give them the kind of superman treatment they desired. For that reason it may be necessary for the leader to keep his guards up at first, and slowly ease the group into more mature and democratic responses through a gradual process of letting down the barriers.

It is also true that when the leadership and contributor roles are combined in one person, there is danger of overdomination taking place. The leader may use whatever advantages and prestige his position of leadership gives him to endow his personal interests and ideas with greater weight than those of the average member of the group. He may monopolize more than one man's share of the conversation, and no one is able to prevent it. He may become engaged in personal conflict with another member of the group to the extent that his perspective is lost and his usefulness as a leader undermined. These are serious problems, and we do not want to underestimate their importance. The proper answer is not to be found, however, in silencing or neutralizing the leader. Rather, we must concern ourselves with finding a way for the leader to combine his own interests and opinions with those of the rest of the group in *suitable proportions*.

We suggest for this purpose an attitude of reasonable or *intelligent partiality* on the part of the leader. By this we mean that the leader should feel free to participate in the group as a member of the group; but, to the extent that the group feels he is "different from the others" or to the extent that he has more power than others (such as control over who shall be recognized to speak) he should exercise more restraint than would otherwise be necessary. If others are competing with him for the floor, he should usually let them speak first. If someone in the group is likely to be personally antagonized by what he says, he had best state it very cautiously and objectively. If he is attempting to resolve a heated conflict between two factions in the group and feels that he must take sides, he would be wise to do so in a very tactful way. In short, we are suggesting that *the way in which he contributes* and *the way in which he takes sides* is of more concern than the points of view he expresses.

This is what we mean by *intelligent* partiality. The "how" is more important than the "what." There are some people who can disagree vehemently with you but at the same time give you the feeling that they have complete respect for your right to differ and that they are always willing to give you a fair hearing. There are others who *profess* complete impartiality, but at the same time give you the feeling that it is not quite safe to express certain points of view. Needless to say, we recommend the former approach for effective group leadership. A warm spirit of reasonableness and open-mindedness are far more important than superficial professions of cold impartiality.

There is one other practical aspect of this problem that needs to be considered. You will remember that when we discussed the different types of leadership — executive, advocate, judge, expert, and discussion leader — we pointed out that most individuals in a position of leadership in a group may be called upon at various times to play each of these different roles. A dean, an office manager, or a factory foreman may have to be executive, expert, or discussion leader on different occasions. An effective classroom teacher or social worker must continually shuttle back and forth from instructor to discussion leader roles.

Whenever the same person must, at different times, exercise both authoritarian and democratic leadership in the same group, confusion on the part of group members is almost inevitable. It is not easy for people, psychologically, to make the differentiation. Hence, when the leader expresses his views in the democratic situation, his contributions may have more impact than is warranted by their intrinsic worth. The carry-over influence of his authoritarian status in the group may thus negate the whole spirit of democratic procedures. And, vice versa, in making a shift from the democratic to the authoritarian relationship he may, by virtue of a loss in status, find it difficult to exercise effective control.[17]

The ideal solution would be to train the group to make a differentiation. This would require that the leader always clearly identify his role of the moment and that he demonstrate his good faith in the democratic role by repeatedly encouraging disagreement with his views and never holding what a person says against him. It is a difficult and long-range task to develop such fine discrimination of emotional responses, on the part of both leader and group, and one that perhaps can never be completely successful. The only reasonable alternative seems to be a compromise with honesty wherein the leader exercises considerable restraint over the expression of his personal feelings, and hence remains somewhat "apart" from the group.

[17] It is interesting that a parallel problem exists in psychotherapy. As Rogers expresses it (*op. cit.*, p. 109): "It seems to the writer that the counsellor cannot maintain a counselling relationship with the client and at the same time have authority over him. - Therapy and authority cannot be coexistent in the same relationship. . . . There cannot be an atmosphere of complete permissiveness when the relationship is authoritative. Is the student free to tell the college counsellor that he cribbed on his last examination, if that same counsellor is responsible for discipline? . . . Attempts to mix the two functions nearly always turn out badly."

VITALITY

Still another quality of effective group leadership is that set of characteristics which can best be included under the general heading of vitality. This encompasses an entire battery of closely related traits at the root of which lies sheer physical energy. Most biographical and experimental studies of leadership have concluded that factors related to energy — such as vigor, enthusiasm, and endurance — all play a part in the making of a leader.[18] It is certainly reasonable that this should be so, since it is difficult to conceive of a man who is half dead on his feet exerting effective group influence.

Another approach to this matter of vitality is made by an expert who says: "I wouldn't give a hoot for any leader . . . who wasn't himself a child at heart." His point is that men who are effective discussion leaders possess that quality which keeps a man young in mind and spirit, which makes him eager to be continually learning from others, which provides buoyance, exuberance, imagination, and daring.

MELLOWNESS

Vitality without mellowness can be exceedingly ineffective. Those who advocate that good leaders are children at heart do not thereby advocate that children should become our leaders. Exuberance must be tempered with maturity and patience, energy must be conserved and channeled into purposeful activities. Courage and daring must not be reckless, behavior must be reasonably dependable and poised, and above all, a sense of humor must be on reserve to be tapped in moments of tension and distress. There is hardly an author or investigator who has not included a sense of humor as one of the primary characteristics of leadership ability.

SUMMARY

In this chapter we have proposed eight qualities which are desirable in a discussion leader: (1) a well-adjusted personality;

[18] See Stogdill, *op. cit.*, Smith and Kreuger, *op. cit.*, and Merriam, *op. cit.*

(2) a basic respect and concern for human beings; (3) sensitivity to the basic trends and moods of the group; (4) reasonable knowledge of the problems being discussed; (5) facility in verbalizing the ideas of the group; (6) reasonable restraint; (7) vitality; and (8) mellowness. We have emphasized that a sincere belief in human dignity is the most important attitude a leader need possess, and that without such an attitude the skills and trappings of democracy will be so much "sound and fury, signifying nothing." We have also emphasized the dilemma of the "leader as leader" versus the "leader as human being," and have suggested the doctrine of intelligent and tactful partiality as a possible solution.

EXERCISES

1. Hold a discussion on the topic, "What should a person in a position of leadership do with respect to the popular principle that familiarity breeds contempt?"

2. Visit a group discussion in your community. Criticize and evaluate the personal attitudes and traits of the leader.

3. How would you recommend that a very competent and highly educated person of your acquaintance who has a tendency to "look down" on the "unenlightened masses" acquire the respect for human beings which is necessary for an effective discussion leader?

4. "It is unnecessary for a prince to have all the good qualities I have enumerated, but it is very necessary to appear to have them . . . inasmuch as men judge generally more by the eye than by the hand, because it belongs to everyone to see you, to few to come in touch with you. Everyone sees what you appear to be, few really know what you are." — MACHIAVELLI
   What do you think of this point of view?

5. According to the Overstreets, those who tend to have the hardest time to become good discussion leaders are teachers, ministers, lawyers, doctors, and successful businessmen. Those who seem to take most naturally to the role are salesmen, foremen, and journalists.
   Assuming this to be true, how would you explain it?

6. At the conclusion of a discussion in which you have participated or have observed, make some estimates concerning the way group members feel about the meeting, the leadership, and some of the basic issues relating to the problem discussed. Check the accuracy of your social sensitivity by balloting the membership on these same matters and comparing the results with your guesswork.

7. If it is true that a democratic attitude is more important to the leader than skill in democratic techniques, then why need a person with a healthy attitude bother learning any techniques? Discuss.

6

Leadership in Interpersonal Relations

*Applaud us if you like the music, throw potatoes at us
if you don't — but don't just sit there.*

THESE WERE THE WORDS of Composer Gian-Carlo Menotti, speaking
to a New York Women's City Club about his Broadway opera, *The
Consul*.[1] They might just as well be spoken by a discussion leader
to the members of his group. But it would be more easily said than
done. For one of the most difficult functions of democratic leadership is to stimulate and encourage *full, frank, and friendly* participation from the members of a group. This requires that a warm and
permissive atmosphere be established in which people feel comfortable and secure. It means that opinions must be freely expressed
and vehemently argued, while at the same time a basic spirit of
cooperativeness and flexibility is preserved. It implies that the
members must become emotionally involved in the group's proc-

[1] *Time*, May 1, 1950, p. 69. Courtesy of *Time*; Copyright Time, Inc., 1950.

esses while at the same time not succumbing to irrationality. Over-dependence on the leader must be reduced. Reticent members of the group who have something valuable to contribute must be drawn out. Overdominant participants must be curbed. In short, a healthy and mature interpersonal situation must be achieved. It shall be our purpose in this chapter to explore some of the techniques for accomplishing these results.

THE NEED FOR DIPLOMACY

The very first principle we should recognize is that a leader can do none of these things until he has himself become personally acceptable to the membership. He cannot hope to modify or influence the interpersonal patterns of a group unless he first adapts himself to its established customs and mores, and proceeds from there with tact and diplomacy.

Ferenc Merei reports an experiment in support of this principle. Merei studied the behavior of a group of children in a play situation. These children, in the course of time, had worked out certain traditions or procedures of play. "Institutionalization" had taken place. Into this situation an older, aggressive child was introduced and his leadership behavior observed. It was discovered that although the new leader was stronger than any one member of the group, he was not stronger than the group tradition. Overt, brusque, undiplomatic attempts to change or modify play procedures were unsuccessful. It was only by the round-about, diplomatic approach — through accepting the customs of the group at first and then working from within — that the older child was able to make any modifications in the group tradition.[2]

This same phenomenon was quite evident in an Air Force heavy bombardment group in which we served for two and one-half years during World War II. The size of the group varied periodically from between 800 to 1500 men. During the course of its existence, it had seven different commanding officers — all distinct personalities. The first of these men, under whom the group was organized

[2] Merei, Ferenc, "Group Leadership and Institutionalization," *Human Relations,* II (1949), pp. 23–40.

and originally trained, fulfilled the stereotyped picture of an air corps flying colonel — squashed-down cap, adventuresome spirit, and total lack of interest in the formalities of military discipline. During his brief period of leadership (four months), a tradition or group standard grew with respect to military discipline which was, to put it mildly, most unmilitary. It was a tradition that six other leaders, some of them quite strong-willed, were never in the course of two years able to alter. This in spite of the unusual power that goes with a military command and in spite of the fact that all but one (who was much like the first) did make deliberate efforts in that direction.

As we learned in an earlier chapter, social pressure is a powerful force which tends to resist change in group standards. If a leader is to have any real influence on interpersonal relations, his actions must receive enough social support to overcome any barriers that may stand in the way. This will be true of all attempts at leadership on the interpersonal level. Alone the leader can do little. By adapting himself to the group and enlisting the aid of social pressure he can do a great deal.

CLIMATE-MAKING

The primary function of the leader in interpersonal relations is that of "climate-maker." It is he, more than any other member of the group, who sets the mood, tone or atmosphere within which the group operates. In order to attain and maintain the best possible climate, there are several details to which he should attend. Although each may seem minor and unimportant in itself, it is a combination of just such factors as these that can make the weather "warm" or "cold."

The first consideration is that of physical facilities. Nothing can cool the atmosphere of a discussion more speedily than an uninviting room, uncomfortable chairs, unpleasant surroundings, or the inability of each member of the group to sit facing all the others. The only way to avoid having people with their backs to one another, and to avoid having some members in more physically dominant positions than others, is to seat the individuals in a complete circle. Square-shaped arrangements put the people who sit at the corners slightly out of things. Rectangles, elipses, and other non-circular arrangements all place some members at more focal points than others. A little foresight and planning on the leader's part can overcome these physical obstacles.

Another consideration is to make sure that all the group members are not only acquainted with one another, but are given a chance to learn a little about each other. Personal introductions and a little "chit-chat" before the meeting begins can accomplish the purpose. This should be followed up by the use of people's names when addressing them. To facilitate this process it is helpful to ask each individual to write the name he likes to be called by in large letters on a piece of paper, and "hang out his shingle" on the desk, table, or floor in front of him.

It is wise to distribute those persons who are known to be the most talkative around the circle, so that the conversation will not become centered in any one area of the room. If it is known that the group is split into two camps over the issues to be discussed, it is well to avoid their lining themselves up on opposite sides of the table or the room, thus physically intensifying the mental barrier which already exists.[3] If the leader has prior indication that one member of the group may prove overtalkative, he can sometimes get him seated in a location where it is easier to "overlook" his requests for recognition when and if his participation gets out of hand. One author terms such a location the "blind spot," and suggests that in round-table conferences the blind spot is immediately to the right or left of the leader.[4]

Insofar as formal recognition by the leader before speaking can be dispensed with conveniently, it should be so eliminated. Members ought to feel free to break into the conversation at will, observing, of course, the common rules of courtesy and respect for others.

The mood of an entire discussion may be set by the leader's open-

---

[3] A research project recently conducted under the writer's supervision at Northwestern University by Lee Mehlig lends tentative support to the hypothesis that the greater the physical distance between individuals in a face-to-face group, the more likely they are to disagree with one another.

[4] Hannaford, op. cit., Chapter 10.

LEADERSHIP IN INTERPERSONAL RELATIONS

ing remarks. If he talks too long, if he speaks dogmatically, if he fails to be informal and put the group at ease, an icy atmosphere will develop which may be difficult or impossible to defrost. If, on the other hand, he is comfortable, secure and relaxed, he can impart that feeling to the others and, by contagion, they will be encouraged to follow suit. If his own behavior is such that it encourages people to talk freely, it is likely that he will stimulate others in the group to a similar willingness to hear and encourage their fellow members.

In our chapter on the dynamics of a group we saw that one of the principal causes of an uncomfortable atmosphere is the existence under the surface of a large number of unresolved personal tensions. So long as those tensions remain on the hidden agenda rather than the open agenda they will make for an atmosphere of artificiality. It is therefore necessary that the leader do what he can to bring the hidden agenda into the open by providing the members with the time and the opportunity for psyche-group activities. Although it is unwise to provoke such sessions prematurely by tactlessly calling the group's attention to specific interpersonal difficulties that the members are not ready to face, the leader should at least avoid suppressing such discussions when they do begin to occur. It can also do no harm occasionally to throw out a broad, apparently harmless question concerning one of these difficulties on the assumption that if the group feels ready to handle the issue his lead will be followed, and if not it will be promptly dropped. For example, just before the end of a meeting he might ask, "Well, was everyone happy with the participation at tonight's session?" If this happens to be a sore spot which is not yet ripe for lancing, the members will probably nod indifferently and start putting on their hats and coats to go home. But if the leader has guessed the tempo of the group correctly, his question may lead to a constructive airing and solving of several emotional grievances.

To the degree that a leader is able to place himself in the shoes of each participant, and see things from that individual's point of view, he will be able to do a capable job of climate-making. He must keep alert to the many personal reactions and subtle innuendoes of behavior. "John looks bored. He is probably tired and wants to go home. . . . Tony's face showed a brief flush of anger a moment ago. He is probably beginning to get provoked at Ed's remarks." These are the kinds of thoughts that will be flashing through an observant leader's mind.

STIMULATING ARGUMENT

It may seem strange to list as one of the functions of leadership the encouragement of arguments and differences of opinion. Ordinarily we expect the leader to strive for cooperation and agreement within the group and unite the members on common goals and policies. This is by all means his major purpose, and we shall devote two chapters to the processes of resolving conflict. We must remember, however, that unity and agreement are not unmixed blessings. There is something wrong with groups which are unanimous at all times. Either the members have lost every shred of individuality, or else the agreements are superficial and do not represent the best thinking efforts of the group. It frequently happens, in groups that think they have settled on a solution, that a little further probing will explode the supposed agreement. A superficial consensus may have been reached which was not founded on a real understanding of all viewpoints. It did not take all aspects of the problem into consideration. It was perhaps arrived at hurriedly without adequate thought. Hence it will crack under the first bit of pressure that is applied. In striving for a decision the group may have ignored a basic principle set out in Chapter 3 — that there is no particular virtue in social unity unless it has been achieved through diversity and is constantly subject to the ever-changing pressures of individual differences.

The discussion leader, then, in pressing for solutions to the group's problems must not be over-eager for quickly and easily attained agreements. He should be suspicious of unanimity. If solid achievements are desired, he must do as much to instigate conflict and provoke thought as he does to resolve conflict and bring discussion to a close.

There are innumerable techniques at the leader's disposal for stimulating argument. He can play the "devil's advocate" — upholding points of view which the group has overlooked, even though he personally may not believe in them. He can submit information to the group which its members have ignored, and ask them to reconcile it with the stand they have taken. He may describe in vivid terms a specific case which dramatizes the complexity of a problem that the group has oversimplified. He can suggest to a particularly agreeable member the possibility that the group's action might infringe upon his personal interests, in an effort to stimulate that person to examine and possibly contest the agreement. In short, he can do anything within the limits of the group's patience which causes the other members to test and retest the product of their thinking.

OBTAINING EMOTIONAL INVOLVEMENT

One of modern man's greatest problems has been to bring more objectivity, more rationality and more science into the conduct of human affairs. For too long our dealings with our fellow men have been plagued by irrationality and excessive emotionalism. The confusion of disagreement with personal hostility has become a chronic social ill. For these reasons, the emphasis in recent years has been on developing group leaders who can help bring order out of chaos and keep emotional subjectivity to a minimum in group discussion. This is as it should be, and most of what we shall say in succeeding chapters is directed to that end. But like all good things, it can be carried too far. Some perceptive observers are now beginning to realize that a certain amount of chaos is not only inevitable but desirable in a democratic group. It is becoming apparent that no group which makes any constructive progress can be completely amiable and always friendly in its interpersonal relations. There will be times when personal friction is unavoidable and in fact desirable, just as there are times in the lives of the most happily married couples when, for the good of their emotional health, the "kettle must boil over." There are probably no two people in the world who could live in harmony and accord at all times. It is, therefore, somewhat foolish to expect complete emotional stability in our social units, which consist of larger numbers of people. One has good reason to be highly suspicious of the depth of the relationship in a group which lives at all times in an atmosphere of "sweetness and light."

It is in such situations as these that the group leader should become concerned about obtaining emotional involvement. We have witnessed hundreds of meetings at which laudably objective and rational discussions took place, at which verbal agreements were concluded, but at which *nothing really happened* to the basic attitudes and feelings of the people present. They were involved in mind but not in heart, if such a figurative distinction may be made.

Let this argument not be used as a rationalization to justify the constant bickering and emotive behavior that takes place in many groups. We are not advocating or defending the kind of behavior that is so typical of the meetings of many city councils, state legislatures, and congressional committees. There are limits beyond which emotionally-charged disagreements are extremely unhealthy, just as there are limits beyond which family quarrels become utterly destructive. The point we are trying to make is simply this: that unless the members of a group have an emotional as well as an intellectual investment in the discussion, they will receive nothing but an intellectual return. Although this may be profitable, it can hardly be said to realize the full potentialities of a democratic society.

How can the group leader obtain constructive emotional involvement without at the same time provoking excessive and destructive irrationality? This is a problem to which we still have few answers. It is an area where much research needs to be done. A few tentative suggestions can be made. Beyond that the leader will have to feel his own way through the problem, until more definitive answers have been discovered.

Negative Involvement

One idea, suggested by some people, is a concept which might, for want of a better name, be called "negative involvement." Simply stated, the technique is for the leader, through deliberate inactivity and refusal to "show the way," to make the members so thoroughly frustrated that they become emotionally disturbed and strongly motivated to do something constructive about the situation. Another possible reaction, of course, is that they will simply turn away from the group in disgust. But if they stay, the technique may work.

Nathaniel Cantor, a professor of sociology at the University of Buffalo, has used this approach with apparent success in his classes. He operates on the theory that if, in the first two or three weeks of the term, students become sufficiently confused and frustrated about the course they will be challenged to straighten themselves out, and real emotional learning will take place. Professor Cantor finds that rarely does a student drop out of the class in those first harrowing days, even though he makes it clear to them that they are completely free to do so.[5]

We have tried a similar technique in one of our own courses. Although it places a rather severe emotional strain on both students and teacher and at times appears to be no more than a sure-fire device for losing friends and alienating people, it seems to accomplish its ultimate purpose with unerring effect. At first the student feels resentful toward the teacher for not providing the kind of leadership he is used to. But gradually he finds that he enjoys having the initiative which has been thrust upon him. The student also finds that he has a strong personal stake in the group's success and is thus more highly motivated to take an active part. If the group were not successful the blame could not be projected onto the leader, as is usually the case, because the group member has emotionally accepted a share of the responsibility. Group failure would mean personal failure; and most people will not admit defeat before putting up a good fight.

Negative involvement is an extreme and hazardous technique for motivating a group. It should never be used in situations where a group meets together for just a few sessions. It should not be used in groups that are hard pressed for time or where the external fac-

[5] Cantor, Nathaniel, *The Dynamics of Learning*. Buffalo: Foster and Stewart, 1946.

tors require a high degree of efficiency. It is primarily a device for stimulating individual and group growth, and as such has its most appropriate place in a learning situation.

Personal Attack

Another way to achieve emotional involvement is by placing a member or members of the group under personal attack or by stimulating such an attack on yourself. By personal attack, we mean unabashed verbal criticism of an individual's personal attitudes or behavior. This technique is like a spark which can set an entire group on fire. Some members will identify with the person or persons under attack. Some will rally to the side of the attacker. Others will try to harmonize the crisis, or to avoid it. Of one thing you can be sure: everyone in the room will become emotionally involved. The most real, meaningful and fruitful discussions this author has observed have been those in which personal conflict has released the feelings of the group and precipitated an honest facing of the issues.

As with any method of obtaining emotional involvement, this one is fraught with danger. To deal with people's emotions is to play with fire. It may be easier to start the blaze than to put it out. But the solution will not be found in avoiding fire altogether, as so many sterile textbooks recommend that we do. Fire, under proper control, is man's greatest source of energy and power. Certainly we run a risk when we use it, just as we run the risk of getting out of hand with any of our emotions — our loves, our hates, and our fears. But this does not cause us to give up loving, hating and fearing, any more than we can give up fire. Rather we must learn to keep these emotions intelligently controlled, so that we may gain the value of their energy while checking their powers of destructiveness.

Role-Playing

A third way of stimulating emotional involvement is through a method called role-playing. Role-playing may be used to provide the group with a concrete sample of the problem they face so that the issues are personalized and made to come alive. The members can then discuss the problem in terms of a common experience. For example, at a school board meeting in your town one of the members may raise the question of racial discrimination among the students. To some of the board members this may not seem a vital issue. It has not affected them personally. It is somebody else's problem and does not stir their interest deeply. In such a setting the leader might well propose a role-playing scene to stimulate and clarify the discussion. One member of the group might be asked to play the role of a classroom teacher, another might play the role of a Negro boy, and two others might play the roles of white boys who have been in trouble with the Negro. The problem portrayed in the role-playing scene should be a fairly typical one, such as a playground argument; and each of the members taking part will need to have enough imagination and enough familiarity with the feelings of the persons they are portraying to project themselves into the roles and react as those persons might react to the scene played. After each of the role-players has been "briefed" by the leader on the imaginary background of events leading up to this particular episode the scene is spontaneously acted out.

As soon as the personal issues involved have been sufficiently dramatized the leader may "cut" the scene and throw the matter open to the group for discussion. All the members will now have had a common experience to talk about. Many of them will have emotionally identified themselves with one or another of the persons involved in the scene. The issues will have come alive and the group will be more strongly motivated to solve the problem.

Other Methods

If role-playing is not practical in a given situation, the leader can sometimes accomplish the same ends by other methods which also help to dramatize a problem and give it personal meaning. The "case-study" method of discussion is one example. Each member of the group is provided with a detailed, written account of a specific instance of the problem. After all have read the case they are ready to discuss it. This technique has been used for years in the teaching of law, and is currently enjoying an upswing of popularity as a method of studying and solving problems of labor-management relations.

Another method of dramatizing a problem for the purpose of obtaining emotional involvement is for the leader simply to describe a concrete personal experience in a detailed and vivid way. Still other methods are to show the group a film, or play them a tape recording which illustrates specific instances of the problem. All of these techniques have the same effect — they stimulate the individual to personally and emotionally identify himself with the group's activities. That this may not be at all necessary in some groups where emotional involvement is already high (such as a United Nations Security Council meeting) goes without saying.

ENCOURAGING MUTUAL RESPECT AND UNDERSTANDING

If the emotional involvement obtained through the methods described in the preceding section (or naturally present in the situation) is not to get out of hand, steps must be taken to encourage mutual respect and understanding among the participants. When people become emotionally involved in a discussion they are quick to doubt the sincerity and intelligence of those with whom they disagree. *We are swift to judge others but slow to understand them.* If the democratic process is to work effectively we must somehow overcome that tendency. An atmosphere of mutual respect must be developed. So long as such an atmosphere does not exist, participants will hesitate to express honest feelings for fear that they will not be dealt with objectively. One of the most significant insights we have gained from the field of psychotherapy is that if emotional problems are to be solved constructively people must be free to air their feelings without fear of condemnation. One of the hardest lessons we yet have to learn in our day-to-day human relations is that people cannot "help feeling" the way they do. They will not be changed by condemnation. What they need is respect and understanding. Then, and then only, are they likely to change.

But what can a leader do about this problem? What could have been done in a situation such as the following?

On December 6, 1949, Senator Styles Bridges and Professor John K. Fairbank of Harvard University were arguing the question, "Should We Recognize the Chinese Communist Government?" on Town Meeting of the Air. Professor Fairbank believed we should. Senator Bridges was violently opposed. In his first statement following Fairbank's talk, the Senator made these comments, among others:

> My answer . . . is NO! Whether they know what the word "no" means up at Harvard, where Professor Fairbank comes from, or not, I don't know. But I say "NO". . . . [If we recognize the Communists] we remove a friend and substitute an enemy. Why, even a moron in this country should be able to understand that.[6]

During the question period Senator Bridges injected the following statement after an answer given by Fairbank:

> Well, of course, we've got to excuse that as coming from Harvard.[7]

When the audience laughed *at* him, the Senator rebuked them:

> All right, you pro-Communists can laugh, but . . .[8]

(You should realize that none of these comments was made with a vocal inflection that would imply the Senator was jesting.)

It is obviously impossible and undesirable for a leader to censor the thoughts and words of group members. He can, however, "throw his weight and influence" against bigoted behavior in an attempt to discourage its repetition. Fair-minded members of the group, who are usually in a majority, will back him in such a stand. Those in a group who, by their intolerance, would destroy the very bases of human dignity upon which democracy is built must either be

[6] *Town Meeting.* Bulletin of America's Town Meeting of the Air. XV (December 6, 1949), pp. 11–12. Reprinted by permission.

[7] *Ibid.*, p. 19. Reprinted by permission.

[8] This comment does not appear in the Town Meeting bulletin. It was, however, definitely a part of the original radio broadcast.

brought to understand the disruptive nature of their behavior or, failing this, be made to feel the full force of social pressure.

REDUCING OVERDEPENDENCE

An effective democratic leader must at all times resist the efforts of his group to abdicate responsibility for its problems. He must struggle against the tendency of group members to take a "Let George do it" attitude toward the leader. He must encourage them to do as much as they are capable of handling. How can these ends be accomplished?

In the first place, he should make it clear by *word and deed* that he is not hostile to the assumption by them of leadership functions. Nothing destroys the democracy of a group more rapidly than a leader who makes people feel that to assume leadership responsibility is to "muscle in" on the leader's territory and that to question the leader's procedures is to usurp authority which does not belong to them. It is not enough for the leader to *tell* them that they are expected to help him lead. He must also *react* to their aid in such a way as to make them *feel* that his words were sincere. The leader who tells the members of his group that this is *their* discussion, and then appears to be annoyed or hurt when somebody disputes his authority will not be able to build a truly democratic group.

The second step the leader must take in order to develop an independent group is to remove himself from the focal point of group activity. As we learned in Chapter 4, a discussion in which the paths of conversation all run to and from the leader is an over-dominated discussion. The leader must tell the members of the group to speak directly to each other. He must encourage a great deal of spontaneous interplay among them. Above all, he must *not* cut into the conversation with comments of his own before and after every contribution is made. Recognition of members by the leader in order to obtain the floor should be used only when absolutely essential — for instance, when the group is rather large, or at those points in the discussion where many people wish to speak at once.

The extent to which a leader should concern himself with reducing overdependence depends upon the purposes of the group with which he is working. In the case of pure action groups he may not be justified in allotting a great deal of time to training for individual and group growth. However, most organizations in a democratic society are devoted, in part at least, to the development of individual abilities. To some extent, nearly every group leader must play the role of a trainer. Just as all of us set aside a portion of our earnings for insurance premiums to protect ourselves and families against the hazards of an uncertain future, so must the democratic leader take time from the day-to-day functions of the group to build an ever-broadening base of leadership.

DRAWING IN THE NON-PARTICIPANT

Drawing non-participating members of a group into a discussion is a delicate matter. Some experts "solve" the problem simply by recommending that the leader put questions to these individuals. Others take quite an opposite stand:

> After putting the opening discussion question to the group, say nothing more until some group member responds. Keep quiet even though a deathly hush falls over the group. . . . If you wait them out, someone will speak and the ice is broken. . . . They may need an opportunity to think. . . . Calling on group members for responses is strictly taboo at any time and any circumstances. . . . [It] puts them on the spot.[9]

We feel that both of these positions oversimplify the problem. What the leader should do depends entirely upon the goals of the group and upon the specific reasons for the non-participant's reticence. If the purpose of a particular meeting is to arrive at a decision in the quickest possible way, and if there is no real need to hear numerous points of view on the subject, the leader may count it a blessing rather than a hindrance to have a few non-talkers around. Under such conditions he will not even concern himself with drawing in the non-participants. But circumstances such as these are the exceptions rather than the rule. If a group is operat-

[9] From *How to Conduct Conferences*, by Alfred Cooper. Copyright, 1942. Courtesy of McGraw-Hill Book Co., Inc., New York, pp. 26–28.

ing on a discussion basis the presumption is that a large degree of democratic action is being sought. Hence, all views should be considered and everyone should take part, to the upper limit of his abilities, in helping to formulate group decisions.

That people in discussion situations do not necessarily participate in proportion to their ability is obvious to anyone who observes group behavior and explores this issue. There are a multitude of causes for non-participation. Here are just a few possibilities, along with typical comments exemplifying each: [10]

1. A lack of confidence in one's own ideas: "It doesn't make any difference whether I say anything or not, because I never have anything original to contribute."
2. A lack of emotional involvement in the matters being discussed: "I just didn't feel excited about the subject."
3. A lack of skill in verbalizing ideas: "The others can state their ideas so much more clearly than I can; so I'd rather just listen."
4. An inability to think rapidly enough to keep up with the pace of the discussion. "By the time I've mulled over a point long enough to have something to say on it, the rest of the group has moved on to something else."
5. A deeper reflection of ideas: "Some people just seem to think out loud; but I prefer to think to myself a while before speaking."
6. An attitude of detached observation: "I just like to hear what other people have to say about these things."
7. Habitual shyness: "I never talk very much."
8. A lack of sleep, or other physical disturbances: "I could hardly keep my eyes open."
9. Distraction to more pressing personal problems: "The reason I didn't talk today was because I was worrying about a mid-term exam I have next period."
10. Submissiveness to more aggressive members: "A guy can never get a word in edgewise in this outfit, so I just keep quiet."
11. An interpersonal conflict: "I knew that if I ever got started I'd have told that —— off, so I decided not to say anything at all."

[10] This list is based upon the testimony of students who have been the least talkative members of their class discussion groups.

12. A non-permissive atmosphere: "I don't feel free to speak when Miss —— is around."
13. An overdominant leader: "He doesn't care what I think. He just wants an audience to make big speeches to."
14. Fear of being rejected: "I'm afraid everybody will think that what I have to say is silly."
15. A solidified pattern of participation: "Everyone in the group has gotten used to my not talking much, so I feel uncomfortable — as though everyone were surprised — when I do speak."
16. A feeling of superiority: "That was such a pointless discussion and nobody really knew what they were talking about. What a waste of time."
17. A disbelief in the value of discussion: "Talk never changes anybody's mind, so why bother?"
18. Lack of knowledge or intelligence: "The discussion was way over my head."

It should now be clear why no single technique or magic formula can be recommended for drawing in non-participants. In the first place, the leader must consider, in the light of the 'group's goals, whether he should do anything at all about the problem. If he decides that something should be done, he must next attempt to determine the causes for non-participation that are operating in each case. Sometimes this information can be picked up from overt verbal and physical clues. (Lack of confidence may be revealed by a person's voice; lack of sleep by a yawn.) It may also be obtained by the leader in private conversations outside of the meeting or by questions on post-meeting reaction sheets. One of the most effective methods is for the members of the group themselves to openly discuss the matter as a group. This approach not only reveals the causes of non-participation to the leader, but it provides all of the members of the group with increased insight into the problem — which is in itself a strong first step toward achieving a more healthy balance of contributions.

What other steps can a leader take to improve the situation? Those members of the group who hesitate to talk because they lack self-assurance should be given encouragement whenever they do speak, so that their confidence will be bolstered and they are made to feel that their contributions are respected. A brief comment after their contributions, such as "That's an interesting point," or "I'd never thought of that before," will go a long way to motivate future participation. We do not suggest that this be done if it means being insincere. Frequently, however, we are not as generous as we might well be.

For those whose non-participation is due to a feeling of superiority, an attitude of detached observation, or a disbelief in the value of discussion, a challenging question by the leader may serve to get them involved. Questions may also be used successfully with the habitually shy person — *provided* that the question does not put him "on the spot." Asking him for a personal opinion on a matter which is vital but not too controversial is probably the safest way of helping him to get his feet wet.

For the benefit of those who think slowly or who like to reflect more deeply than others, the leader might well take a lesson from the Quakers, who provide periods of silence at their business meetings for the purpose of private deliberation. Perhaps if "talking groups" would sometimes do a little less talking they might be able to achieve a little more solid thinking. This issue brings us, quite logically, to a consideration of another category of problems — those pertaining to the overtalkative member.

CHECKING OVERAGGRESSIVE PARTICIPANTS

To check an overtalkative or overdominant group member and at the same time retain his good will is one of the most taxing problems of diplomacy a group leader can face. Such a person rarely responds to hints and takes offense quite easily at attempts to muzzle him. The path of least resistance is to let him talk. This, however, leads to several undesirable results. It tends to stifle contributions from those who are less aggressive. It works counter to the maintenance of a free and permissive atmosphere. Most important, it may block the group's progress or slow it down immeasurably. It may force the group to resort to "steam-roller" tactics. It may lead the members of the group to "quarantine the aggressor"

— to put him in a state of social isolation which only causes him to become more obnoxious.

In dealing with this problem as with that of non-participation, a leader will do well to understand the causes of overaggressiveness and also to consider rather carefully the needs and purposes of the group. With respect to the latter issue it should be pointed out that a democratic leader has certain obligations to fulfill.

First, he must help protect the group from any single individual or small clique of individuals who try, either consciously or unconsciously, to "take over" power. As Rousseau said, "If we have a prince it is to save ourselves from having a master." Although experimental evidence is inadequate on the point, there is some reason to fear that a democratic group is peculiarly vulnerable to exploitation by intelligent and skillful members who desire to manipulate the discussion for their own ends. The frank and permissive nature of the situation, encouraging people as it does to let down their defenses and expose their real thoughts and feelings, may be highly desirable for the purposes of democratic action but it also sets up a rather naked target for those who are not interested in democracy. One of the primary functions of democratic leadership, therefore, is to block the would-be tyrant — and to do it without becoming "undemocratic!"

The leader's second obligation or goal is to help provide the discipline that is necessary for accomplishing group action. Democracy is not the same as anarchy. Individualism cannot simply run rampant. Some degree of conformity — and hence group discipline — is essential. Everyone cannot talk when he likes or as much as he likes. Everyone cannot come to meetings and leave as and when he pleases, nor carry on little side conversations that disrupt the group. Democracy is a compromise between no discipline (anarchy) and total discipline (totalitarianism), and the leader must see it as such. Non-conforming behavior must be tolerated and even encouraged, but at the same time not allowed to disrupt essential group activities. With respect to disciplining deviant members, the leader must constantly walk a tight rope between these basically conflicting goals.

The overaggressive or overindividualistic members must be kept from stalemating the group's processes and stifling others, but at the same time, any attempts to steam-roller a dissident man or idea through powerful social pressures of conformity must be discouraged. No matter how divergent, obnoxious or insincere a man's behavior may *appear to be,* every reasonable effort should be made to get the group to understand him and to help him become a useful and constructive participant. So far as is humanly possible, he should be aided rather than condemned. It may be that he has potentialities for becoming one of the group's most valuable members, and that his overaggressiveness is simply due to an eagerness to help the group.

What other causes might be motivating his behavior? We have already discussed the most important ones in Chapter 4 when we described the frustration-aggression formula and also talked about the phenomenon of overcompensation. To recapitulate briefly, we might say that overaggressive behavior can be classified in three general categories of causes: (1) that which arises from a sincere but over-eager desire to help the group; (2) that which results unconsciously from a psychological need to dominate the situation or to gain recognition; and (3) that which is a deliberate effort to control and manipulate the group for anti-group purposes.

With regard to the third category the leader's job is to attempt to expose the would-be dominator's motives to the rest of the group, for when he is exposed he is undone. This should be handled carefully, for the leader may be wrong in his analysis, and a man is innocent until proved guilty. Probing questions designed to test the individual's consistency or which force him to make constructive suggestions may help to reveal his hand.

Persons in the first two categories usually are not even aware of their overaggressiveness or of its effects upon the group. Talking with them privately and revealing the group's feeling toward them may, therefore, help to modify their behavior. Giving such a person a position of responsibility, such as recording and summarizing the group's work, may provide his ego with the attention it demands and at the same time keep him relatively quiet. Asking him to help draw out the less verbal members may turn his energies to constructive purposes. In a group where the problem is acute and the time can be afforded, a role-playing scene, designed to dramatize the interpersonal relationships in a hypothetical discussion group which is disrupted by overdomination, may help to focus group attention on the problem and stimulate a re-evaluation and modification by the group itself in its own participation patterns. Only as a last resort, in emergency situations, should members be forcibly silenced and thus lost completely to the group.

SUMMARY

A leader's handling of interpersonal relations is aimed at the ultimate goal of frank, friendly and sensibly balanced participation by the members of the group. This requires that a warm and permissive atmosphere be established in which there is freedom from overdependence upon the leader or overdominance by any of the members of the group. It requires that issues be argued vigorously and that participants become emotionally identified with the problems of the group — though not to the extent of irrationality. It further requires that individuals who are not participating to the utmost of their ability be helped to do so, and that attitudes of mutual respect and understanding among the members be encouraged.

A number of techniques for achieving these goals have been suggested. The appropriateness of any one of them in a given situation will depend upon the purpose of the group and the causes of the interpersonal difficulty being dealt with. We feel that if the group as a whole can face and solve these problems through such techniques as role-playing and open discussion of interpersonal issues the effects upon group behavior will be more real and enduring than if they are handled by the leader through questions, suggestions, or personal conferences. Nevertheless, these latter techniques, and others like them, may frequently be the most expedient methods for achieving some degree of improvement in the situation.

EXERCISES

1. Pick out the two most talkative members and the two least talkative members of a discussion group and arrange individual interviews with them. Try to find out how they feel about the group and their role in the group. Compare the answers of the talkers and non-talkers to see what, if any, significant differences are apparent.

2. How can a group which is culturally conditioned to over-dependence upon authority and autocratic leadership be brought by its leader to an acceptance of greater group responsibility? Discuss.

3. Compile a "gripe list" of all the persons and situations which bother you when you participate in discussions. Attempt to analyze the reasons why these particular problems irritate you, and lay out a plan of action for dealing with them.

4. What can a democratic leader do about a member whose hidden agendum is to sabotage the group's leadership and whose position on every issue is determined by that aim? Discuss.

5. What can a democratic leader do to retain the support and wise counsel of a senior member who becomes uncooperative if not given privileged status and recognition within the group? Discuss.

6. Assuming that a group wishes to operate as democratically and effectively as possible, what would be an ideal balance of verbal participation?

   a) Should everyone in the group talk just about the same amount?

   b) Should one's amount of participation be in proportion to one's ability to contribute valuable ideas to the group? If so, who is in a position to decide what is or is not valuable?

   c) Should some members be encouraged to talk even though they have nothing of value to give to the group simply for the training value to them as individuals?

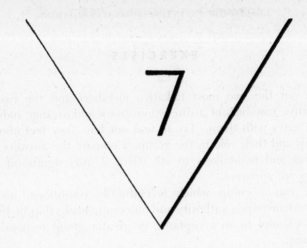

Leadership in Scientific Method

BECAUSE OF THE IMPORTANCE of developing healthy interpersonal relationships in all phases of human activity, and because of our serious leadership shortcomings in that area, most of the attention of investigators at the present time is focused on the psychological problems that arise in group discussion. This is a wholesome sign, for progress in that direction is badly needed. No society can expect to do a good job of cooperative and democratic living until interpersonal relations have been brought under effective control.

There is some danger, however, that in our enthusiasm for overcoming the psychological difficulties, we may assume that once these matters have been worked out effectively, all problems which confront the group will be automatically solved. It is important that we not allow ourselves to be lulled into such complacency. Even though a group may be friendly, cooperative, and devoid of unhealthy psychological barriers to discussion, it will still face joint problems of great magnitude — problems, which, if they are to be solved, necessitate effective group thinking. Successful group thought cannot be achieved simply by creating an atmosphere of warmth and rapport. It requires, in addition, experience and skill in joint reflective thinking. As one book puts it:

> We have been so happy to see people escape from loneliness and inarticulateness that we may have only tardily come to recognize that . . . people who are thinking together must be thinking, not merely talking.[1]

We can best describe the leader's function in this realm by saying that the initiative for creating order out of chaos rests with him. Thomas Huxley has said that "science is nothing but organized common sense." A scientific method of discussion is simply a logical, well-organized and constructive method of group thinking. Any group which sets out upon the task of jointly solving a problem is always first confronted with the question of how to proceed. How can its thinking, based upon a wide variety of facts and viewpoints, be kept orderly and constructive, and continually move forward toward a solution? These are questions to which the competent leader must be able to provide an answer. He should be prepared to guide the group's efforts in a systematic way and must help the members of the group to keep their thinking clear and uncluttered. This requires some knowledge on his part as to what constitutes a good pattern of thinking. Although he must be flexible and willing to adapt that pattern, perhaps a great deal, to the special needs of any particular group or problem, it is essential that some leadership in scientific method be provided.

A number of authors have set forth their ideas of what constitutes a good, scientific pattern of solving problems and have recommended these procedures to conference leaders because, in their own experience, they have found them to be useful. As we examine these recommendations we find them all to be a little different. This finding leads us to believe that no single pattern is *the right one. Any systematic approach which provides order and clarity*

[1] Overstreet and Overstreet, *op. cit.*, p. 28. Reprinted by permission.

will aid the group thinking process. We do find, however, that all
of the proposals made by various experts have striking similarities.
Though they may use different terminology, they are all similar to
the "pattern of reflective thinking" originally proposed by Dewey,[2]
and adapted to the group situation by such authors as McBurney
and Hance. The recommendations we shall make are derived from
this school of thought and can be investigated more fully by the
reader in the original sources.

We have said that the leader must understand what constitutes
a good pattern of thinking before he undertakes to deal with a
group and its problems. We should like to make it absolutely clear
that this does not mean he should have a preconceived notion of
what constitutes the best solution to their problem or problems.
Having a preconceived *methodology* is quite different from having
preconceptions about what the group should or should not *decide*
about its problems. He may determine ahead of time *how* they
might best decide, but not *what* they should decide. When either
a leader or member has pre-judged the problem itself the very
essence of cooperative thinking is destroyed. Cooperative thinking
means *thinking together toward a solution.* This is impossible
when a member of the group has already made up his mind before
the group meets.

This is a crucial matter. Too often men who are really executives,
advocates, or instructor-leaders operate under the guise of cooperative thinking, and thus seek to gain acceptance for preconceived
ideas of their own. There are even books and research articles
written on how to do this.[3] It becomes increasingly obvious to those
who work with group discussion that, when cleverly and subtly
perverted in this way, it can become one of the most powerful
tools of persuasion ever known. It is much more powerful than
straightforward propaganda because the members of the group,
thinking that they are participating in the decision, lay all of their
cards honestly on the table, and then are caught completely off

[2] Dewey, John, *How We Think*, Revised. Boston: Heath, 1933.

[3] Cooper, *op. cit.*; and Maier, Norman R. F., "The Quality of Group Decisions as Influenced by the Discussion Leader," *Human Relations*, III (1950), pp.
155–74.

guard without even knowing what has happened to them. The ethics of such procedures are highly questionable. A group discussion leader is not supposed to be an advocate or teacher, and cooperative thinking is not supposed to be persuasion or instruction. Discussion assumes that *everyone,* including the leader, is open to the possibility of change.

There are some skeptics who maintain that real scientific thinking, reasonably free from prejudice and preconception, is an impossible dream, in a group situation. We shall refer these skeptics to the experiences of a group of men who faced one of the most difficult problems the world has known — a problem laden with all sorts of fears and prejudices — "What should the United States do about atomic energy control?"

Shortly after the first atomic bomb was dropped on Hiroshima and World War II had ended, President Truman asked the State Department to make recommendations to him concerning this nation's policy with regard to atomic energy. He wanted a plan which this country, shouldering the bulk of responsibility for the bomb, could present to the United Nations. A Board of Consultants, composed of five outstanding men led by David Lilienthal (later to become the first chairman of the United States Atomic Energy Commission), was asked by Dean Acheson, who was then Under-Secretary of State, to do the job. Here is what one of the members of that board had to say about the way in which the problem was approached:

> At the first meeting . . . the group agreed the subject was too important to be subjected to the hazards of the push and pull of the committee approach. And so, even before we studied the problem of atomic energy, we studied committee techniques. . . .
>
> Our first joint decision . . . was to liberate all our discussions from idea-possessiveness . . . we agreed that we should attack the problem inductively. . . .
>
> We were not going to get into the usual type of barter system, trading off one pet idea against another. . . . We agreed that we would issue five reports if any of us felt that the group report lacked directness and honesty.

You might call this a sort of search for individual and group objectivity. At the least it meant that each of us was pledged to attempt to emancipate himself from the tyranny of his own ego. We were trying to create a collective wisdom. At first it was hard to do this. Every now and then the discussion would break down just because one of us found it difficult to get used to the science of joint thinking and would lapse into the role of prosecutor or defendant. But little by little the preconceived ideas dropped out; the clash of conflicting personalities became less and less apparent. . . . [4]

This committee finally submitted a unanimous report to the president, which became the basis of the United States plan for world-wide atomic energy control presented to the United Nations by Bernard Baruch (known popularly as the "Baruch plan"). In a crucial test it had been clearly proven that the "science of joint thinking" can be mastered effectively if men of intelligence and goodwill make an honest effort to use it. The fact that the United Nations did not adopt the American proposal in no way detracts from the thoroughness and competence with which it was drawn up. On the contrary, the manner in which the United Nations has handled this particular issue is vivid proof of the need for more open-mindedness in that organization.

Assuming that a group is willing and able to free itself from prejudice and to do an honest job of scientific thinking, the leader must be ready to provide guidance in that undertaking. He must know where to begin and in what direction to proceed so that an orderly sequence of reflective thinking may take place. What is this scientific pattern which the experts have found to be effective? In what way should the leader proceed?

LIMIT THE PROBLEM

The first step is to have the group agree upon the limitations of the problem — to have them draw a boundary line around the area in which they are to work. This is essential if one wishes to avoid

---

[4] Cousins, Norman, and Thomas K. Finletter, "A Beginning for Sanity," *Saturday Review of Literature*, XXIX (June 15, 1946), pp. 8–9. Reprinted by permission.

the danger of dissipating the time and energy of the group on irrelevant matters or on matters which are beyond the scope of its proper concern. By bringing the problem into focus, by clearly staking out the ground that must be covered, endless hours of waste and confusion can be avoided. For example, the atomic energy consultants floundered helplessly for days in a maze of seemingly insoluble problems until they discovered a way in which they could delimit the task. This occurred when they came to realize that, since uranium was the only source of atomic energy, then or in the forseeable future, and since it was available in relatively few places in the world, their problem could be limited to figuring out ways and means of controlling the world's supplies of uranium. Similarly, a group which is concerned, let us say, with combatting juvenile delinquency in its community should decide at the outset whether it intends to concern itself with both preventive and curative measures or whether it wishes to limit its endeavors to one or the other.

CLARIFY THE CONCEPTS INVOLVED

Having built a fence, as it were, around the problem, the next logical step is a clarification of the concepts with which the group is likely to be dealing. We have seen earlier that the democratic process is a verbal affair. Since language is the principal means by which the members of the group will communicate with one another, this step involves primarily a definition of terms. Its purpose is to make certain that the members of the group understand one another and have a common understanding of the meaning of the concepts with which they are working. Referring again to the atomic energy committee, before they attempted to solve the problem itself it was necessary that the members learn what was meant by "atomic energy," "nuclear fission," "isotope," "U-235," and a host of other concepts. For this purpose they asked Dr. J. Robert Oppenheimer, an atomic physicist and member of the group, to "brief them" on the meaning of such terms.

Similarly, the members of the executive committee of a labor union, discussing the problem of communist activities within their union, must clarify their thinking and agree at the outset on what they mean by a "Communist" and by "Communist activity." Do they consider a Communist to be one who is a card-holding member of the party, a member of a so-called Communist-front organization, or simply one who is sympathetic to some of the Communist doctrines? Is anyone who speaks in tune with the party-line engaged in Communist activity, or does Communist activity refer only to acts of force and violence? These are vital questions upon which understanding must be reached before the group can proceed logically to the next step in its pattern of reflective thinking.

DETERMINE THE GROUP'S OBJECTIVES

Having taken as many precautions as seem reasonable by way of limiting the scope of the problem and clarifying the meaning of the concepts to be dealt with, the group's next job is the determination of its objectives. Toward what end is it striving? What goals does it seek? What are its motives and desires? What basic values does it hope to achieve? These are critical questions in the functioning of any society.

Often the answers are clear and simple. To increase the family's income, to wipe out crime, to improve the nation's health, to achieve world peace may be the obvious goals and desires of groups of people working and thinking together in those areas. But often the answers are neither simple nor obvious, and in such situations the leader must encourage his group to discover what it is that it really wants. Until people know clearly where they are going, it is rather difficult to figure out the best way of getting there.

For example, here are the members of the local board of education trying to decide whether religious education should be introduced in the public schools of their community. The discussion is a lively one, but seems to be getting nowhere. There are those who favor the suggested plan of religious education and those who oppose it. All of them are being reasonable and are trying honestly to work out a mutually satisfactory course of action. Yet they are making no progress. The trouble is that they have not yet clarified the goal or goals toward which they are striving. They have not brought their personal motives out into the open to discuss and examine with the others. Perhaps some of them are not even consciously aware of their own basic values and objectives. In short, this group is trying to decide upon a course of action without having first agreed upon the ends which its course of action is designed to achieve. In the words of a well-known expression, "We don't know where we're going, but we're on our way."

A competent leader would recognize the difficulty and would seek to remedy the situation. He would ask questions in an attempt to discover the desires each member of the group is seeking to satisfy and would then work for agreement on a common goal. Without understanding and agreement on the ultimate ends which a group seeks, nothing better than shaky and tentative compromise solutions can be achieved. For without this understanding, there are no criteria by which the possible solutions can be evaluated intelligently — no yardsticks by which they can be measured. How can we decide if religious education in the schools is a good idea until we understand and agree upon what we are trying to accomplish in the public school system?

If, as some people believe, church and state should be kept completely separate, we have one approach to the problem. If, as others believe, separation of church and state is not as important as indoctrinating our children with religious faith, we have another approach to the problem. And if, as still others believe, religion is a matter of personal choice and education a matter of public necessity, we have quite another approach to the problem. Our decisions depend upon the goals we seek, and without an intelligent understanding of those goals we cannot hope to make intelligent decisions. This is basic to scientific thinking.

ANALYZE THE PROBLEM-SITUATION

Many groups, though unaware of the technicalities of scientific method, are guided by their own good common sense to follow the three steps which we have outlined. It is in moving forward from this point that common sense often fails to provide an adequate formula. Too often, having done what has been suggested thus far, people suppose themselves ready to plunge headlong into a consideration of possible solutions to the problem. Such a move is extremely unintelligent. No one is adequately prepared to solve any kind of problem until he has made a thorough analysis of the situation in which he finds himself. This should include both a survey of the situation as it is (what are the facts?) and a diagnosis of the causes which have given rise to it.

A competent group leader will no more guide his group to a consideration of solutions prior to proper analysis than will a competent physician write a prescription without first examining the patient and discovering the causes of his illness. How can a congressional committee write a good labor-management relations bill without having first examined the industrial scene objectively and discovered the causes of labor-management difficulties? How can the United States eliminate racial and religious discrimination until we discover the basic causes of the problem and go to work on them? How can the nations of the world hope to achieve a workable and lasting peace until they have discovered and dealt constructively with the situations and circumstances which give rise to war?

What are the facts? How did the situation get the way it is? These are the kinds of questions which, in the realm of medical research or any other natural science, are so commonplace as a necessary first step in curing any disease or solving any problem that we take them for granted. But in many of our social units we have not yet seen the light! It is to be hoped that with more effective group leadership in the future those questions will become as commonplace in society as they now are in science.

RE-EXAMINE THE GOALS

Having made an analysis of the situation it is often, though not always, necessary to undertake a re-examination of the goals which have been set up earlier by the group. It is necessary whenever the analysis shows the objectives previously agreed upon to be unrealistic, unattainable, or perhaps even undesirable. Since this is often the case, and since some knowledge of the facts is required before sensible goals can be worked out, many experts recommend holding off completely on the consideration of objectives until after an appraisal of the situation has been made. Hence, instead of re-examining the goals at this point in the pattern, they set them up for the first time.

Either procedure works well. The kind of problem which the group is dealing with should govern their choice. For instance, if the problem being discussed is that of racial and religious discrimination, the group's goals are not likely to be influenced very much by an examination of the situation as it exists. For that reason the group might just as well clarify its objectives at the outset, thus giving more purpose and focus to its investigation of the problem-situation. Judging from their report, that was precisely the procedure followed by the President's Committee on Civil Rights.[5]

On the other hand, a group of sociologists might be discussing the tremendous number of marital difficulties in this country in an attempt to alleviate the problem. Prior to an analysis of the situation they might have hoped to find means for entirely eliminating divorces and separations. After a careful investigation into the extent and causes of the problem, they might conclude that they should seek only to reduce the number of cases. In the course of analysis they may have discovered that some separations are inevitable and, in some situations, even desirable. Throwing light on a problem may significantly influence our attitudes toward it. That is why a re-evaluation of objectives, in the light of the facts, should usually take place before a group proceeds to the next step in reflective thinking.

DISCOVER AND DESCRIBE THE POSSIBLE SOLUTIONS

The next step involves the discovery of possible solutions. Here again the process may be obvious and routine, or it may be extremely complex. A family group may be attempting to decide whether or not to go out of town for two weeks on a summer vacation. The alternatives may be clear and simple and require no elaborate investigation — either they go out of town or they stay home. For other problems, the possible solutions are not quite so

[5] *To Secure These Rights.* Washington, D.C.: U.S. Government Printing Office, 1947.

simple to discover. For example, how can we protect the United States against totalitarian conspiracies without becoming totalitarian ourselves in the process? Here are very clear-cut objectives, but if anyone has found a satisfactory solution which adequately accomplishes both of those goals he must be keeping it secret from the American public.

It is important to satisfactory reflective thinking that the step we are now discussing not be confused with the step which follows it, namely the evaluation of possible solutions. The present step is designed merely to *discover* the possible courses of action and *learn* what they mean — it is not intended to involve an appraisal of them. Appraisal and attitudes must be reserved for later. Unless these functions are carefully kept apart, cooperative thinking may soon degenerate into competitive wrangling. The discovery and description of possible solutions can and should be an objective process. Whether or not the members of the group approve of the suggestions is not relevant here. The purpose is to *understand* all the possibilities available. Most of the world's progress has been made by people who were willing to learn about new ideas which, when first suggested, seemed foolish or impractical. Most of the world's lack of progress has been due to those whose prejudices caused them to attempt to evaluate ideas before understanding them, or to refuse to evaluate new ideas at all.

How often the history books tell the story of people like Christopher Columbus, Susan B. Anthony, Alexander Graham Bell, and the Wright brothers, whose ideas were laughed off as foolish, impractical dreams but who each lived to see their dreams come true. And how often, today, we see people condemning, rejecting or scoffing at modern architecture, modern music, psychoanalysis, or the Kinsey Report without understanding in the least what each entails.

The group leader should be firm at this point. He should insist that all conceivable points of view be brought before the group and given a fair hearing. He should discourage the group from "laughing off" new ideas or from ridiculing them to death, as many people are so prone to do. Though he may have to stand against the tide of majority opinion in order to accomplish this, in the long run his efforts will be appreciated. History shows that human beings have a peculiar habit of resisting unconventional nonconformist points of view when they are first advanced, while coming to appreciate them and even becoming grateful for them if, in spite of the opposition, they eventually manage to gain widespread acceptance.

EVALUATE THE SOLUTIONS

We come now to evaluation of possible solutions, the final step in the pattern of reflective thinking. All of the steps which have preceded it are designed to prepare the group for this phase of its activity. It is here that each of the courses of action that has been suggested is "weighed and measured." The goals which were set up earlier are used as the yardsticks of measurement, and the analysis provides the raw materials with which the group works. The basic questions to be asked at this point are: "Will these means accomplish the ends for which they are intended?" "Will these answers solve the problem?"

All the evidence, values and reasoning powers which are at the group's disposal must be brought to bear on those questions, so that a decision may be reached. That decision need not be final and unalterable. In fact, it is far healthier if the group recognizes the limitations of its thinking process and realizes that only by *trying out* the most reasonable solution can the questions be answered conclusively. In other words, discussion can at best answer those questions only tentatively. It can only say, "This solution is *probably* the best one." The rest is left to experimentation, for the "proof of the pudding is in the eating thereof." A wise leader will do all in his power to keep the group from becoming complacent and dogmatic about its decisions. He will do all he can to encourage an open-minded, experimental attitude.

ADAPTABILITY

It is not enough to know the scientific pattern and to utilize it as a basis for group leadership. The competent leader also knows when *not* to use it as it stands. He is prepared to modify it and adapt it to the needs of a given situation. If, at the very outset of a discussion, the limitations of a problem are clear, the concepts and objectives well-defined, the causes obvious, and the alternatives plain, it would be a foolish leader who encouraged his group to labor its way through all of those steps. Such a group is ready for evaluation.

The leader should recognize what is already apparent to everyone and try to focus the group's attention on what still needs to be done. Scientific method in group discussion should be viewed as an aid, not as a strait-jacket. It should be used with flexibility and common sense. Perhaps the only aspects of the whole pattern that should be adhered to rigidly are the principles that, in any group problem-solving activity, understanding should precede evaluation, and clarification of the terms employed should precede both.

SUMMARY

We have pointed out that one of the functions of leadership is to guide a group through a systematic or scientific approach to its problems. This usually involves the following steps: (1) limit the problem, (2) clarify the concepts involved, (3) determine the group's objectives, (4) analyze the problem-situation, (5) re-examine the goals, (6) discover and describe possible solutions, (7) evaluate the solutions. We have also emphasized that this pattern should be adapted to specific situations, and need not always be utilized in full.

EXERCISES

1. Visit a group discussion in your community or a class in group discussion. Keep a record of the problem-solving pattern used there and evaluate the leader's methods of guiding the group's thinking process.
2. Lead a small group discussion in which your immediate job is to:
   a) Help the group define and delimit a hazy problem
   b) Help the group diagnose a problem
   c) Aid the group in determining its ultimate objectives
   d) Release the creative talents of a group which is confronted with a clear problem that has no apparent solution
   e) Lead a group in the evaluation of possible solutions to a problem when the possibilities, criteria, and analysis are already given.
3. Conduct a "brain-storming" session on some problem of interest to your group in which members suggest all the possible solutions they can think of — foolish or not — and in which no one is allowed, by word or gesture, to indicate any evaluation.
4. Imagine that you have been called in to moderate a labor-management dispute. How might you go about reducing preconceived opinions and inducing scientific methods?
5. Most people are not accustomed to solving their individual problems in a logical or systematic way. In view of that fact, aren't we hoping for too much when we expect them to be scientific in *group* problem-solving situations? Discuss.
6. Frequently attempts by leaders to discipline group thinking processes along lines similar to those indicated in this chapter result in killing the spontaneity of the discussion and in stifling the creative talents of the group members. Can such undesirable results be avoided? If so, how? Discuss.

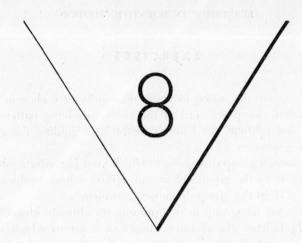

Leadership in Cooperative Thinking

GROUP LEADERSHIP IS NOT SIMPLY a matter of promoting healthy interpersonal relationships and encouraging scientific procedures. Whenever two or more people attempt to *think together,* they become easily confused. Constructive thinking is a complicated enough process for most of us when carried on privately, let alone in groups. In group situations we must coordinate our own thoughts with those of others, many of whom think at different speeds, different levels, and in different ways. Some people grasp ideas quickly, whereas others are slow to assimilate new thoughts. Some people tend to think in more concrete terms than others. Some are highly methodical. Others tend to be "scatterbrains." One of the big problems of leadership is to pull these divergent types together and coordinate them into a thinking team. This requires the performance of many functions which we include here under the general heading of leadership in cooperative thinking.

Each of these is a leadership service which must be performed by someone in the group if the other members are to be enabled to think their problems through together.

INITIATING DISCUSSION

The group leader's first task is to get the cooperative thinking process under way. He must open the discussion and start the ball of conversation rolling. His opening remarks should accomplish three purposes.

First, they should establish a warm and friendly climate. We have already discussed the importance of this matter, and have noted that if the leader talks too long, speaks formally, or appears dogmatic, the group will get off to a weak start. His remarks should be brief and informal. They should convey the impression that frank and free participation from the members will be encouraged, and that the leader has no intention of dominating the discussion or dictating its procedures.

The second purpose of the leader's introductory remarks is to stimulate as much interest in the problem as he can in a few words. People do not think unless they are disturbed about something. The leader should help to get them disturbed. Any statements he can make which dramatize the problem in concrete, vivid terms will serve this function.

The leader's third purpose, as he opens the discussion, is to start the members of the group talking together. To do this it is necessary to conclude his remarks with a question — preferably directed at a specific member of the group and one that *cannot* be answered by a simple "yes" or "no." If the question is put to the group in general, everyone hesitates to be first in responding. (This does not apply to a group that is already well-acquainted.) Eventually somebody will talk, just as someone will always be first on the dance floor. But the tension of that initial awkward moment of silence can be avoided if the leader will direct his query to a specific individual.

Questions with simple "yes" or "no" answers should be avoided, because they do not get the ball rolling by itself. If the leader asks such a question it is quickly answered, and the discussion is right back in his lap to initiate again. Of course, this may even happen with a good question. Most groups, particularly new ones, warm up slowly. The leader may have to light several matches to the first stick of wood before other twigs will catch fire directly from it. He has to make the first one burn a bit — talk a bit — before that can happen. The leader should not be discouraged if this requires three or four attempts, for that is normal; but after that he had better use a bigger match — a more provocative question. Sometimes he may even need a "stick of dynamite," in the form of a highly explosive idea.

Whether at the beginning of the discussion, or later on, questions are the most vital instruments at a leader's disposal. If it were necessary to sum up all the skills of group leadership in one phrase, we would say that a leader must be a master of the art of questioning. Much of the material in Part Two of this book is designed to help him know what kinds of questions to ask. But in addition to the content of the question, its form is important enough to warrant some of our attention.

For one thing, the leader's questions should be clear and concise. There is nothing more bewildering in discussion than long, involved questions with vague meanings. Furthermore, two or three questions should not be rolled into one. This is an exceedingly common habit, and one that group leaders should learn to overcome. Finally, questions should be phrased in such a way as to indicate that an answer is sincerely sought. They should not be public speeches followed by a question mark! If the reader will study some of the samples given in the exercises at the end of this chapter he will see some of the differences between good and poor questioning techniques.

SUMMARIZING AND TRANSITION-MAKING

Having gotten the discussion under way successfully, the next leadership function is to keep it moving in such a manner that the members of the group are clear as to what they have accomplished, where they are at the time, and where they are going next. This requires occasional interruptions on the part of a group leader for the purpose of summarizing and providing transitions from one major point to another.

One of the things that a leader can learn only from experience is to sense when a group is ready for summaries and transitions. This becomes evident from clues such as bafflement on people's faces and restlessness in their bodily movements. Occasionally they will even verbalize their confusion and impatience. Summaries and transitions should be simple and to the point. They should not be a repetition of everything that has been said, but should attempt to pull it all together. They are designed to correlate and review what has been decided, and to suggest what logically might be considered next. An example follows:

> I believe we have all agreed that the mental institutions in this state do not have sufficient funds to do an adequate job, and that the legislature should provide more money. But even if we get the money, are there enough trained people to fill the necessary positions? How about that, Doctor Brown?

It often happens that the leader is not quite sure what, if anything, the group has agreed upon. In such cases, he should phrase a summary which he *thinks* represents the feeling of the members accurately and then ask: "Now, is this the way everybody feels? Is there anyone who differs? O.K., then, let's move on." He then proceeds to initiate discussion on the next phase of the problem.

RECORDING THE DISCUSSION

To provide summaries, and to do it well, one cannot always rely on memory. Another responsibility of group leadership, therefore, is to provide for the taking of notes so that a record may be kept, not of everything that is said, but of those contributions which seem to be significant in the thinking process of the entire group. It is sometimes helpful, if a blackboard is available, to put these notes on the board where everyone can see them and where they can serve as the group's memory. One member of the group may be asked to perform this particular leadership service.

Frequently, however, the use of a blackboard is an inhibiting influence on the members of the group, for they are constantly aware that something is being written down and are thus working under a certain amount of unnatural pressure. For that reason it may be better for the recorder to work unobtrusively, taking the necessary notes on a piece of paper and reviewing for the group when that service becomes necessary.

CLOCK-WATCHING

Any group which is to function effectively must occasionally be reminded of the amount of time it is spending on a particular point and of the necessity for finishing its work by a certain hour. Otherwise the members lose perspective and fail to apportion their efforts reasonably. It is tempting for people to pursue fascinating ideas which are actually irrelevant to the problem at hand. It is also easy for a group to get bogged down on a minor point, hence never getting to the core of the problem. Someone must assume leadership for reminding the group of its responsibilities.

If the man officially called leader, or any other individual in the group, were to be the one who constantly performed this leadership service, it can readily be seen how such a person might become obnoxious to the group. Although recognizing the merit of his suggestions, the members might feel that he was "spoiling their fun." This is true of many other functions discussed in this chapter, and it is a potent argument for the philosophy of diffused leadership. If, on different occasions, various members of the group were to perform the clock-watching function, the stigma would be removed from any one individual.

SIDE-TRACKING IRRELEVANCIES

One of the difficulties which occurs repeatedly in discussion groups is the contribution by individuals of statements which are irrelevant to the point being discussed, or premature in terms of scientific method. Such comments are often simply passed off by the group and thus do no harm. But more often than not someone else will pick up the trend of thought introduced by this member and the entire group is soon seduced into following a path which leads away from the original target.

In our experience with discussion groups we have found this phenomenon to be *the most important single cause* of breakdowns in the cooperative thinking process. The average group member seems to be a "sucker" for exploring every bypath that is proposed. Perhaps this is due to the power of suggestion exerted by the one who introduces the irrelevancy. Or it may be a desire on the part of the others not to seem discourteous by ignoring the comment. It may even represent a hidden desire on the part of group members to free themselves from the confining discipline of systematic thought. Or it may simply be that they are unaware of getting off the beam. In any case, one of the most necessary and psychologically unpopular leadership services is to get the group back on the main track. This must be done in a tactful way, so that nobody's feelings are injured. For instance:

> That's a very interesting point, Mrs. Turner, but I'd like to get back to the question Miss Byers raised a moment ago.

or

> That's a good idea, John. Let's come back to it later, after we get this other matter settled.

ELABORATING CONTRIBUTIONS

Sometimes a participant in discussion will have an excellent idea which he cannot formulate or verbalize and make understandable to the rest of the group. A valuable leadership service is performed when somebody else enters the discussion and says, "Is this what you mean, Phil . . . ?" and then proceeds to restate the point in his own words, or to give an apt illustration of the idea. Unless this is done, individuals in the group will continue to think on different levels, and no meeting of minds will take place.

SEEKING FURTHER OPINIONS

There are always some members of a group who take a position without presenting adequate reasons for their attitude. This makes it impossible for others to understand why they feel as they do. In order to overcome this barrier, someone must assume the leadership in probing this individual for additional statements of opinion. One would think that to ask a simple question such as, "Why do you feel that way, Bill?" does not require much skill. To be sure, it does not. Still it is amazing how few participants in a typical discussion are sufficiently group-centered to be concerned about exploring the other man's beliefs. If the discussion process is to mean anything at all leadership must be exerted in encouraging group members to become less egocentric and more interested in one another.

SEEKING FURTHER INFORMATION

One of the most common causes for stalemates in discussion is a lack of sufficient information. Frequently, certain members of the group have the background which would enable them to contribute the necessary facts. They fail to do so, either because they do not recognize the pertinence of their knowledge or because nobody bothers to ask them, and they are not eager to take the initiative. It may be necessary for a leader, who recognizes the possibility of getting help for the group from this individual, to put questions to him which draw the information out. "Joe, do you happen to know how long ago that plant was built?" "How many members do you have in your organization, Jane?" These are the sorts of questions which fall into this category.

TESTING THE VALIDITY OF CONTRIBUTIONS

In our eagerness to get people to participate in discussion, we must not lull ourselves into believing that everything which is said is worthwhile. The hallmark of intelligence is discrimination, whether in the individual or group thinking process. Everything that is said may be valuable in that it helps us to understand the contributing members and reveals their thought processes, but in terms of helping to solve the group's problems it may be worthless. Consequently, a vitally necessary leadership function — one in which every single member of a group should share — is to question and critically evaluate the ideas brought forth. "Where did you get those facts?" "Who is this so-called expert you are quoting?" "Is that a typical example?" "*How* do you know that what you are saying is true?" Without such probing as this the democratic process might just as well go out of business, for it will accomplish no worthwhile purpose.

REALITY TESTING

Closely related to the previous point, but worthy of a separate category all its own, is the question which forces a group to face reality. It is extremely easy, when people are sitting around in a comfortable room talking over their problems, to become abstract and unrealistic — to oversimplify the difficulties and ignore reality. The individual who says, "Is this as simple as you would have us believe?" "That sounds like a mighty fine plan, but will it work?" or "How would you apply that principle in this specific case?" performs an essential leadership service.

SETTING STANDARDS

Not only should a group be made to face reality, but it should also be encouraged to live up to its professed ideals. In the confusion of discussion or heat of argument it is easy for people to lose sight of the very purposes for which the group exists. That is why it becomes necessary for group leaders to remind the membership, "Doesn't this proposal ignore our ultimate objectives?" "Aren't we forgetting our obligations to those we are supposed to be protecting?"

POINTING OUT SIMILARITIES

It was suggested at the outset of this chapter that one of the reasons for group leadership is the need to coordinate the ideas of individuals who think in different ways. Therefore, the group leader frequently finds it necessary after several members have made their contributions to say, "Now it seems to me that you four people are all suggesting just about the same thing. Isn't this the basic idea . . . ?" He then proceeds to synthesize and asks for their approval.

POINTING OUT DIFFERENCES

Not only do group members who have similar ideas express them in different ways, but sometimes people who have different ideas describe them in a way that sounds the same. For example, one member of the group who is a staunch advocate of free enterprise makes the statement that he is much in favor of further power developments in the Missouri Valley (meaning development by private capital). Another member, who believes strongly in government enterprises like the Tennessee Valley Authority, agrees whole-heartedly that further power developments in the Missouri Valley are desirable (meaning a Missouri Valley Authority).

In such a situation a leader is necessary who can point out, "I don't think that you two are really talking about the same thing," and who then goes on to explain why.

RESOLVING CONFLICT

This is a major field in itself. We shall devote the next two chapters to the specific problems involved in resolving conflict.

CONCLUDING THE DISCUSSION

The leader's final duty in the cooperative thinking process is to bring the discussion to a satisfactory close. He should do this by summarizing what has been accomplished. He should point out what has been agreed upon, where there are clear disagreements, and what remains confused and unresolved. It is well to remind the group not to be discouraged at having failed to solve all the world's problems in two hours and to suggest, when warranted, that if every group could do as much as their group has done to reduce misunderstanding, perhaps some of man's most burdensome conflicts could be resolved.

SUMMARY

Leadership in cooperative thinking involves a series of services, most of which are performed as well by members of the group as by the officially designated leader. They include (1) initiating discussion, (2) summarizing and transition-making, (3) recording the discussion, (4) clock-watching, (5) side-tracking irrelevancies, (6) elaborating contributions, (7) seeking further opinions, (8) seeking further information, (9) testing the validity of contributions, (10) reality testing, (11) setting standards, (12) pointing out similarities, (13) pointing out differences, (14) resolving conflict, and (15) concluding the discussion. Special attention must be given to the form in which questions are phrased. They should be clear and concise, they should contain only one question, and they should indicate that an answer is sincerely sought.

EXERCISES

1. Divide your study group into small sections of three or four persons each. Have each unit choose a problem of real significance to its members. Each of these sub-groups, functioning as a committee outside of class, should then hold deliberations on its problem and submit a written report to the total group. Every member of each sub-group should also write up his own evaluations of the committee's cooperative thinking procedures. Those evaluations should then be discussed in class.

2. Visit a group discussion and copy down verbatim every question that is asked of one member by another. Classify these questions in terms of the categories discussed in this chapter. Evaluate each question in terms of its form.

3. Here are some sample statements which group leaders have used at the conclusion of their introductory remarks in order to start the discussion moving. Rate these questions as Excellent, Fair, or Poor, and give reasons for your ratings.

    a) "This is a big problem, so we better get started. Does anyone have any ideas?"

    b) "Ladies and Gentlemen, there is absolutely no question in my mind that the Administration has blundered badly on this issue. It is for us — the honest, upright citizens of America — to repair the damage before it is too late. Mr. Nelson, tell us your views on this deplorable situation!"

    c) "Bill, as you see it what is the basic issue here?"

    d) "Mrs. Phillips, if you were confronted with a choice between salvation and degradation, which would you choose?"

    e) "There are apparently two schools of thought as to the best psychology for publicizing our civilian defense plans. Does anyone happen to know what the U.S. Council of Mayors has said about this?"

    f) "Jane, do you believe that college sororities have a right to exclude certain girls from membership because of their race or religion?"

g) "Economists, government officials and other experts are apparently all agreed that the only thing we can do is raise income taxes. Now, what do you people think?"

h) "George, do you think that it's right for the colleges to place such an emphasis on football and to subsidize their athletes, or would you rather have them put more money into the academic program — hiring more professors, giving more scholarships to needy students, and lowering tuition rates?"

i) "Apparently we have three alternatives: we can double our dues, cut out half of our activities, or disband the organization. Sally, what reaction do you think the members would have to doubling the dues?"

j) "As you understand it, Mr. Martin, what is involved in this proposal for consolidating our departments and how do you feel about it?"

k) "It would probably be a good idea to start off here by getting some agreement on what we mean by 'fellow-travellers.' Sam, what kind of picture comes to your mind when you hear someone say that Joe Axelrod is a Communist fellow-traveller?"

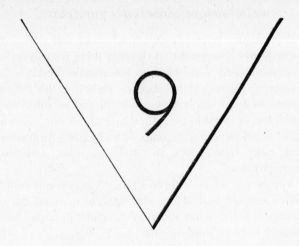

Resolving Social Conflict: Integration

In the little city of Leon one night last week,
brothers Ignacio and Manuel Vargas, aged 18 and 20,
went from the open-roofed adobe Margot theater,
where they had seen the sultry story of White Cargo
to a bar, where they discussed the film's star, Hedy
Lamarr, over glasses of guaro (rum). *"A paragon of*
rectitude," said Ignacio. "A lady of little virtue," said
Manuel. Both whipped out knives. Both died in a
Leon hospital next day.[1]

THIS IS ONE METHOD of handling conflict and eliminating differences
of opinion. We do not recommend it to the group leader! A second
method, which we also do *not* recommend, is to ignore the conflict.
This might be all right for cases in which the difference is incon-
sequential, such as one person liking mashed potatoes and another

[1] *Time,* January 23, 1950, p. 26. Courtesy of *Time.* Copyright Time, Inc.,
1950.

preferring french fries. But on serious social matters, ignoring conflict leads to bottled-up emotional tensions, misunderstanding, intolerance and perhaps eventually to the method of Ignacio and Manuel Vargas.

This does not mean that all important differences among individuals in their beliefs or attitudes can or should be eliminated. There are many instances in which social agreement is unnecessary — even undesirable — because cooperative group action is not required. That is the case with regard to religion in the United States of America. We do not all have to agree on religion because we do not have to act as a single, unified group on this issue. Nevertheless, the differences are too important to ignore completely. In such matters, the healthiest approach is to talk the issue out, understand the differences, and then agree to disagree. This method is as sound in marriage as in inter-faith relations. It uncorks emotional tension, relieves misunderstanding, and paves the way to tolerance of irreconcilable differences.

METHODS OF RESOLVING CONFLICT

But we are concerned in this chapter with intra-group conflicts that *must* be resolved because united group action is necessary. Killing one another, ignoring the differences, or agreeing to disagree are methods which fail to fulfill this need. Agreement on a single course of action must be achieved. There are only three known methods by which this can be accomplished: (1) force, (2) arbitration, and (3) integration.

Force

The first of these methods implies that the member or members of the group who possess the most power (physical, military, economic, etc.) will resolve the conflict according to their own desires and will coerce the rest of the group into compliance. In other words, the issue will be settled by everyone accepting the course of action favored by the most powerful. Group leaders may sometimes have to resort to this expedient, but in so doing they depart from the realm of democratic leadership. Hence, we are not concerned here with a study of the techniques of this method.

Arbitration

Arbitration is a method of resolving conflict in which the parties to the dispute voluntarily agree to abide by the decision of some specified authority. They debate their cases as persuasively as possible and then abide by the judgment rendered by that authority — whether they like the decision or not. There are many kinds of authorities to whom conflicts may be submitted for arbitration. The term "arbitration" usually is used in reference to disputes between management and labor which are submitted to a board of three impartial experts for judgment. But this is using the term in its most narrow sense. The process is fundamentally the same whether the arbitrating authority be a board of three experts in a labor dispute, a judge in a civil court trial, a jury of twelve laymen in a criminal court case, or a vote of the majority of the entire society. The latter type of arbitration — decision by majority vote — is common practice in face-to-face groups, and we shall discuss it in the next chapter.

Arbitration may result in a complete victory for one point of view or it may result in a compromise whereby each side gives up a little and gains a little. In either case, disappointment and frustration follow, and conflict may re-occur at a later date. The parties to the dispute will not have changed their minds about the issue. The differences which gave rise to the conflict will still exist. The decision will be accepted only because of a recognition by all concerned of the need to work together on some basis — even though that basis may be distasteful to many members of the group. The dissatisfied individuals will simply bide their time until they can win enough support or build a strong enough case to effect a change in the decision. This phenomenon is certainly typical of the behavior of our national political parties as well as of labor and management.

To speak of force and arbitration as methods of "resolving" conflict is to use the term "resolving" loosely. Actually the differences that gave rise to the conflict are not eliminated. It would be more accurate to say that a temporary settlement has been achieved. This may be all that is needed or wanted for the purpose of social action. People can frequently act together effectively on the basis of a "working agreement" even though they are not one-hundred percent satisfied with the situation.

Integration

The third method of resolving conflict, by integration, is the only one that can truly be described as *resolving* conflict, and hence is of great concern to the democratic leader. It is a process in which we attempt, through discussion, to work out an agreement (not a compromise) which incorporates the thinking of all parties to the dispute — a solution or product of cooperative effort with which they are all quite satisfied. Such agreements cannot always be achieved, for they presume *a willingness and ability to change* on the part of the participants. Sometimes differences are truly irreconcilable or individuals are completely inflexible, and hours or years of discussion will not bring about any change. In social conflicts which are irreconcilable by discussion and integration we must resort to debate and arbitration. But wherever possible, integration is to be preferred, for it is based upon solid understanding and does not involve the kinds of sacrifice which lead to dissatisfaction and the breaking of agreements.

As we begin our study of leadership techniques for resolving conflict through integration, it will be helpful to recall the distinction made earlier between extrinsic and intrinsic conflict (see Chapter 4). Both are usually present in any dispute. Extrinsic conflict is the psychological or emotional element. Intrinsic conflict is the rational, ideational, or intellectual content. The distinction is somewhat artificial, for it is much easier to separate these two elements on paper than in real life. It is useful to us here, however, for purposes of clarity in analysis and explanation. It will be seen that leadership in resolving intrinsic conflict requires analytical keenness, whereas leadership in resolving extrinsic conflict requires social tact and diplomacy. It is because these two qualities are so rarely combined in the same person to a high degree that successful "integrators" like United Nations Mediator Ralph Bunche and Federal Mediator Cyrus Ching are worth their weight in uranium.

INTRINSIC CONFLICT

Resolving intrinsic conflict is a continual process of finding, isolating, and clarifying the areas of agreement and disagreement in a dispute. It requires that the items of agreement be carefully ferreted out, set aside, and "nailed down," thus constantly narrowing the field of disagreement until it has been wiped out or reduced to its most basic elements. The leader in this type of conflict resolution is a clarifier and coordinator par excellence. But what does he clarify and coordinate? How does he proceed? He proceeds by working through as many of the following four categories as is necessary to settle the difference: (1) conflict in meaning, (2) conflict in evidence, (3) conflict in reasoning, and (4) conflict in values.

Conflict in Meaning

Conflict in meaning arises when members of the group use the same term in different ways, consequently appearing to be in disagreement when actually they are not. We referred to this problem in Chapter 4 when we spoke of difficulties in communication. For example, two men get into an argument over religion. One maintains that there is a God, the other maintains that there is not. The conflict *appears* irreconcilable. But the leader is not willing to give up so easily. He asks each man to explain what he means by God. The one who claims that there is a God explains that, to him, the term "God" refers to some vast and mysterious force which maintains order in the universe. The other man, who claims there is no God, explains, that, to him, the term has always referred to a kind of personal being who sits on a throne somewhere in the heavens and governs the lives of men. The leader questions these men further and discovers that the disagreement was only a verbal difficulty. For according to the definition given by the first man, the second agrees too, that there is a God. And according to the definition given by the second man, the first agrees that there is no God. The conflict has been resolved.

To be sure, things do not always work out so smoothly. People tend to cling emotionally to their own definitions as though theirs were *right* and others were wrong — as though a definition were sacred.

> "When I use a word," Humpty Dumpty said in a rather scornful tone, "it means just what I choose it to mean — nothing more nor less."
>
> "The question is," said Alice, "whether you can make words mean so many different things."
>
> "The question is," said Humpty Dumpty, "which is to be master — that's all." [2]

We have had a great deal of difficulty adjusting our students to the idea of using the term "leader" to refer to the democratic type, so accustomed are they to identifying leadership with autocracy. One student even suggested that this obstacle was too ingrained to overcome, and that we should find another word to describe the democratic type of leader. But these are extrinsic problems and do not always occur. There are thousands of times when a simple clarification of meaning will prevent endless hours of fruitless disagreement. The stand once taken by A. B. Johnson may be unreasonably extreme, but it has much merit to it. Johnson said, "I am so confident that nearly every proposition is true, in the manner intended by the speaker, that I never contradict." [3]

Conflict in Evidence

The second type of intrinsic conflict is due to a clash in evidence. By evidence we mean the facts and expert opinions upon which the members of the group base their discussion. For illustration of this point we can look at almost any of the labor-management conferences of the past four or five years. Labor has consistently based its demands for higher wages on statistical evidence (sup-

[2] Carroll, Lewis, *Through the Looking Glass,* Chapter 6. *Complete Works of Lewis Carroll.* Garden City, N.Y.: Garden City Publishing Co., 1942.

[3] Johnson, A. B., *The Meaning of Words.* Milwaukee: John Windsor Chamberlain, 1940, p. 182.

plemented by the testimony of experts in economics) which purports to show that industry can afford to grant wage increases without raising prices. Management has opposed labor's demands on the grounds that it cannot afford to grant wage increases without also raising prices. Moreover, statistical evidence and expert testimony have been marshalled to support this contention. The "facts" apparently do not agree. Obviously something is wrong somewhere. Both sets of evidence cannot be correct. It will be the job of the mediator who attempts to resolve this conflict to help discover the flaws and find the real facts. Until, and unless, agreement can be reached on what the facts are, no mutually satisfactory solution can be achieved.

Conflict in Reasoning

Conflict in reasoning occurs when different people, reasoning from the same set of facts, arrive at different conclusions. Here are two men who agree that socialism has worked well in Great Britain. One of them feels, therefore, that it should be tried in the United States, because if it has been good for Britain it will be good for us too. The other man maintains that its success in Britain does not mean it is suitable for the United States, because the two countries are not comparable economically. The first man has attempted to draw an analogy — one of the most common types of reasoning. The second man has attempted to point out a fallacy in that reasoning process. If the leader is alert to the rules of sound reasoning, he will be able to suggest to these gentlemen that unless the first man can show that the two nations are economically comparable, the second man's objection is a valid one and the analogy does not hold. By testing the validity of the reasoning processes used — analogies, generalizations, syllogisms, etc. — conflict in reasoning can often be resolved.[4] Nevertheless, we must recognize that sometimes different interpretations of the same facts

[4] For help in testing the validity of reasoning the reader is referred to: Larrabee, Harold A., *Reliable Knowledge*, Boston: Houghton Mifflin, 1945; Mander, A. E., *Logic for the Millions*, New York: Philosophical Library, 1947; and Werkmeister, W. H., *An Introduction to Critical Thinking*, Lincoln, Neb.: Johnsen, 1948.

can be made which both appear reasonable — in which case neither party to the conflict will be willing to concede greater truth to his opponent.

Conflict in Values

The fourth and most difficult type of intrinsic conflict is due to a clash in values. A doctor and a lawyer are engaged in a controversy over socialized medicine. As is suggested by the pattern of reflective thinking, they are trying to reach an understanding on ultimate objectives before actually discussing any specific proposals. The doctor says that, whatever we do, we must not in any way limit the freedom of people to choose their own physicians. The lawyer feels it is more important to improve the health standards of the nation, even if it means limiting that freedom of choice somewhat. In other words, the lawyer places less value on freedom to choose a physician than the doctor. What can a leader do about such conflicts in value?

Many people say he can do nothing. "De gustibus est non disputandum" — there is no disputing tastes. If one man likes mushroom soup and the other does not, all the talk in the world is not going to change the mind of either. These are usually the same people who advise us never to discuss politics or religion — for the same reasons.

We do not entirely agree. Certainly we must admit that in many cases nothing can be done. Individual values and preferences do differ. It would be a dull, static world if they did not or if all those differences were to be resolved. There are many times, however, when leaders despair long before it is necessary. There are all sorts of reasons why people's tastes and values differ, and in some cases those differences are reconcilable. It depends upon how they have originated and upon how the leader attempts to deal with them.

Some psychologists believe that there are a few personal preferences which have their roots in the individual differences of physical and biological structure among men. They cite as an illustration of this point the fact that, due to different reactions of the taste buds located on the tongue, the chemical substance phenylthiocarbimide is bitter to some people, sweet to others, salty to others, and taste-less to still others. We might question whether it is the biological difference alone which accounts for differences in preference, or *learned cultural attitudes toward* sweetness, bitterness, and salti-ness. Be that as it may, we can hardly question the fact that such preferences are so deep-seated as to be hardly distinguishable from innate responses.

Most social values and preferences cannot be traced even indi-rectly to differences in the chemical or physical make-up of the body. They are clearly the result of a long conditioning process which begins in childhood and continues throughout life. The kinds of personal experiences that an individual has, the kind of environ-ment in which he grows up, the political party his parents belonged to, and a host of other influences will determine the nature of his social values and preferences. There are also some values which men acquire through thought processes rather than direct experi-ence. These are the kinds of ideals which we learn from inspiring teachers and books.

What does all this mean to the man who is a leader in a situation where a conflict of values has arisen? It means that if the conflict is due to deeply ingrained preferences, there is little hope of resolving it by integration. The group either will have to agree to disagree or debate the issue and settle it by majority vote. It also means (since anything that has been learned can eventually be unlearned) that rarely is there absolutely no hope of resolving it — given sufficient time. It will depend on how deeply rooted the preferences are, and on how important they are to the disputants. In those cases where the leader thinks there is some possibility of integration, how shall he proceed?

> If two men conflict over preferences which are assumed to be good without further proof, the only way agreement can be reached is if, by further clarification they can both be brought to agree on some *common further end* — and then the best means can be reflectively determined. If no such more ultimate end can be found, agreement is impossible, and it is decided by force, majority rule, etc . . .

Ends can be evaluated reflectively only when they are regarded in the light of still further ends to which they may contribute . . . In any given process of evaluation some preferred end must remain unquestioned . . . If there is any common ground whatsoever, it is possible to introduce reflective thinking into the great field of values just as into every other branch of knowledge.[5]

In short, the leader should seek to discover some basic value upon which the members of the group will agree and then, in the light of that common goal, attempt to work out rationally and cooperatively with them the intermediate goals or means which are most likely to achieve that ultimate end.

Let us suppose, for example, that two people disagree over the value of organized religion. One says that organized religion — whether it be Protestantism, Catholicism, or Judaism — is a good thing. The other claims it is not, and he is therefore opposed to any kind of religious education in the public schools. The basic issue here is obviously not religious education, but whether or not organized religion itself is good. Until that issue is settled, the more superficial one will also remain in conflict.

We have here a question of rather deep-seated values, but it should not discourage the leader. The first step he might take is to ask the man who believes in organized religion *why* he feels it to be good. The man may be quite willing but unable to answer this question. Perhaps he has always taken it for granted that religion is a good thing and has not thought about it as a disputable subject. If this is the case, the leader can help the man to explore the problem and to explain himself. The leader can do this with questions beginning, "Is it because . . . ?" It may be that the man can explain it without any help. In any event, the leader, through such a process, will be able to expose the more basic values upon which this man's belief in religion rests. He will then do the same with the other man. He may find that both individuals are basically interested in developing an increased feeling of brotherhood among

[5] Columbia Associates in Philosophy, *An Introduction to Reflective Thinking*. Boston: Houghton Mifflin, 1923, pp. 217–27.

men. The first person feels that organized religion is aimed at that goal. The second believes that organized religion is a barrier to that goal. But they both agree on the goal.

We now have a situation in which a "common further end" has been agreed upon. If both men are openminded we are in a position to sit down and rationally figure out what seems to be the most likely means to accomplish their end. Should everyone join in support of organized religion as it now stands? Should organized religion be modified in certain ways so as to be more effective as an instrument for accomplishing its avowed purposes? Should we eliminate all the differences among religious groups and have one world-wide religion? Should we throw out religion altogether and substitute psychiatric counselling in its place? To be sure, it might be difficult or impossible to find a mutually suitable answer to these questions, but such issues would be due to conflicts in reasoning — to be dealt with as such — or emotional blockages, to be treated as extrinsic conflict.

Let us now suppose that the first man responds differently to the leader's initial probing. Let us assume that when asked why he believes organized religion to be good he responds, "Well, I just do. It's a matter of faith. I don't need reasons." In other words, religion is something he values in and of itself. He assumes it to be good without further proof. It is not something which is good *because* it serves a larger purpose. It is itself a purpose or goal. He is not interested in the whys or wherefores.

It may be that he is afraid of exploring the question, lest he begin to doubt the value of his faith. This would again be an emotional problem and would have to be dealt with as such. But we should not assume that to be the case. It may simply be a personal preference with which the person is quite satisfied and which he is not at all interested in questioning. As we have already pointed out, such a position is not amenable to integration. If the problem were one which required united social action, the conflict would have to be battled out and settled by arbitration or force.

EXTRINSIC CONFLICT

One would have to be an unabashed idealist living in an ivory tower to believe that social issues can ordinarily be resolved by dealing with intrinsic conflict alone. Rather, we are confronted at every turn with emotional barriers to agreement. People refuse to use definitions which differ from their own, even after being shown that there is nothing sacred about the word. They deny the validity of facts which negate what they want to believe. They cling to their own arguments long after the fallacies have been pointed out to them and their defenses have been logically shattered. They persist in adhering to values which are shown to be valueless. Why?

The Need to Save Face

One of the basic causes of extrinsic conflict is the need to "save face." It is not easy for an individual in social situations to modify his attitude on the spot and thus, by implication, admit that he was wrong. He must defend his ego. He does not wish to appear to have been stupid, foolish, illogical, uninformed, unenlightened, misdirected, or what have you — even though he may admit it to himself. Rather than appear in such a light he will either (1) persist emotionally in a rationally untenable position, (2) refuse to discuss the matter further, or (3) find some loophole through which he can crawl out of the dilemma without losing prestige.

It is the last alternative which provides us with the first clue to effective leadership techniques in resolving extrinsic conflict. The *leader can help provide "face-saving" positions to which members who find themselves in difficulty can retreat.* If this is done skillfully, chances are good that the person involved will seize this opportunity to escape from the "hot-seat." We shall illustrate the point.

A discussion is taking place among a group of people on the question of whether or not the United States Congress should enact a program of compulsory national health insurance. One of the members of the group, Mr. X, violently opposes the scheme and, at the outset of the discussion, strongly commits himself to that position. The arguments which he presents are forceful and reasonable, but all are based upon the assumption that this plan is the same thing as an all-out program of socialized medicine. As X proceeds to unfold his line of thought it becomes increasingly obvious that he is unaware of the differences between the two plans. He thinks, for example, that under the national insurance plan all doctors are required to work for the government and that private practice is entirely wiped out. He thinks that patients would no longer be allowed to go to doctors of their own choosing. He apparently does not know that the legislation for health insurance does not provide for these things at all, but merely provides a method for the payment of medical bills by the government. So far as one can gather from his remarks, he apparently is not in agreement with the position of the American Medical Association on this subject and seemingly would have no objections to compulsory health insurance if he knew the facts about it. We might add that Mr. X is a somewhat aggressive and dogmatic individual. How might one handle this situation?

One way would be to point out his ignorance of the subject to Mr. X and frankly tell him the difference between socialized medicine and compulsory health insurance. Since his arguments were all directed against the former, you could then assert that he does not have a leg to stand on and must agree to the latter! How would you expect X to react to this? Would he freely confess his lack of knowledge to the group and agree to a program of health insurance? Or having so vehemently committed himself against the program, would he frantically search around for new arguments to bolster his sagging position and save face? If he is like a majority of the people we have observed in discussion, he will do the latter.

There is another way to handle the situation. Suppose one were to take this approach to our friend.

Mr. X, I understand that there have been at least five or six different health bills introduced into Congress in the past two or three years, under all sorts of different titles, and the whole thing has gotten *me* very confused. I was just wondering if we are all talking about the same bill. It seems that this health insurance bill which you are objecting to is different from the one I've read about. The one I'm thinking of provides for . . . (etc.), and doesn't provide for those things to which you are opposed. Now, if we could have a bill like this one I've described, rather than like the health insurance bill you've been reading about, how would you feel about it?

If Mr. X is not really opposed to the principle of health insurance, but simply to that of socialized medicine, there is now little danger of his refusing to go along with you. Why? Because you have taken the trouble to help him preserve his ego. You have not shown him up to be ignorant of the bill, even though down deep both you and he may know that that is precisely what was wrong. You have provided an "out" for him by suggesting that not only might there be another bill such as he has described, pending in Congress, but that it *might* even be referred to as health insurance. You have made it unnecessary for him to cling to an untenable position simply for the sake of saving face. You have won agreement on an important issue simply by being generous and diplomatic. If you are terribly conscientious about the "proper" meaning of the term "health insurance," and dislike compromising your principles even that much for the sake of diplomacy, perhaps you can straighten him out on that matter in a subtle way at some later date.

The Appearance of Free Will

Nobody likes to be pushed around — at least, not if others know about it. Most of us are egotistical enough to wish to appear as free-thinking, unfettered, unmanipulated individuals. Therefore if someone implies that our opinions have been bought and paid for — by Wall Street, Moscow, the labor unions, the oil companies, our in-laws, or anybody else, we resent it. Even if it is true, we resent it. We respond emotionally, and are so thoroughly antagonized that agreement is impossible — even if, logically, all the grounds for dispute have been removed.

The same thing happens when a group "gangs up" on one of its members and attempts to "shove an opinion down his throat" by high-powered persuasion and social pressure. It can also happen if the high-powered persuader is simply one other member of the group who cleverly traps his victim into a vital concession and does not care who knows it. Even though the individual on the receiving end of these manipulations clearly recognizes that he is in error, he is likely to persist in it because he refuses to be pushed around. It is a matter of public record that many of the disputes between John L. Lewis and the coal operators have been prolonged due to reactions such as these by both parties.

What is the leader's role with respect to this type of extrinsic conflict? He must do everything in his power to discourage members from making unkind implications about the sources of their colleagues' opinions. He must restrain those who would press too hard and fast for agreement. He must discourage members who succeed in their persuasion from gloating over those who have changed. It is best for him to prevent these activities before they go very far, else the situation will be irretrievable. People whose self-respect and pride have been wounded in front of a group are not easily placated by the diplomatic somersaults of a leader.

Supercharged Emotions

It is a physiological fact that we do not digest our food properly when we are emotionally upset. The same thing can be said for the digestion of ideas. When emotional involvement in a group discussion gets out of control, reason flies out the window, making integration impossible. Supercharged emotions are thus a basic cause of extrinsic conflict.

There are numerous leadership techniques for helping to keep the emotions of group members from getting out of hand.

1. Objectifying Antagonistic Contributions. Probably the most frequent precipitating cause of irrationality is the contribution which is stated in such a way as to arouse intense antagonism on the part of other group members. These contributions usually contain highly loaded language, extreme generalizations, and uncomplimentary innuendoes against the opposition. The group leader who can step into the breach before the antagonists have a chance to respond and rephrase this statement in a more objective manner may succeed in getting the respondents to react to the leader's statement rather than to the original.

There is another variation of this technique. Many times in a group where prejudices against a certain idea are very deep-rooted the leader may desire to get that point of view at least introduced for consideration. He is wise enough to know that if it is introduced as his own idea, personal antagonism will be created and irrationality will develop. He therefore objectifies the contribution by making this approach: "You know, some people maintain that . . . (etc.)" or "I have a friend who believes that . . . (etc.)" Is this a cowardly and deceitful thing to do? That, it seems to us, depends on the circumstances. Certainly it is undesirable if it is really unnecessary, or if used for the purposes of self-defense rather than in an honest, constructive attempt to broaden the viewpoints of others. If the use of this technique is confined to situations where it is the only way in which an idea can gain a fair hearing, then it seems justifiable.

2. Delaying Highly Controversial Issues. Another useful method for avoiding supercharged emotions is one that has been suggested in the mediation of labor-management disputes by Major Charles Estes, a member of the staff of the United States Conciliation Service. It involves, first, classifying all the issues in the dispute into two categories: "less controversial" and "more controversial." Having done that, the leader then proposes dealing with the less controversial matters first. The psychology behind this is sound. If, through discussing less controversial matters first, the group can grow into the habit of arriving at agreement rather than disagreement, a spirit of cooperation is built up which makes it easier to handle the more difficult problems. This principle should prove valid in any situation where it is possible to get the group working together on something which is not so freighted with emotional coloring before they tackle the problems which are "nearer and dearer to their hearts." Along these same lines, it has been suggested by experts working in the field of race relations, that if you can get inter-racial community groups working together on matters that have nothing to do with race — such as an art exhibit — this is the best approach to the problems of racial discrimination.

3. Humor. There is nothing more effective than humor for easing strained relations in a group and breaking the tensions created by excessive emotional conflict. The ability to inject a light note into a tense discussion is one of the most vital leadership techniques we know. We say little about it here only because we are aware of no ready-made formula for developing a sense of humor.

4. Diversion. If two members of a group become involved in an argument which begins to generate unhealthy personal antagonisms, a leader might well encourage the group to drop that point and *divert to another matter*. If the question at issue is an important one, the group can always return to it later with a fresh and calm approach.

It is possible also to employ *diversion to other participants*. If a storm is brewing between certain members of the group, it is well to make sure they do not get a chance to speak again until they have "cooled off." Meanwhile the discussion is diverted to other members of the group.

Still another aspect of diversion, and a somewhat risky one, is that of *diversion to the leader*. When two participants have begun to generate excessive emotionalism, the leader might step in and say, "I think you are both all wrong," thus causing them to team up in a cooperative attack upon himself. If all that this accomplishes is to make it a three-way antagonism instead of two, it is certainly unwise. However, the theory behind it is that the leader is a popular person, well-liked and respected by the parties to the conflict. Consequently, when they shift their hostility from each other to him, they will at the same time, without realizing it, be shifting from extrinsic to intrinsic conflict. In other words, if they are both on good personal terms with the leader, they will now tend to concentrate more on the ideas at issue than the personalities involved. A leader who is not sure of the state of health of his own interpersonal relations with either of the disputants should not employ this technique.

5. Breaks and Recesses. Once in a while emotional conflict gets so completely out of hand that no useful purpose is served by continuing the discussion. The members of the group are too upset to be mollified by any of the techniques discussed in this section. In that kind of a situation, the wisest thing a leader can do is to suggest that the meeting be adjourned until such time as everyone has calmed down enough to approach the problem more rationally.

Seeing Horns on the Opponent's Head

A fourth and final cause of extrinsic conflict may be traced to the fact that in many conflict situations — particularly where members of the group are strange to one another — an individual will tend to see his opponent not as a warm, likeable human being, but as the devil himself. When we become excited about something which we feel is important it is easy to believe that those who oppose us are fiends. It takes no great effort on the part of a coal miner in the midst of a strike to visualize a company owner as the bloated, greedy vampire that Communist cartoons make him out to be. It is not difficult for the alumni of American college fraternities and sororities to imagine that those who seek the removal of racial and religious barriers to membership are wild-eyed, horn-rimmed, long-haired radicals. Certainly they could not be clean-cut, wholesome American youths! These examples may be a bit extreme, but the point we are making is not. When people become involved in social conflict, they forget that those on the other side of the fence may be just as sincere, just as decent, and personally just as attractive and likeable as themselves.

There is a rather obvious leadership technique for combatting this aspect of extrinsic conflict. It consists, simply, of providing an opportunity, before serious discussion takes place, for the participants to get to know one another personally. A good dinner, a couple of drinks together, some conversation about baseball, L'il Abner, or women (assuming a male gathering) — in short, anything which provides a chance for people to socialize a bit and discover common bonds of fellowship — will aid in removing the horns from the other fellow's head. With rare exceptions (we would even maintain with no exceptions), the better we understand a person and the more we know about him the harder it is to dislike him. The leader who seeks to resolve extrinsic conflict will do well to give ample attention to this most fundamental of all human relations — the process of making friends.

SUMMARY

Differences of opinion which lead to conflict among human beings can be handled in many ways. If the differences are insignificant it is probably best to ignore them. If they are important, but unified group action is unnecessary, it is well to discuss them and agree to disagree — thus developing understanding and making tolerance possible. It is when group action is required that means must be found for reaching a settlement of differences. One method is for those who are most powerful to coerce those who disagree with them into accepting their decisions. Another method is for the parties to the dispute to debate their cases before an arbitrating authority — judge, jury, or majority vote — and to abide by the decision then made. These two methods do not eliminate the differences; they merely provide temporary settlements as a basis for group action. Conflict can only be resolved, in the narrow sense of the word, through discussion and integration. Integration must reckon with both intrinsic and extrinsic conflict. Intrinsic conflict arises from differences in meaning, in evidence, in reasoning and in values. If they can be resolved at all, differences in meaning may be reconciled by clarification; differences in evidence by finding the true facts; differences in reasoning by applying the tests of logic; and differences in values by discovering common further ends. Extrinsic conflict arises from the need to save face, the need to maintain an appearance of free will, supercharged emotions, and the tendency to attribute evil to one's opponents. Numerous techniques, both preventive and curative, have been suggested for dealing with each of these sources of difficulty.

EXERCISES

1. Keep a log for one week of the intrinsic conflict you run across in all sorts of informal discussions. Identify the type in each case: meaning, evidence, reasoning, or value.
2. Select two of your friends or acquaintances who have a personal antagonism towards one another. Analyze the causes of their extrinsic conflict and outline a course of action you might undertake to alleviate the difficulty.
3. Hold a group discussion in which two people who are known to have opposite views on some subject of interest state their respective positions at the outset. Have all the rest of the members of the group act as a team of leaders — questioning these two people for the purpose of attempting to resolve the conflict by integration.
4. What, if any, effect should the difference between learning and action groups have upon the leader's eagerness to achieve integration? Discuss.
5. Do we, as democratic group leaders or members, have any right to attempt to change or modify another individual's basic values? Discuss.
6. Set up a role-playing scene in which six people hold a committee meeting to discuss a controversial issue with which they are (in real life) familiar. The committee has been asked to make recommendations on this problem to a larger organization of which they are a part. Brief each individual on his role while the other five are out of the room. Set up the scene so that two members will be taking a strong positive stand on the issue, two will be in opposition, and two will be seeking to resolve the conflict. Assign some of the role-players personality traits that will lead to extrinsic conflict with some of the others. Ask half the audience to watch particularly for the types of conflict, both intrinsic and extrinsic, that arise; and ask the other half to concentrate on the techniques of the two conciliators. Play the scene through, and then have the members of the audience present and discuss their analyses of the conflict and their evaluations of the leadership techniques employed.

Sample Casting

Meeting in Dean's Office of small liberal arts college. Campus has been stirred up by agitation in behalf of plan for student evaluation of teachers. Dean Douglas has asked the following people to serve as a committee to make recommendations to the President and Board of Trustees:

Professor Moore — 60-year-old chairman of economics department. Crusty old man. Feels that all students are wet behind the ears. Faculty knows best what is good for them. "I have taught for thirty years and know how to teach." Opposes the plan.

Mr. Niedenthal — 28-year-old debate coach. Likeable, democratic person. Popular with students. Is in close touch and sympathy with student views. Is aware of considerable faculty opposition to evaluation plan and hopes to help resolve the conflict.

Miss Kallman — Bright student. Inclined to be a bookworm. Economics major. Doing work under Professor Moore. Agrees with him that students' place is to do what they are told. Thinks the plan for evaluation is an attempt by poor students to browbeat faculty members who are too hard on them.

Miss Morgan — Serious student. Bright. Has had Professor Moore in class and thinks he is a very bad teacher. Did good work for him but got a poor grade. Heads student committee which has been organized to promote evaluation plan.

Mr. Schroeder — Student council president. B.M.O.C. One of Niedenthal's star debaters. Has also had Moore in class and does not like him. Favors evaluation plan more because of campus political reasons than because of a deep personal conviction on issue.

Dean Douglas, a middle-aged man, is open-minded on the subject, but generally tends to be conservative. He is mainly interested in promoting and preserving satisfaction among both faculty and student body and will work for integration of conflict.

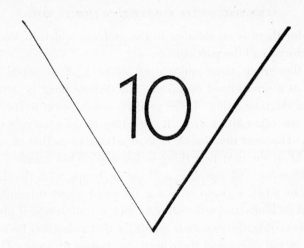

Resolving Social Conflict:
Majority Vote

It SHOULD BE APPARENT after reading the preceding chapter that, for many reasons, a group cannot always resolve its conflicts to the mutual satisfaction of all its members. Integration is not always attainable. Evidence may be contradictory and there may be no conclusive way of determining which of the purported facts is correct. Conflicting chains of reasoning may fulfill the requirements of valid logic and yet differ in the substantive interpretations at which they finally arrive. Conflict may be due to an irreconcilable difference in the basic values or interests to which the members of the group adhere. Extrinsic conflict may be of such magnitude that rational, cooperative effort is impossible. Time may be too short to explore all the facets of the conflict. The group may be too large for a thorough and detailed examination of all the variations in attitude. In any of these cases, the integrative method breaks down, for there is no solution to the problem which is completely satisfactory to all the participants.

Yet the group must unite upon some kind of social policy. Action as a group must be taken. The dispute must be settled, at least for the time being. If the group is not to resort to force there is only one other alternative. It must turn to the processes of arbitration. The most democratic type of arbitration is that of majority vote. This is the next best thing to integration but entails a significant difference. All members will not be happy with the decision. Therefore, when a group arrives at the point where integration has reached its limits and where the conflict, for all practical purposes, is irreconcilable, the members recognize that a decision by majority vote is in the offing and their flexibility begins to wane. They are naturally disposed to do all they can to make their views prevail. As a result, they begin to argue persuasively and dogmatically for their own side. Cooperation goes out the window. Competition and vigorous debate come in. Middle grounds and shades of gray disappear. It is now a black and white, either-or proposition, to be accepted or rejected by the group.

As the transition from cooperative problem-solving to competitive debate takes place, the leadership needs of the group also begin to shift. The group is no longer one unit working together, but now consists of two or more sub-units struggling against each other for the upper hand. The willingness with which the losing faction will accept its defeat and go along with the majority decision will depend upon how impartially the arbitration process has been conducted. If each faction believes it has had a just and equitable hearing and that the decision has been made fairly by majority rule (and if the participants have willingly agreed to live by the democratic way of life), they may grumble about the outcome, but they will not refuse to abide by it. The vital problem of democratic leadership in such situations is to insure that the processes of debate and decision are fair so that no one can have any legitimate complaints.

Therefore, the leader under whose guidance arbitration is to take place must play a different role from that discussed in the preceding four chapters. He is not interested in scientific method, cooperative thinking, or integration, for presumably those possibilities have either been exhausted or time and circumstance do not permit their full application. He is not particularly concerned with extrinsic conflict, for there is little that can be done about it at this advanced stage. He has no responsibility for climate-making, drawing in reticent participants, or stimulating argument — for each faction is on its own and has its own advocate-leaders. The group leader's job is that of an impartial referee.

If the group is exceptionally small and congenial the leader may be able to fulfill this function in quite an informal way. Usually, however, it will be necessary to resort to more formal procedures. Just as any competitive sport or card game must have established rules which insure justice to the participants, so must a competitive discussion group be operated according to some set of established principles. It does not matter so much that the leader adhere specifically to the letter of the law, but he should observe the basic spirit and intent of these principles.

Leadership in the type of situation we are now discussing is not a new concept. The leader has at his disposal several hundred years of historical precedent in the conduct of parliamentary procedures. Debate in the public forum is as old as freedom of speech itself, and rules for its proper conduct have been worked out in great detail and have become almost a matter of second nature to people who are experienced in democracy. The difficulty is that not enough of our people have had this experience at first hand. As a result, you will often find that no one in the group is adequately prepared to conduct a parliamentary session. This need not be. The basic principles are simple to understand and relatively easy to master. We shall review them briefly in this chapter.

The set of procedural rules under which debate takes place in a democratic assembly is known as "parliamentary law." This term originally referred to the rules and customs for conducting business in the English parliament, but has come to have broader reference to the procedures of any formal, democratic gathering.

Although these procedures may vary in detail and degree of formality from one place to another and although any social unit has a right to set up its own rules, there are certain universal principles which are generally observed. We suggest to group leaders that it is more important to understand these broad principles and be flexible in their application than it is to adhere rigidly to mechanical details. Nothing causes people to turn away from parliamentary law in disgust more quickly than an insensitive use of formal procedures which are utterly unadapted to the needs of a particular situation. It is not a heinous crime for a group leader to employ a *few* aspects of parliamentary procedure which he finds helpful and to ignore the rest. There is no law (except in the minds of unreasoning purists) against originality and creativity on the part of an intelligent group leader.

RULE OF THE MAJORITY

The first basic principle of parliamentary law is that of majority rule. According to this doctrine, which is basic in democratic life, the power of final decision and control in a social unit rests in the hands of a numerical majority of the membership. To be sure there may be, and usually are, special circumstances in which action cannot be taken by the majority. There are sometimes organizational constitutions or by-laws which require that, on certain matters, the vote must be unanimous. Such is the case on the admission of new members to most college social fraternities and sororities. Often a certain length of time must pass before particular actions, such as amending its constitution, can be taken by a group. Frequently, a two-thirds vote is required on a proposal. But such special rules, providing for various curbs on the immediate will of the majority, exist only because, at one time, the majority believed them to be wise and voluntarily accepted them. Though it rightfully might take time and entail complicated processes to change those rules, in the final analysis the ability to do so lies in the hands of the majority in a truly democratic group.

Unfortunately, in accepting written curbs on its power, a majority sometimes ties its own hands and the hands of future generations. One example of this is the United Nations. Any proposal for changing the rules so as to eliminate the veto power of the "Big Five" in the Security Council could be vetoed by one of the five — because a principle of unanimity is written into the United Nations Charter. Another example is the Constitution of the United States, or any of the numerous organizational constitutions in this country which have been patterned after it. Changes in these documents are impossible without a two-thirds vote.[1] Whether the requirement be two-thirds, three-fourths, or unanimity, to whatever extent a majority permanently abdicates its power, to that extent it gives up pure democracy.

If the reader doubts this reasoning let him look to the history books to find out why the fathers of the United States Constitution conceived the two-thirds requirement. He will discover that it was because they distrusted the will of an uneducated majority and sought to safeguard the nation against what they saw as a danger of unlimited democracy.

A more timely example is that of the filibuster — a device which has, on more than one occasion, frustrated the will of a majority of the United States Senate. Under Senate rules which were designed originally to protect a minority of members from being "steamrollered" by the majority, action on certain motions can be delayed by those members of the minority so long as they wish to continue talking. Many people feel that this privilege of filibuster has been abused — that it is no longer merely an instrument whereby the minority prevents the majority from taking hasty action, but that it also has become a weapon with which a few men can permanently block legitimate decisions of the majority. As a result of this feeling, frequent attempts have been made to change the rules. The most recent of these efforts occurred in the opening days of the Eighty-First Congress in January, 1949, and like earlier attempts, met with defeat.[2]

[1] In the case of the United States Constitution, amendments must be approved by a ⅔ vote in both houses of Congress and then be ratified by ¾ of the states.

[2] A modification of rules was achieved which reduced somewhat the area in which filibustering is allowed. But at the same time the majority accepted

Because of the complicated chain of motions that was involved, and because some of the steps required a two-thirds vote which could not be mustered, many people were led to believe that the situation was hopeless and that without two-thirds support nothing could be done. This is undoubtedly what many senators who participated in the unsuccessful attempt wanted the public to believe, but its truth is questionable. Had there been a solid majority, standing together from beginning to end, the rules might have been changed. On a crucial ruling from the chairman, Vice-President Alben Barkley, which required a simple majority backing, some of the senators deserted the cause and Barkley was overruled. There was not a majority which desired the change sincerely enough to stay with it to the end and to face the possibility of retaliation from the minority. The filibuster remains, apparently not because a majority was legally *unable* to eliminate it, but because a majority was *unwilling* to pay the political price. It was the same problem of "political expediency" which confronted the founders of the United Nations. Had the delegates at San Francisco refused to accept the veto power they might not have had a United Nations at all.

PROTECTION OF THE MINORITY

A second principle of parliamentary law has already been implied in our reference to the origin of the filibuster. As a corollary to the concept of majority rule, democratic procedures demand that those who are numerically in the minority should be afforded certain protections. Among these are the right to a fair hearing, and the right to delay action or to make action difficult on matters of vital concern to everyone. This latter right is based upon the theory that a majority in haste and carelessness might attempt to adopt proposals which would not stand the test of thorough consideration. That is one reason it was made so difficult to amend the Constitution of the United States. It is the reason that a two-thirds vote is required on many matters by parliamentary law. It is the

even more curbs on its future right to tamper with the filibuster in the vital areas where it remains.

reason that any member of an assembly has the right to stand up at any time and question the procedures that are being used, question or appeal a decision of the chairman, question the presence of a quorum, or make a motion to adjourn. Under democratic procedures, a minority of even one man is given every *reasonable opportunity* to try to win others over to his point of view. Who knows but what the minority opinion of today may become the majority opinion of tomorrow?

The difficult problem is to determine what constitutes a reasonable opportunity. Parliamentary rules were not devised for the purpose of providing a minority with a means of obstructing business — although they are frequently used in that way. There is a difference between protecting the legitimate rights of a minority and letting a minority ruin a social unit with obstructive tactics. The question is how and where to draw the line.

This is basically similar to the question which confronted the United States Supreme Court in the Terminiello case. Terminiello had been convicted by the Illinois courts of inciting a riot in Chicago by a speech described as fascistic. The United States Supreme Court, in a bitterly contested five-to-four decision, reversed the Illinois tribunals and held that Terminiello did not exceed the constitutional limits of free speech guaranteed to Americans. Writing the majority opinion, Mr. Justice William O. Douglas declared:

> Freedom of speech, though not absolute . . . is nevertheless protected against censorship or punishment, unless shown likely to produce a clear and present danger of a serious substantive evil that arises far above public inconvenience, annoyance, or unrest.[3]

This doctrine of "clear and present danger" was first propounded by Justice Oliver Wendell Holmes in *Schenck* v. *U.S.*, 249 US 47. In the dissenting opinion, Mr. Justice Robert Jackson wrote:

> This court has gone far toward accepting the doctrine that civil liberty means the removal of all restraints. . . . There is danger that if the court does not temper its doctrinaire logic

[3] Official Reports of the Supreme Court, 337 US 272, p. 4.

with a little practical wisdom, it will convert the constitutional Bill of Rights into a suicide pact.[4]

Actually, the disagreement here was not one of principle but of degree. No one doubts the principle enunciated by Justice Jackson — that a society has a right to try to prevent its own suicide. We are sure that everyone also agrees with Justice Douglas that a society should be extremely cautious in the curbs it places on free speech and should be certain that they are really necessary for the protection of that society from a "clear and present danger." The disagreement lies in the application of those principles to specific cases. Four members of the court thought Terminiello went too far; five members did not.

The problem which confronts the leader of a parliamentary session is similar in principle to the one just discussed. It is similar in that the group leader must decide in each specific case which arises (as the Supreme Court had to decide) whether a highly aggressive and obstructive member of the group is exercising his legitimate minority rights when he speaks or is deliberately trying to disrupt the society. If it is the former, the leader must protect those rights. If the leader believes it to be the latter he may rule the individual out of order and, if necessary, eject him from the meeting.

The group leader's situation is different from that of the Supreme Court in two important respects. In the first place, his responsibility is less weighty than that of the court because his decision, if questioned, can be sustained or overruled by a vote of the membership. In the second place, he is not deciding whether the man shall be sentenced to prison but merely whether he shall speak in one particular meeting. The general principle of protecting minority rights, however, is similarly involved in both instances.

MAKING MOTIONS AND OBTAINING THE FLOOR

Before any debate takes place in a parliamentary session, a motion should be presented to the house so that the issue being argued is clearly defined. According to *Robert's Rules of Order*,

[4] *Ibid.*, p. 37.

which is the most universally recognized authority on parliamentary law in this country, a motion is "a proposal that the assembly take certain action, or that it express itself as holding certain views." [5]

In order to get a motion before the house, so that it may be debated, or in order to participate in the debate itself, a member must first "obtain the floor." This means that he must be "recognized" (called upon) by the leader. The procedures for getting recognition, and thus obtaining the floor, vary according to the customs of different organizations. In a formal setting it may be necessary to stand up and say "Mr. Chairman!" (the title used by leaders in a parliamentary situation). In an informal meeting, one can simply raise his hand.

It is the right and the responsibility of the chairman to recognize members and thus grant them the floor. It is within his discretion to determine whether he shall call upon Joe Smith first or Bill Baxter. However, there are certain principles of fairness which should govern, and in some instances must govern, that decision. If Bill Baxter has already had the floor several times to make motions, and if Joe Smith has been silent, it is only right that Smith now be given the first chance to speak. If a motion is already on the floor and being debated, *Robert's Rules* require that the chairman not allow anyone to speak a second time until all who desire to do so have spoken once. Furthermore, it is only fair that the chairman try to alternate speaking opportunities between the advocates and the opponents of the motion. If he happens to know what each member's position is on a particular motion he can do this most readily. If he does not know he simply may say, "We have heard from the opposition. The chair would now like to recognize someone who wishes to speak in favor of the motion." It is presumed that, after such a request has been made, only members who favor the motion will hold up their hands for recognition. If no one wants to speak in favor of the motion at that point the chairman is then justified in allowing the opposition to continue holding the floor.

[5] Robert, Henry M., *Robert's Rules of Order*, Article I, Section 4. Chicago: Scott Foresman, 1943.

When a member of the group gets the floor and makes a motion, his proposal is *not* then automatically open for debate. Most motions must be seconded, and all motions must be restated by the chairman before they are open to debate. Even then there are some motions which are not debatable at all, but which must be put to an immediate vote. These will be discussed later.

With few exceptions, such as motions nominating a person for office, proposals must be seconded before they may be debated. The theory behind requiring seconds for all motions is that the assembly's time should not be consumed by consideration of a motion in which only one person is interested. If his proposal cannot win the support or even arouse the curiosity of at least one other person, it is foolish to waste time debating it.

ORDER OF PRECEDENCE OF MOTIONS

We are now ready to consider the principle of the order of precedence of motions. We can approach the problem best by means of an illustration. Let us suppose that a college student council meeting is in progress, and that someone has moved that $100 be appropriated for Homecoming Decorations. The motion has been seconded and restated by the chairman, and debate is now in progress. This proposal is termed a *main motion,* because it is the main problem being considered by the group. During the course of debate someone who gets the floor stands up and says, "I am in favor of this proposition but do not believe that the amount of money proposed is large enough. Therefore, I move that the motion be amended to read $150."

Is such a motion in order at this point? Can someone make a motion when there is already another motion on the floor which has not been disposed of yet by a vote? The answer is "yes" to both of these questions — *provided* that the second motion is of the type that takes *precedence* over the first. If it is not the kind of motion which takes precedence then it should be ruled out of order by the chairman, and consideration of it must wait until the first motion has been voted upon or otherwise taken care of.

It so happens that an amendment takes precedence over a main motion. If an amendment to a main motion is introduced as in our illustration, the chairman must recognize it, allow the group to discuss it, and return to finish consideration of the previous motion only after the amendment has been voted upon. This same procedure applies whenever any kind of motion is made which takes precedence over the kind of motion that is on the floor at the time.

Main motions are at the bottom of the list in the order of precedence of motions. They are "outranked" by all other kinds of motions, and must give way to them. They are outranked, not because they are less important (in fact, quite the contrary is true) but because it is more logical to settle the other issues first. A chairman should be familiar with the entire list of the precedence of motions so that he will know the order in which they take priority over each other. A list of the precedence of the most common motions is as follows:

1. Fix the time to which to adjourn, if that has not already been provided for. For example, "I move that we adjourn until 3 p.m. tomorrow."
2. Adjourn, provided the motion is not qualified in any way. For example, "I move that we adjourn."
3. Take a recess. For example, "I move that we take a break for fifteen minutes."
4. Lay on the table. This means that the matter is dropped until called up again by majority vote.
5. Close debate. For example, "I move that we stop debate and take a vote now."
6. Limit or extend the limits of debate. For example, "I move that we debate the question for one more hour, and then vote."
7. Postpone consideration of the matter to a stated time. For example, "I move that we postpone consideration of this issue until our August meeting."
8. Commit or refer. For example, "I move that the whole problem be submitted to a committee for further investigation."
9. Amend.
10. Postpone indefinitely.
11. Main Motion.

Each motion in this table takes precedence over all those which are listed below it. Each gives way to all those above it.

In our illustration of the student council meeting, the motion to amend the one-hundred dollar figure is in order because an amendment (Number 9) takes precedence over a main motion (Number 11). The debate must now center on the question of whether the figure should be $100 or $150. Not until that question is settled will the group return to the main motion and vote on whether the appropriation should be made at all.

Let us suppose that before a vote is taken on the proposed amendment, another complication is introduced. Someone suggests that the group does not really have enough information to make the decision between the two sums of money being debated. He thinks that the matter should be referred to a committee for further investigation and recommendations. He so moves. According to our table, this is a type of motion (Number 8) which has priority over both amendments and main motions. It is, therefore, in order. The group argues for a while on whether to send this matter to a committee or settle it here and now. A vote is taken and those who want it referred to a committee are found to be in the majority. Having settled that, what does the chairman do next? Does he return to consideration of the amendment? To the main motion? Obviously not, for the group has just decided not to consider the matter further at this meeting, but to await the recommendations of a committee. Therefore the chairman moves on to the next piece of business.

Let us now suppose that the motion to refer the matter to a committee was not made or was defeated. The council is in the process of debating the amendment to change the amount to $150. A heated argument is taking place. All of the members seem to have a great deal to say. But it is getting late, and there are many other problems to be considered at this meeting. Realizing this, the chairman interrupts and suggests that it might be wise to limit the debate. He asks if someone would care to make a motion to that effect. One of the members obligingly responds and moves that debate on this amendment be limited to two minutes for each person who wants to speak. The motion is seconded, restated, put to a vote, and passed. The group now returns to its debate on the amendment, operating under the limitations that have been imposed. After everyone has had his two minutes, the chairman automatically puts the matter to a vote, and the amendment is defeated.

The council is now ready to return to its consideration of the main motion. It is very late, and everyone is tired. Debate on the main motion has been resumed. One of the members obtains the floor and says, "Mr. Chairman, I call for the question." This means that he wants debate to be stopped and the matter put to a vote immediately. It is not in the form of a motion, but simply a suggestion. If the chairman discovers (perhaps by asking, "Are all of you ready for the vote?") that there are no objections, he may take it upon himself to shut off debate and put the question to a vote.

But over in the corner is Abner Brown, who does object. He wants to debate the matter some more. In such a case — and this is a common occurrence — it will require a formal motion to close debate and obtain a vote. One of the members must obtain the floor and say, "Mr. Chairman, I move the previous question." (This is synonymous with, "I move that we close debate and take an immediate vote." In groups which are unfamiliar with parliamentary law it is wise to use the simpler language.) Since this motion (Number 5) takes precedence over the others which are before the house, it is voted upon immediately. The motion is passed. Abner is silenced and goes back to his corner. The main motion is put to a vote and passed. The chairman then moves on to the next order of business.

UNDEBATABLE MOTIONS

For the purpose of expediting business, most assemblies follow the recommendations of *Robert's Rules* that certain types of motions are undebatable and, when made, must be put to an immediate vote. The first six motions on the table given earlier are of this type. Only the last five are debatable motions.

Undebatable	*Debatable*
Fix the time to which to adjourn	Postpone to a certain time
Adjourn	Refer to a committee
Take a recess	Amend
Lay on the table	Postpone indefinitely
Close debate	Main Motion
Limit or extend limits of debate	

MOTIONS REQUIRING A TWO-THIRDS VOTE

As was pointed out earlier, there are certain matters which an assembly should consider with more caution than others. A brake must be placed upon what might become the "reckless will" of the majority. For this purpose, the requirement of a two-thirds vote has been evolved. An organization can provide in its rules for a two-thirds vote on anything it wishes to. For example, the United States Constitution states that in order to propose amendments to the constitution a two-thirds vote of both Houses of Congress shall be necessary (Article V); that a two-thirds vote is necessary before either house can expel one of its members (Article I, Section 5, Part 2); and that a two-thirds vote of both houses is necessary to override a presidential veto (Article I, Section 7, Part 2). It further requires that treaties must be ratified by two-thirds of the United States Senate (Article II, Section 2, Part 2).

There are three important motions which, according to *Robert's Rules*, ought always to be subject to a two-thirds vote. They are:

1. Motions to limit or extend the limits of debate
2. Motions to close debate
3. Motions to suspend the rules

The apparent reason behind the selection of these particular motions is that, in each case, important minority rights are at stake and should be carefully guarded.

APPEALS FROM THE DECISIONS OF THE CHAIR

Occasionally, at a large and important meeting, a group will enlist the services of an expert parliamentarian to advise the chairman on matters of procedure. Most of the time, however, the chairman will have to handle the situation himself. Unless being a parliamentary leader is his full-time profession he is not likely to have at his fingertips all the details set forth in *Robert's Rules of Order* or any other manual of parliamentary law. This is expecting too much. Nevertheless, if he has a real understanding of the basic principles outlined in this chapter, and if he "uses his head" he should be able to do a creditable job of meeting specific problem-situations. He may not have exactly correct answers nor use the precise technical terms available, but more important than either of these are sound principles and a fair-minded attitude. If he is not certain what to do in a particular situation, he should do that which seems most reasonable. He should feel perfectly secure in so doing, because if any member of the group does not like a ruling of the chairman that member has the right and opportunity to appeal from the decision of the chair.

Any decision of the chair may be appealed so long as that appeal is made immediately — that is to say, right at the time the disputed ruling is made, and not after other business has intervened. A member need not obtain recognition to make such a motion, and he may interrupt someone else who has the floor. He need only announce, "Mr. Chairman, I appeal from the decision of the chair." If there is a second to the appeal, the chairman must put the matter to the group for argument. Just before debate is concluded the chairman has the right to state a defense of his position. He then asks, "Shall the decision of the chair be sustained?" and puts this question to a vote. If a majority of the assembly votes unfavorably, the chair is overruled and its decision reversed. Otherwise the chairman's ruling is sustained.

The importance of the right to appeal from the decision of the chair cannot be overestimated, for it goes directly to the heart of the relationship between a democratic leader and the group he leads. It clearly demonstrates that in the final reckoning, he is a servant of the group. Without the backing (explicit or implied) of a majority of the members, he is powerless. On the other hand, with the unwavering support of a majority behind him, there is actually little that he cannot do. This was the key to the fabulous power held by such colorful Speakers of the United States House of Representatives as Thomas B. Reed and "Uncle Joe" Cannon. With a well-disciplined party machine behind them, their rulings on "procedure" were frequently of crucial importance to the fate of legislation itself. Certainly these men are not to be emulated as examples of democratic leadership. Rather their careers clearly illustrate the way in which an irresponsible majority may allow the democratic process to be abused.

There really is not much that a minority can do by peaceful means to protect itself when the group leader and his loyal supporters of the majority are not interested in observing the democratic rules of fair play. The minority's only protection lies in the good sportsmanship and faith in democratic procedures of the members of the majority, plus the hard-headed realization by members of that majority that some day they too may be a minority dependent upon the decency of other people.

This problem is not unique to parliamentary law. In any social unit, the survival of a minority of any kind in the last analysis depends upon the goodwill and civilized behavior of those who hold the power of social control. In a democracy that power is held by the majority. It is a basic assumption of democracy that the majority is decent and civilized. If that assumption is not valid for a particular group, then democracy itself is not valid for that group. The leader can encourage and promote democracy, but he cannot by himself create it.

SUMMARY

Integration as a means of resolving social conflict is not always practicable. Differences may be irreconcilable, time may be too short, or the group may be too large. In any of these cases, unless we are to resort to force, we must turn to arbitration by majority vote. This method requires a different set of leadership skills than those discussed heretofore. The leader's job is to serve as an impartial chairman who assures that the debate and vote-taking processes are carried out fairly. It is more important that he understand the broad principles of parliamentary law and apply them with flexibility than that he be a master of technical details. The leader should know that parliamentary procedure rests upon the foundations of rule by the majority and protection of the minority. He should understand the processes of obtaining the floor and making motions. He should be generally familiar with the order of precedence of motions, and should know which ones are un-debatable and which require a two-thirds vote. Finally, he must have a thorough appreciation of the right of appeal from decisions of the chair, for this right defines his role as a servant of the group.

EXERCISES

1. Fill the role of chairmanship in a mock parliamentary session, and practice the rules discussed in this chapter.
2. Visit a meeting of your city council or state legislature. Note examples of the principle of:
   a) majority rule
   b) protection of the minority
   c) order of precedence of motions
   d) undebatable motions
   e) motions requiring a two-thirds vote
   f) appeals from decisions of the chair
3. Attend a meeting at which parliamentary procedures are used.
   a) Keep an account of the instances in which you think the chairman violated the rules of good procedure.
   b) Keep an account of the instances in which you think procedural rules got in the way — serving to hinder rather than expedite group progress.
4. Cite two examples of situations you have observed in which:
   a) Discussion was used, but parliamentary debate would have been more appropriate.
   b) Parliamentary debate was used, but informal discussion would have been more appropriate.
5. To what extent do most groups to which you have belonged use parliamentary law more because it is "the thing to do" than because of its appropriateness to the situation? Discuss.
6. "Under majority rule one vote is as good as another. Under the two-thirds requirement, a member of the minority has twice as much say as a member of the majority. Under the rule of unanimity, one person has more power than all the other members combined. Therefore, anything other than majority rule is undemocratic."
   Do you agree? Discuss.

Part Three

The Future of Group Leadership

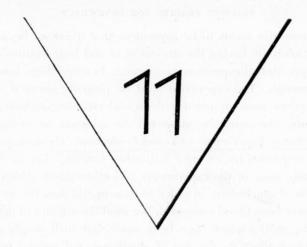

Training Leaders for Democracy

A QUESTION WHICH INVARIABLY ARISES when advice is being given on leadership skill is whether or not a person can *do* much about it. Is it possible to develop the ability to handle problems like those which have been discussed in this book? If so, how can it be done? Is it enough to read about leadership? Is experience necessary? Can experience alone do the job? What proof is there that leaders are made and not born? In view of the widespread amount of research that has been done in the past few years and is going on in many places at the present time,[1] we are now in a position to begin proposing answers to some of those questions.

There seems to be general agreement among the experts in this field that democratic leadership ability can be enhanced by train-

[1] To mention but a few: Ohio State Leadership Studies, Columbus, Ohio; Research Center for Group Dynamics, Ann Arbor, Michigan; National Training Laboratory in Group Development, Bethel, Maine; Laboratory for Social Relations, Harvard University, Cambridge, Massachusetts.

ing. There also seems to be agreement that it cannot be accomplished solely by having the student read and hear lectures about leadership. Actual experience is essential. Practice alone, however, is not enough. The experience must be properly oriented — that is, the trainee must go into it with an understanding attitude. The experience also must be subjected to criticism or evaluation. *Orientation — Experience — Critical Evaluation.* These, in general, are the requisites for effective leadership training. Let us review specifically some of the experiments and other efforts which have led to these conclusions, in order to gain insight into the methods which have been found successful. We shall not attempt to describe all of the studies which have made, but shall simply report those which illustrate the use of significant and unique training techniques.

ON-THE-JOB TRAINING

An experiment which has become a classic in the new area in which we are working was that described by Bavelas and Lewin in 1942.[2] The experiment was conducted in a summer day camp and centered around the four women and two men who were the recreational leaders in that camp. The women were leaders in handicraft classes, the men in outdoor games. Before retraining, the leadership methods of these six people were largely authoritarian, and the morale of the children *and* the leaders was low.

Three of these leaders were given a course of training planned by the experimenters. Through a type of "clinic-on-the-job," rather than by lectures, an attempt was made to change their attitudes and techniques. The first step was to make them more sensitive to the ways in which a leader can meet various situations. This was accomplished by having them observe many leaders, both good and bad, in action; by having them critically observe each other and the trainer in action; and by showing them films of other experiments in democratic, authoritarian and laissez-faire leadership. Then they were constantly observed on the job, and their behavior was evaluated for them. The results of the experiment showed that

[2] Bavelas and Lewin, "Training in Democratic Leadership," *loc. cit.*

those who received this training exhibited a marked change in their behavior with children. Prior to training, over 70% of their methods had been authoritarian. After training the figure was less than 10%. The morale of the retrained leaders shifted from definitely low to definitely high, and the morale of the children also improved. Meanwhile, the leaders who received no training remained the same or grew worse in methods and morale.

ROLE-PLAYING

Another interesting and pertinent experiment is that reported by French.[3] It makes use of the method known as "role-playing" as a leadership training technique. It is actually a case study of one application of this method. The study centered around a Mr. Smith, who gave training courses for scoutmasters and who "could be characterized as an unsuccessful autocrat." Smith placed his trainee scoutmasters on an inferior level, lectured to them in a dull way, and kept the determination of policy for the group in his own hands. The group was bored and apathetic, and by the end of one of his courses, all but two members had dropped out.

A leader training institute, conducted by Alex Bavelas, was set up for Mr. Smith and a few other teachers of scoutmasters. The basic principles upon which this program was planned were: (1) that a leader must experience during the training process the kind of leadership and the style of group living which you wish him to use as a leader, and (2) that he must receive on-the-job training which permits the trainer to influence his behavior in the real-life situation. The training program consisted of five meetings and a total of thirteen hours. The first two and one half meetings were devoted to a group discussion which Bavelas led in a democratic way. During and after this session, the trainer illustrated the ideas he wished to get across by pointing up and discussing his own behavior, and the reactions of the group. This provided an example and ideology for the rest of the training program.

The next one-and-a-half sessions were devoted to role-playing.

[3] French, John R. P. Jr., "Retraining an Autocratic Leader," *Journal of Abnormal and Social Psychology*, XXXIX (April, 1944), pp. 224–37.

Mr. Smith was asked to play the role of a scoutmaster trainer and the others in the group were to play the role of green scoutmasters. He started out for ten minutes in his old authoritarian manner, but he was then stopped and criticized in a friendly way. The others took turns in functioning as the leader, during which time Smith enacted the role of a green scoutmaster and thus gained some insight into such a person's reactions. The next time his turn came around for leadership there was a noticeable change in his attitude and methods. Once in a while he began to slip back into his old pattern, but every time he did so he was stopped and corrected. Each time he used a new technique especially well, it was pointed out and praised. French concludes that after training, "Smith's behavior had changed so markedly that the observers spoke of it as a 'metamorphosis'." [4]

French also points out three advantages of the role-playing method:

1. The trainee practices what he will have to do later on.

2. The trainee has knowledge of his results.

3. There is a close connection in time between behavior and reward or punishment.

Psychologists will agree that all three of these factors are vital in any learning process. No skill — whether it be playing golf or making a public speech — can be learned without practice. Furthermore, if the golfer never knows whether he got the ball on the green or the speaker never finds out if his message got across, the experience is useless to him. Finally, a high score for the golfer or a vigorous audience response for the speaker will provide incentives to adopt the techniques which brought these rewards; whereas a dozen lost golf balls or people walking out of the auditorium will discourage repetition of the behavior patterns which produced such results.

Since practice in a variety of real situations is not always possible, especially in group leadership training, the next best thing is role-playing — the setting up of make-believe situations. That is virtually what the practice golfer does when he lines up the ball

4 *Ibid.*, p. 234.

on the living-room carpet, or what the businessman does when he practices his speech on his wife, two kids, and the dog. Role-playing is nothing more than an attempt artificially to create for practice purposes situations which approximate as closely as possible the conditions that may be encountered in real-life.

The terms "psychodrama" and "sociodrama" are sometimes used to refer to the role-playing method which we have been discussing. Lippitt tells of an interesting application of psychodrama to leadership training.

> It is recognized that each leader has a certain range of situations where it is particularly difficult for him to be objective and intelligent in his own reactions. . . . (People and situations that) set him on edge.[5]

Lippitt goes on to recommend a psychodramatic technique for working on such problems. First, each leader composes a "gripe list" of these provoking people and situations. Then, when he leads the discussion, other members of the group play the roles he has described. At the conclusion of the discussion, or perhaps during it, an analysis is made of his reactions to these people and of the ways in which he attempted to deal with them.

Still other uses and values of role-playing are discussed by Benne, particularly as regards the training of children for democratic leadership.[6] He suggests that for a child who has been brought up in a basically undemocratic home or gang atmosphere, cooperative democratic group behavior will be unfamiliar and may consequently be resisted, like any new pattern of relationships tends to be resisted, as a threat to himself. Confidence in trying out new styles of group membership and leadership, says Benne, "requires a free and permissive atmosphere in which the ego threat is reduced to a minimum." This, he feels, can be accomplished by role-playing, where the child regards it as a game and does not feel his ego to be at stake. Benne also believes that leadership can

---

[5] Lippitt, Ronald, "The Psychodrama in Leadership Training," *Sociometry,* VI (August, 1943), p. 291.
[6] Benne, Kenneth, "Leaders are Made, Not Born," *loc. cit.*

be learned by children only if they can practice it in a variety of group situations, and if the groups have opportunities for self-evaluation. Role-playing again seems to provide the most practical way of accomplishing these objectives.

TRAINING IN COLLEGES

For several years valuable training in group leadership has been provided in a number of ways by many of our colleges and universities. One method has been the establishment of Speakers' Bureaus which send students out to church groups, adult forums, fraternal organizations, and the like, to serve as discussion leaders and to receive evaluations of their work. An outstanding example of this has been the Western Reserve University Rostrum, a college group which has served the Greater Cleveland area since 1923. Speech departments in many institutions have offered courses in group discussion and group leadership which provide the student with experience and criticism in the use of democratic techniques. Student government and other extracurricular activities have aided in the training process, though too often without benefit of adequate orientation and evaluation.

Unfortunately not many experimental studies have been conducted to measure the effectiveness of these college training experiences. There is one, however, now under way at the Northwestern University School of Speech which merits considerable attention. This study, being conducted by Dean Barnlund as a doctoral research project, has already produced significant results.

Barnlund's first step was to set up nine leaderless groups of five students each from the freshman classes in group discussion. Each group was assigned to a separate room and given fifty minutes to arrive at a set of written recommendations on a problem of concern to all students. The trained observers in each room kept a record of every action or remark made by any member which could be construed as an attempt at leadership. On the basis of these observations a list of leadership functions which occurred frequently and persistently in these groups was compiled. From this list Barnlund selected four functions to be used in his training experi-

224

ment: (1) initiating discussion, (2) directing group thinking, (3) summarizing, and (4) resolving conflict.

The second step in the experiment, several days later, was another round of fifty-minute discussions (nine groups, five members each) on a problem similar to the first one. This time, however, Barnlund appointed a leader for each group. Six of these leaders were people who had been chosen on secret ballots by their classmates and their instructor as the least effective discussion leaders in their respective classes. The other three were people in the middle bracket of their respective classes, chosen neither as most effective or least effective leaders. The discussions at which these nine leaders presided were again watched by trained observers who, at the end of the meeting, rated the leader on a preliminary version of the Barnlund-Haiman Leader Rating Scale contained in Appendix A (page 237) of this book.[7] Needless to say, none of the leaders did very well.

Following this round of discussions, six of the nine leaders (four from the poor category and two from the middle category) were pulled out of their discussion classes for two weeks (nine days — fifty minutes a day) and given intensive training in the four group leadership functions listed above. The other three leaders continued with their regular class work, which included some references to leadership but no concentrated attention on it.

Barnlund's training procedure for the six student leaders was as follows:

a) A training manual was prepared and given to the students which contained a brief introduction to the philosophy of democratic leadership and a lesson (about five pages long) on each of the four leadership functions to be dealt with — initiating discussion, directing group thinking, summarizing, and resolving conflict.

b) The group read (all reading was done out of class) and discussed for one session the material on democratic leadership.

c) The group read the lesson on initiating discussion and spent

[7] The preliminary form did not contain a section on Climate-Making. Otherwise it was the same as this one. Seven quantitative and seven qualitative judgments were called for.

about ten minutes asking questions about it. Two class meetings were then devoted to role-playing exercises which gave each trainee actual practice in initiating discussions. Their techniques were discussed and evaluated by Barnlund and the group.

d) The same procedures — a brief discussion of theory, a series of role-playing exercises, and evaluation — were used for two days each on directing group thinking, summarizing, and resolving conflict.

At the conclusion of this two weeks' period another round of fifty-minute discussions like those held prior to training was again scheduled. The same nine leaders were used, the personnel of each group was the same, the problem to be discussed was similar, and the same observers rated the leaders on the Barnlund-Haiman Rating Scale. *The observers did not know which of the nine leaders had received training.*

The results were startling. For the group of three leaders who had not been in Barnlund's training group there were no significant changes in any of the fourteen judgments made by observers on the rating scales. For the group of six who had received training, the following statistically significant changes were recorded:

> Gain in providing proper amount of effort to stimulate thinking
> Gain in the quality of effort to stimulate thinking
> Gain in providing the proper amount of effort to resolve conflict
> Gain in the quality of introductory remarks
> Gain in the quality of effort to regulate amount of participation
> Gain in the quality of over-all leadership ability

In addition to these statistical findings a few subjective reactions to the trainees are worthy of note. Several observers came back to Barnlund after the final round and expressed amazement at the change that had come over the leader since the meeting that had been observed two weeks earlier. The participants in one of the groups wanted to know "what on earth" their leader had been doing while he was out of class for the past two weeks to cause such a change. One of the instructors of the freshman discussion classes involved in the experiment noted a definite increase in self-confidence and sensitivity of participation on the part of the trained leaders during the remainder of the term following their return to class. These results have been so encouraging that follow-up experiments are in progress as this book goes to press. The ultimate findings will be reported in Barnlund's dissertation.

BUSINESS AND ADULT EDUCATION PROGRAMS

Experiments in training for discussion leadership have not been confined to the research of psychologists and professors. Businessmen, adult educators, and others close to the "grass-roots" problems of discussion have done an impressive amount of work in this area. Organizations such as the "Great Books" movement and the Parent-Teachers' Association have established courses or workshops to train democratic leaders. Training programs for conference leadership are being set up all over the country in business and industry.

Typical of the kind of work being done is the Conference Leadership Training Program outlined by Hannaford.[8] In any given industry this includes a two-week program for the training of key men to train leaders; a five-day program for conference leadership in supervisory levels above the first line; a three-day program for first-line supervisors and foremen; and a four-hour "Cook's Tour" program, not designed to equip for conference leadership, but to provide the top executives with an appreciation of the program. Hannaford's basic procedure is to hold discussions among the trainees, which are carefully checked by observers. Three sets of observations are made. The first provides a detailed history of the content of the discussion, and is termed a Discussion Flow Diagram. The second is a check on the leader's techniques — the extent and kinds of questions he uses, the amount of undirected discussion he permits, etc. The third observer watches the over-all effectiveness of the discussion and the general reactions of the

[8] Hannaford, *op. cit.*

group. These three sets of observations are then used as the basis upon which the group evaluates the leader's work.

This procedure is similar to that of the training conferences which have been held in the field of adult education and have been described from time to time in the *Adult Education Bulletin*.[9] Most of these sessions are two weeks long and are built around small group discussions. Each group is provided with a staff — leader, recorder, and observer — which has been selected and trained before the conference itself gets under way. The recorder keeps track of the content of the discussion. The observer keeps a check sheet on group interaction and plays a "feed-back" role — that is, he provides the group with an evaluation of its procedures, so that it can discuss, revise and improve them as it goes along.

This process of self-analysis by the group — discussing the discussion — is of the utmost importance in training leaders. Under democratic guidance by the observer, the members of the group state exactly how they feel about the leadership they have had. In this way the entire group becomes more alert to its own leadership needs and becomes more mature in the conduct of its own business. We have seen earlier in this book how group self-analysis can be a valuable aid in the resolving of interpersonal difficulties. What we did not emphasize at that point is that any such process of self-evaluation not only helps solve the immediate problem but also sensitizes people to the kinds of problems that a group faces and hence develops in them more leadership competence for the future.

These methods of "self-training" are still in the experimental stage, and are being tested and further developed each summer at the annual sessions of the National Training Laboratory in Group

[9] Howard, Palmer, and Ronald Lippitt, "Training Community Leadership Toward More Effective Group Living," *Adult Education Bulletin*, X (August, 1946), pp. 168–74.

Barron, Margaret and associates. "The Vermont School for Training in Group Leadership," *Adult Education Bulletin*, XII (June, 1948), pp. 140–48.

"California Leadership Training," *Adult Education Bulletin*, XI (June, 1947), p. 147.

"A Tale of Three Conferences," *Adult Education Bulletin*, XII (February, 1948), pp. 79–93.

Development at Bethel, Maine. The results are already encouraging, however, and have led Professor Benne to suggest that history is being made by the methods employed at these training conferences.[10]

Only history can tell whether Benne and the rest of us engaged in various types of leadership training are overstating our case. For the present we must be satisfied with the immediate, observable results which have been produced. The evidence indicates that these results are significant and well worth continued effort.

In summarizing this evidence there are three principles which we would do well to bear in mind:

1. Effective leadership training is as much a matter of developing the proper attitudes toward leadership as it is a matter of teaching specific skills.
2. The more group experience, in both amount and variety, that the student of leadership receives, the better will be his training.
3. His group experience should be such that his methods can be criticized and evaluated by others on the spot.

OVERCOMING THE RESISTANCE TO CHANGE

There can be little doubt of the necessity for the extensive training of democratic leaders in our society. If the problem of developing effective leaders was of grave concern to Plato and Plutarch in classical times, how much more so is it today when the complexities of society have increased a millionfold, and when participation in social action has come to include the great masses of men. It is this latter fact which makes leadership in our day a real problem and a real challenge. As more men become literate and educated, and as social and political participation is extended to an ever-increasing number and variety of such people, leadership must become more widely distributed, more competent, and more democratic. A civilization such as ours cannot long survive with weak and unskillful leadership.

[10] Benne, Kenneth, "The Future of Work-Survey Conferences," *Adult Education Bulletin*, XII (February, 1948), pp. 93–96.

There are many persons who oppose the growth of the new concept of democratic leadership and resist any training in its skills. We had best be prepared to understand the nature of their resistance in order to combat it.

Their first charge is that democratic leadership is an excuse by the leader for his own laziness and incompetence. It is much more difficult, they argue, for a teacher to prepare a lecture, for a clergyman to give a sermon, for a judge to write a verdict, or for an executive to plan his strategy than it is for any of them to lead a discussion.

We must admit that when responsibility is shared among a number of people, the work is easier for everyone. We merely ask, "Is that bad?" Moreover, we cannot agree that the democratic leader is necessarily lazy or incompetent. Though these *might* be his motivating characteristics, there is good reason to believe that an *effective* democratic leader can be neither lazy nor incompetent. The abilities discussed in Part Two of this book are not easy to master. Human relations skills are not acquired overnight. They are developed by dint of hard work and constant experience with human behavior. True, the democratic leader need not sit up all night before a specific meeting preparing his speech or planning his strategy. But he has done *his* planning and preparing over an entire lifetime. Lazy or incompetent people are *afraid* to expose themselves to the unpredictable twists and turns of a democratically operated meeting. The professor who permits no interruptions in his carefully planned classroom lectures or the executive who will not discuss his policies with others does not subject himself to unforeseen hazards. Could it be that he is afraid of a freer situation? Let us challenge the arguments of the autocrat who smugly charges democratic leadership with laziness and incompetence. Let us point out that it requires far greater effort and competence to guide a group of active, educated individuals who are thinking for themselves than to push around a group of passive, ignorant poeple.

The second source of resistance to being trained in democratic leadership is rarely spoken aloud or even consciously recognized.

Nevertheless it operates as a powerful factor in the autocrat's behavior. Many leaders subconsciously feel that by becoming more democratic they will lose the highly gratifying ego-satisfaction which comes to persons of authority. For the minister to come down from his pulpit or for the executive to come out from behind his mammoth mahogany desk would destroy the rewards they derive from that type of prestige.

If we are to be realistic, we must admit the fact that ego-satisfaction is a prime mover of man. We must recognize that unless there are psychological rewards of a personal nature there is no motivation for an individual to be a leader. What we must do is demonstrate to the autocratically-inclined person that democratic leadership *does not* entail a loss of ego-satisfaction. Quite the contrary, it is a far headier wine to drink. Once tasted, it makes the ego-pleasures of authoritarianism pale by comparison. Granted, it provides a different kind of gratification, which is less immediate and more subtle. It is the fore-sighted, intelligent ego-satisfaction that a democratic parent gets by watching his children grow strong and independent under his guidance, as contrasted to the greedy, immediate ego-satisfaction the autocratic parent gets from beating or barking his kids into line. The personal thrill that comes from stimulating and guiding a free discussion is of more solid stuff than the standing applause of an adoring audience. A teacher who can make his students feel free to challenge him on any ground may take a beating now and then but will be a more secure and happy person than one who is never quite sure what the members of his class are really thinking. The autocratic leader who can be brought to experience the richer satisfactions of democratic behavior will not resist them for long.

The third cause for resisting democratic leadership is closely related to the second. Thomas Carlyle, if he were alive today, would be appalled at our apparent attempts to deflate his "great man." Carlyle still lives in many people. More of us than care to admit it are in love with the power and glory that is a part of the "strong man" concept of leadership. This in spite of the fact that the shallowness and inadequacies of this doctrine have been pointed out for centuries. Its refutation lies at the very heart of Christ's teachings. Great poets have dramatized its weaknesses. Thomas Gray, for instance, in his well-known *Elegy Written in a Country Churchyard*:

> The boast of heraldry, the pomp of pow'r,
>   And all that beauty, all that wealth e'er gave,
> Await alike th' inevitable hour:
>   The paths of glory lead but to the grave.

And Percy Bysshe Shelley, in *Ozymandias*:

> I met a traveller from an antique land
> Who said: "Two vast and trunkless legs of stone
> Stand in the desert. Near them, on the sand,
> Half sunk, a shattered visage lies, whose frown,
> And wrinkled lip, and sneer of cold command,
> Tell that its sculptor well those passions read
> Which yet survive, stamp'd on these lifeless things,
> The hand that mock'd them, and the heart that fed:
> And on the pedestal these words appear:
> 'My name is Ozymandias, King of Kings:
> Look on my works, ye Mighty, and despair!'
> Nothing beside remains. Round the decay
> Of that colossal wreck, boundless and bare
> The lone and level sands stretch far away."

Why is it that we have not listened to these prophecies and words of advice? Perhaps it is because the poets, and even the religionists, have preached warnings which are based on sentimental idealism and which ignore the basic ego-needs of man. To follow the advice they give would seem to require that we be selfless and self-abasing to an extent that no healthy human being cares to go. The only alternatives to power and dominance that they leave us would seem to be humbleness and weakness. We have heard Christ himself characterized in some quarters as a "sissy." Certainly no healthy person wishes to be like the frustrated "schoolmarm" whose only joys in life are the vicarious thrills she gets from watching her students succeed, or like the parents whose only pleasures come from witnessing the triumphs of their children. Is that what democratic leadership is? If so, it neglects the natural, selfish human impulse to accomplish, to succeed, to grow strong — and most of us, quite properly, want no part of it!

Those who believe that this is what democratic leadership is have missed its basic significance and have missed the point of this entire book. Democratic leadership is built upon foundations that are more firm and real than selflessness and self-abasement. It fulfills, more than any other philosophy, the leader's human desire to grow and be strong, for it enables him to fulfill that desire *with the help of others. The democratic leader is engaged in a reciprocal process.* He not only gives, but he takes. As others in his group grow stronger and more independent, he grows with them. When students disagree with the teacher this does not spell his doom but his growth. For his ideas are put to a test and, if he is open-minded, he can thrive on such conflict. He can learn as much from the students as they can learn from him, and thus become more capable than he was before. The authoritarian leader, on the contrary, becomes progressively weaker, because his followers continually sap away his strength and give nothing in return. Those who, for selfish reasons, resist training in democratic leadership should be shown that they are amateurs at selfishness, and that there is no greater influence for good in the world than the *enlightened self-interest* embodied in a democratic leader.

CONCLUSION

Leadership in society may reside in an Abraham Lincoln or an Adolf Hitler. It may be a helpful or a harmful role, but unless there is anarchy, it is an inevitable one. Leaders may command, they may manipulate, they may persuade, or they may guide — but they cannot be suppressed. Wherever people live and work together there will be leadership, and the destiny of the group will depend in large part upon the kind of leadership it has.

We need no longer wait, as Carlyle would have done, for Providence to send us our leaders. Although the process is still shrouded with much mystery we have made a firm beginning in the deliberate development of the sort of leadership which can satisfy our real needs. As we move forward to still deeper insights and discover better training techniques we can reasonably hope to achieve a state of affairs in which democratic leadership will be more than an academic theory.

Appendices

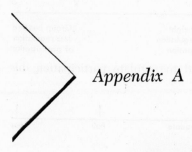

Appendix A

BARNLUND-HAIMAN
LEADER RATING SCALE [1]

INITIATING DISCUSSION

3	2	1	0	1	2	3

| Group needed more help in getting started | | | Group got right amount of help in getting started | | | Group needed less help in getting started |

The quality of the leader's introductory remarks was:

Excellent	Good	Adequate	Fair	Poor

CLIMATE–MAKING

3	2	1	0	1	2	3

| Group needed more help in securing a frank, permissive atmosphere | | | Group got right amount of help in securing a frank, permissive atmosphere | | | Group needed less help in securing a frank permissive atmosphere |

With regard to the establishment and maintenance of a frank and permissive atmosphere the leader's behavior was:

Excellent	Good	Adequate	Fair	Poor

[1] This scale may be reproduced without permission of the publisher or author *provided that* it is reproduced in full, with the title *Barnlund-Haiman Leader Rating Scale,* and that it is used only for educational purposes by non-profit organizations. Permission must be obtained for other purposes.

REGULATING AMOUNT OF PARTICIPATION

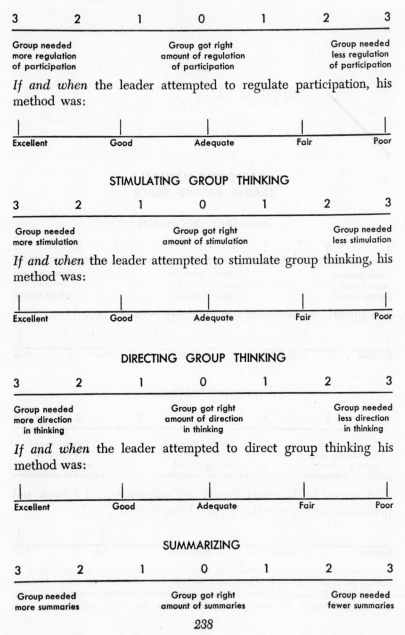

3	2	1	0	1	2	3

| Group needed more regulation of participation | | | Group got right amount of regulation of participation | | | Group needed less regulation of participation |

If and when the leader attempted to regulate participation, his method was:

Excellent	Good	Adequate	Fair	Poor

STIMULATING GROUP THINKING

3	2	1	0	1	2	3

| Group needed more stimulation | | | Group got right amount of stimulation | | | Group needed less stimulation |

If and when the leader attempted to stimulate group thinking, his method was:

Excellent	Good	Adequate	Fair	Poor

DIRECTING GROUP THINKING

3	2	1	0	1	2	3

| Group needed more direction in thinking | | | Group got right amount of direction in thinking | | | Group needed less direction in thinking |

If and when the leader attempted to direct group thinking his method was:

Excellent	Good	Adequate	Fair	Poor

SUMMARIZING

3	2	1	0	1	2	3

| Group needed more summaries | | | Group got right amount of summaries | | | Group needed fewer summaries |

If and when the leader provided summaries, his method was:

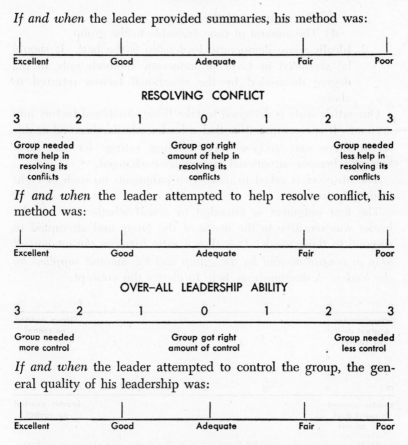

| Excellent | Good | Adequate | Fair | Poor |

RESOLVING CONFLICT

| 3 | 2 | 1 | 0 | 1 | 2 | 3 |

| Group needed more help in resolving its conflicts | | Group got right amount of help in resolving its conflicts | | | Group needed less help in resolving its conflicts |

If and when the leader attempted to help resolve conflict, his method was:

| Excellent | Good | Adequate | Fair | Poor |

OVER–ALL LEADERSHIP ABILITY

| 3 | 2 | 1 | 0 | 1 | 2 | 3 |

| Group needed more control | | Group got right amount of control | | | Group needed less control |

If and when the leader attempted to control the group, the general quality of his leadership was:

| Excellent | Good | Adequate | Fair | Poor |

Instructions for use of the Barnlund-Haiman Rating Scale

This rating scale is designed for use by *trained observers* in evaluating discussion leaders. Its reliability is dependent upon the extent to which observers understand and agree upon the assumptions and criteria set forth in these instructions.

We start with two basic assumptions:

1. Discussion leadership can be evaluated properly only when a number of situational factors are taken into consideration. Some of these factors are:

    a) The purpose of the group

    b) The nature of the problem which confronts the group

    c) The maturity of the group

    d) The amount of time available to the group

2. Ideally, pure democratic leadership is the best. It should be sacrificed in favor of autocratic methods only to the degree demanded by the situational factors referred to above.

Our rating scale is designed to take these situational factors into account. It is constructed so that a leader who is observed at different times may receive very different ratings for the same behavior because situational factors have changed.

The observer is asked to make two judgments on each of eight leadership functions.

The first judgment is intended to reveal whether or not the leader was sensitive to the needs of the group and attempted to respond to those needs. It is thus a *ratio between the amount of help or control needed by the group and the amount supplied by the leader.* A diagram may help to clarify this concept:

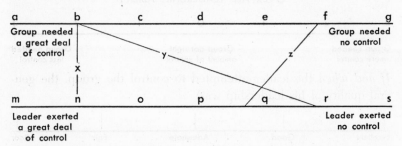

If the group observed is at point "a" on the continuum and the leader is at point "m," we may say that the group got just the right amount of control. This would also be true if the group needed no control (point "g") and got none (point "s"). In short, if a line drawn between any two appropriate points on these continua is perpendicular (such as "x"), the rating scale should be marked at "right amount" thus:

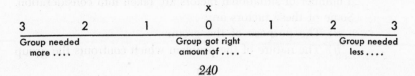

If the line is not perpendicular, the rating scale will be marked somewhere to the right or left of "right amount." For example, if the group is at point "b" and the leader at point "r" (line "y"), the rating scale would be marked almost to the extreme left — "group needed more. . . . " If the group is at "f" and the leader at "s," the rating scale would be marked only slightly to the left of center. Whenever the upper end of the line is to the left of the lower end (such as line "y") the rating scale will be marked somewhere to the left of center. Whenever the upper end of the line is to the right of the lower end (such as line "z") the rating scale will be marked somewhere to the right of center.[2]

The second judgment that the observer is asked to make on each of the eight leadership functions concerns the quality of the leader's methods. Whereas the first judgment simply reflects the leader's awareness of a need as shown by his efforts to provide help, the second judgment concerns the skill with which those efforts are made. Although these two matters are closely interrelated, and the two judgments will sometimes influence each other a great deal, there seems to be considerable merit in attempting to distinguish between them.

In those cases where the leader did nothing in a particular category the observer should ignore the second rating scale for that category.

v   v   v

This rating scale is concerned with eight specific leadership functions. It was believed that this particular classification would be the most useful for helping to train group leaders.

In order to develop a high degree of reliability for the scale, it is essential that uniform standards of judgment be developed among the observers with respect to each of the eight functions. We cannot hope to accomplish that end in these instructions. We can only provide a brief description of each category and refer the observer to the textbook material for further elaboration.

[2] It should be mentioned, in passing, that when the group is at point "g" and the leader at point "s" and the resultant rating is "right amount," there is no way for the observer to know whether the leader's abstinence was due to sensitivity to the needs of the group or to default. This limitation can be overcome only by intuition on the observer's part or by repeated observations of the same leader in a variety of settings.

INITIATING DISCUSSION

This category pertains to the opening of the meeting only. It concerns the way in which the problem or the purpose of the meeting is stated and the way in which discussion is started.

CLIMATE-MAKING

We are concerned here with the establishment of an atmosphere which:

a) Encourages frankness on the part of the group members. Enables them to state their ideas, convictions and feelings with honesty. Is free from artificiality.

b) Is permissive. Provides psychological freedom for the members. Is free from over-domination or pressure by the leader or by any other member. Encourages objectivity in dealing with the feelings of group members.

REGULATING AMOUNT OF PARTICIPATION

This function has to do with the problem of achieving a healthy balance among members in their quantity of participation. It does not require that everyone participate equally, but that there is equality of *opportunity to participate*. It enables the group to make the most effective use of its own human resources — drawing on all the worth-while talents that are available, and protecting the group from undue monopolizing of the conversation.

STIMULATING GROUP THINKING

This category includes such matters as bringing the problem close to the group, obtaining emotional involvement, helping the group to consider all angles, making the abstract concrete, playing the devil's advocate — in short, motivating the thinking processes.

DIRECTING GROUP THINKING

In order to solve problems effectively some measure of discipline must prevail in our thinking processes. Digressions must be kept to a minimum. Tangents and irrelevancies must be reduced. Some kind of systematic procedure or logical method must be followed.

SUMMARIZING

This refers to the pulling together of loose ends. It includes reporting what the group has done (what ground has been covered), and/or re-emphasizing important points that have been made.

RESOLVING CONFLICT

Into this category fall all efforts to reconcile differences. This includes such sub-headings as exploring the differences, clarifying areas of agreement and disagreement, and reducing extrinsic conflict.

OVER-ALL LEADERSHIP ABILITY

We are concerned here with the total impact of the leader on the group. Weighing all factors (both on and off the rating scale) and placing them in perspective, how good a job did the leader do?

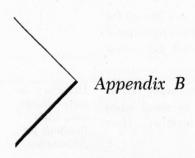

Appendix B

TWO SAMPLES OF SHARED LEADERSHIP

We present here the transcripts of two group discussions. Each demonstrates the way in which leadership functions are shared in a democratic group. As an aid to the reader, every leadership contribution has been *italicized* and has been identified in the margin. The reader can thus see at a glance how leadership passes from one responsible member of the group to another.

The participants in our first discussion, aired over the Mutual Broadcasting System on October 15, 1950 by the Northwestern University Reviewing Stand, are a group of men who both practice and preach the philosophy of shared leadership. They are: Leland P. Bradford, Director, Division of Adult Education Services, National Education Association; Director, National Training Laboratory in Group Development; Malcolm S. Knowles, President, Adult Education Council of Greater Chicago; Executive Secretary, Central Y.M.C.A., Chicago; Paul Sheats, Professor of Education, University of California at Los Angeles; Associate Director, University of California Extension; and Herbert Thelen, Associate Professor of Educational Psychology, University of Chicago; Director, Human Dynamics Laboratory, University of Chicago. Moderator: James H. McBurney, Dean, The School of Speech, Northwestern University.

The participants in our second discussion, aired over Station WNUR, Evanston, are all students of group dynamics at Northwestern University. They are: William Biel, Doris Brown, William Emmennegger, and Cliff Ford. Moderator: Franklyn Haiman.

APPENDIX B

Can We Get People to Work Together?

(Northwestern University Reviewing Stand, October 15, 1950)[1]

McBurney: Our speakers today are in Chicago for the annual national conference of the Department of Adult Education of the National Education Association.

Now, gentlemen, to open this discussion, tell us what kind of situations you have in mind when you talk about people working together. How would you answer that, Bradford?

McBurney initiates discussion. Asks Bradford for delimitation.

Bradford: People work together or meet in groups in all kinds of situations and all kinds of groups. To be specific, we have committees and community councils, we have staff meetings in business or industry or social work or education or family councils. There are certain industrial relations, management-labor meetings. There are international meetings; certainly Lake Success has its share of them. Wherever people get together, where we are facing the need for people to solve problems together, we have group situations which need study. Many problems are too complex for individuals to handle alone.

McBurney: *Do you have anything to add to that, Thelen?*

McBurney asks Thelen for delimitation.

Thelen: Yes, I like this notion of putting it in terms of social problem solving. I would like to extend it to personal problem solving with the concept that every individual is a group, too, and that many of the things that go on among several people also go on with one person. Thus a person can be a Protestant, a professor, a consumer, a father. He has to somehow make a group of all these people, and he has to remember which

[1] Reprinted by permission.

246

particular member of this group is the one that should be leader at any one given time.

McBURNEY: *Why are you men concerned* about the way people work together? Does it make any difference, *Sheats?*

McBurney stimulates discussion by asking significance of problem.

SHEATS: This seems to be pretty fundamental in maintaining the vitality of the democratic system, because so much social action these days depends upon the effectiveness with which groups can work together in solving their common problems.

KNOWLES: I would like to add to that. I am concerned, too, about the effects of group experiences on the kinds of individuals we have in our democracy. In other words, I think that one of the important objectives of group experience to anyone is in terms of helping him to grow into a more mature person.

BRADFORD: I think there is another factor, too, that enters in. In this day of tension, where we are all vitally concerned with the development of democracy as a bulwark against other philosophies, we need to realize that we have to do a lot more than talk about it.

The thing that disturbs me is that, if we want to bring someone in to fix our kitchen sink we call for a licensed plumber, but the process of a democracy, the process of people working together in groups, is a terrifically complex thing, and yet we assume that anybody without thinking about it can lead a group and can be a member of a group. Actually that is something that necessitates clear thinking, study, analysis, research, so that we can improve our basic methods of being democratic.

SHEATS: *Would you men agree* that the problems of working together in groups are much more

Sheats attempts to

247

difficult these days than they were, for example, in the pioneer period? In those days you had concrete problems which a group could get together and solve in a town meeting pattern, for example. Today it is much more difficult to see the relationship between a neighborhood Parent Teacher Association meeting, for example, and the great social issues of our times, and yet fundamentally what goes on in that small face-to-face group may have a great deal to do with the operation of the democratic system and these worldwide issues. *point out area of agreement.*

THELEN: I think it is very important to recognize, Sheats, that groups exist and go on. That is a fact. We don't have any choice whether or not we are going to work with groups. Our only choice is whether we are going to work with groups better and help them be more efficient.

Another point that impresses me here is that when you think about the size and complexity of our problems today and then ask what is that power that can solve them, you get down to an untouched source, a sort of atomic social power. That is the "behavior acts" of each individual. But these individuals do not act alone. They act in groups, and the kind of experience they have in groups determines whether or not this power is going to be enough to solve racial problems, for example, and peace problems.

McBURNEY: *Is this atomic social power to which you refer, Thelen, primarily a matter of communication? Is it primarily a verbal process you are talking about?* *McBurney asks Thelen for definition.*

THELEN: The control system for the release of this power is through the communication process in which many other people are involved. The source of the power itself, I suppose, boils down to the individual psychology of growth and the needs that individuals have to be mature and to be human in working with others in groups.

KNOWLES: I would like to suggest, too, that it seems to me what we are talking about here is releasing people to be productive, to be themselves, to be free from self-defensiveness, and so forth. One of the reasons why groups of people are not working well together now is that the air is so full of tension, and each person feels impelled to defend his point of view rather than to share with someone else, in producing.

McBURNEY: Now, releasing themselves, you say "releasing people," working together effectively — with what ends in view, *Bradford? What are you after here, anyway?*

McBurney asks Bradford for goals or values.

BRADFORD: We are after opportunities for people to solve the problems they are facing. We want to release them from tensions and restrictions which impair cooperative behavior. It is an interesting fact that a group of persons, a collection of people, do not always form a mature group. Very adult people can form a very infantile kind of group. This means we have to look very squarely at how you can help groups grow, just as we have always helped individuals grow, because by helping groups grow you also help individuals grow. The individual becomes much more of an individual and flowers much more as an individual when he has security in belonging and working with other people in a warm group situation.

THELEN: *Aren't you implying, Bradford,* that having a bunch of people together who are really eager to solve a particular problem does not of and by itself insure that the problem will be solved? Certainly we are really here to raise the

Thelen asks Bradford for elaboration.

question as to whether or not there are other things that have to be taken into account besides that one common interest.

BRADFORD: I was about to say that the communication involved in working together is certainly a much more complex thing than the verbal exchange of words. It is a matter of understanding the motives of other people, understanding their needs, helping them to play their parts in a group.

SHEATS: On the other hand, *I don't think we ought to try to cover the whole waterfront in a half an hour.* Taking Bradford's original lead, here, *we ought to begin to define the specific kinds of group situations* with which we are concerned here primarily. Let me give you an example. It seems to me the competency of a group to handle certain problem situations has a lot to do with the effectiveness with which it can work. You wouldn't expect a group of citizens in the Tennessee Valley to decide what kind of construction ought to go into the next dam that is built down there, but you might very well expect that group of citizens to have intelligent, informed opinions on whether this is the kind of direction they want our policy to take in that area.

Sheats suggests delimitation of the discussion.

Points direction.

KNOWLES: *You are suggesting, Sheats, that there are some situations in which group discussions just don't apply?*

Knowles asks for clarification.

SHEATS: Yes, where your need may be entirely for information.

MCBURNEY: *What are the situations in which it does apply?* What are the areas with which you are most concerned here?

McBurney asks for further opinions.

BRADFORD: Certainly where a group faces a problem that is common to the group, that can't be solved alone because it demands interdependence of the members of a group, is a place where you have to have a group situation.

Also we have found as you all know, that groups are places where people sometimes learn best, in terms of just learning or getting information. Groups, too, are the places where you solve conflicts; this matter of mediation or conciliation is involved. We are also finding in this new area of human relationship training that groups provide one of the best ways of training people in the skills of behaving adequately as human beings.

THELEN: I would like to go on with that point a little bit, too, to show the influence of groups on individuals. For example, in the Hyde Park-Kenwood Community Conference on the South Side of Chicago which is concerned with racial problems, there had been a woman who had gone to many tea parties and social gatherings. In many of them she heard prejudiced remarks, remarks that were antisocial, and shouldn't have been allowed to go by, but she had done nothing about it except sit there feeling flushed and guilty for some time. Then she got in with a group of neighbors in this conference program, and found that many of these people felt the same way and were indignant but also didn't know what to do. Just that amount of information was enough to strengthen her hand. The next time she heard a prejudiced remark she said something about it. And she said it effectively, too, because she was backed by a whole group and could feel secure in doing so.

KNOWLES: Mr. McBurney, there has been quite a lot of research going on in this matter of what causes groups to work or not to work well together, and I know that Bradford has been right at the center of a good deal of that research. *I wonder if he could illustrate* from Kurt Lewin's experiments on food habits exactly *how this sort of thing works.*

Knowles seeks further information. Points direction.

BRADFORD: The one study of Lewin's I think of doesn't do that exactly, Knowles. It merely shows the effectiveness of groups in certain situations. In this study of food habits two kinds of methods were used during the war to get housewives to change their food habits from buying meat that couldn't be bought to buying meat they didn't think they wanted, which meant, of course, changing the food habits of their whole families.

In one situation they were given pamphlets to read and given lectures and asked to change. In the other situation they discussed the desirability of changing, the adequacy of the food and came to a decision to do it and committed themselves in front of each other — even though they knew they would not see each other again.

I don't remember the exact figures, but as I recall there was a 2 per cent change in the first situation after reading the usual mass media and hearing lectures; there was a 33 per cent change in the case where people discussed together and decided together and committed themselves.

I wonder if at this point we wouldn't want to move, though, to a consideration of some of the characteristics you see in groups. I am a little concerned lest we give the impression that there is a set pattern or magic answer, that if you once know it you can buy it at the local drug store and then become a good group leader. I would like to stress that groups are complex. The best thing that can be said is that more scientific methods of inquiry are being applied to finding out what happens in groups. We know very little but we are trying to find out a few things. *We might look at some of those things.*

Bradford suggests new direction for group thinking. Suggests analysis.

Bradford reiterates suggestion.

McBurney: *I wonder if we can't get relatively specific on two things. First* why some of these group processes break down, *why groups fail; and then go on from there to take a look at some of the factors that may contribute to success in group meetings. Why do groups fail, Sheats?*

McBurney recommends a further focusing. First look at the causes of the problem, and then some solutions.

Sheats: I would like to take a shot at that. Just by listening to what seems to be one important explanation I have a hunch that we have placed entirely too much reliance on information-giving techniques. Take our national organizations, for example, in the field of international relations. I talked with a man just recently from the Carnegie Endowment for International Peace who says frankly that his organization has been producing materials and information which were rather widely circulated. The organization has absolutely no evidence as to what has happened in terms of the effect on behavior, on attitudes and opinions of the people whom they have reached. The tendency to rely on information-giving techniques as the primary answer to our problem tends to take away from the importance of group process and cooperative group work, it seems to me.

Bradford: I think, moving to another point, Sheats, we could say that one of the factors causing difficulty beyond that certainly is our idea or concept of leadership. We often think of leadership as something that one person does to the group rather than thinking that leadership is something the group has to do with and for itself. Leadership is very complex and calls for a lot of different behaviors, so many in fact that no one person can do it anyway. *You might want to say something about that, Thelen.*

Bradford asks Thelen for opinion.

Thelen: I would say that leadership is a kind of insurance policy, that the things that have to go on for a group to be effective do go on. Sheats has talked about the need for information. I would raise the question as to what kind of information the group needs. The leadership is there to make sure that the group gets that information, but the group has to participate in giving it. For instance, one kind of information the group needs is as to what the problem really is they are working on, that is, its hidden agenda, you might say. If you get a lot of people together, something will happen, that's for sure; but the question is what are they really trying to do, not what do they call it; not what are they allowed to say, but what are they trying to do.

One of the interesting problems, of course, is that so often they are working on the problem of what to do with their leader.

McBurney: *To focus this a bit I suggest that groups fail sometimes because they don't know what they are talking about and because they don't have adequate information; and they fail secondly because they are in the hands of an incompetent leader. What do you say to that?*

McBurney attempts to summarize.

KNOWLES: I would like to suggest, McBurney, that the incompetency of the leader needs a lot of definition. I think that in our society today we have tended to put a premium on what might be called an autocratic or authoritarian leader, a leader who has the point of view that it is his responsibility to see that the group accepts the answer that he himself has arrived at rather than a leader with the point of view of facilitating the group in thinking through the problem, what the possible solutions are, and then allowing the group itself to arrive at the kind of decisions that it wants.

Asks for verification of his summary.

BRADFORD: I certainly agree with you, and I agree with McBurney. I would say, though, that moving from the autocratic leader doesn't mean moving from a strong leader. We want "strong" leadership. Too frequently we think it means that the leader sits back and says, "What do you want to do now, boys and girls?" and no one knows what to do. It seems to me the leader's major functions are in part management, but not the police kind of management we have assumed too much in the past, but largely the role of being a consultant to the group in terms of the problems encountered in working together. We have studies that show in many instances that putting the attention on the part of the leader only on the problem being discussed and having information about it may not really help the group because he becomes only another group member. A better method is putting attention on the rough spots in our working together, why so and so are not talking, what has happened to cause tension, and other such matters.

THELEN: A very good example of that, it seems to me, Bradford, again from this Community Conference I referred to, has to do with getting together a bunch of neighbors, some of whom are strongly prejudiced against Negroes, and some of whom are strongly prejudiced for Negroes. Under these conditions it is very easy for a group to go over into an ideological kind of argument with a lot of tension and name calling, "you so-and-so, you feel this way," and so forth and so on. But the leadership skill here, and this is really an insight for a leader, would be to see that the real problem would not be to settle whether prejudice is good or bad, but to solve a particular problem. So the leader, for example, could say, "Let us all simply accept as a fact the fact that we all have different prejudices. That isn't our fault. And there isn't too much we can do about that immediately. But the real problem we have here is: here are these Negroes who moved in across the street. What are we going to do? Are we going to be friendly? Are we going to talk to them? Or are we going to try to ignore them?"

SHEATS: That would seem to me to be taking this concept of leadership almost to the point of considering it a function and responsibility of the whole group rather than as a combination of personality attributes that rest in one person who is, "capital L," the Leader.

McBurney, you know from your own field of speech that we have had a tendency to list a long list of requirements or technical skills or qualifications which the discussion leader in a group should have, without recognizing that it is almost impossible for one person to do all of the things that we have said it is important to do. Why not look at it as a function and divide it up among the members of the group?

THELEN: I think that is very accurate, Sheats. For example, the behavior I just spoke of which helped the group so much could have come from anyone in the group. People try different things. This particular thing happened to work, and it was done with the group's approval. If it hadn't happened to work, somebody else would have tried something else and he might have in a sense taken over for a short period of time if he had something to contribute that seemed to help the group.

McBurney: *Are you men talking about* a relatively specific method of group behavior?

McBurney seeks further information.

BRADFORD: No, I don't think so. We are talking about the things we are finding as we look critically and as scientifically as we can at the things that happen in groups, and from the results we are getting — as small as they are — we are beginning to say: these things do happen in groups; now what can be done?

Just to give an example . . . if we are looking for the magic method, it doesn't work . . . we have always heard it said that summarizing in a group is a very fine thing to do, and it is. But we have all watched certain situations where a person, usually the leader, gets up to summarize and blocks off some very wonderful thinking which he didn't want to have happen. And after the summary was through no one had courage enough to start again.

For example, as you look carefully at groups you see many things are present that you don't think about. In almost any group there could be and usually is what might be called two agenda, the surface or sophisticated agenda that we are dealing with on the table, and a variety of hidden agenda. Maybe our hidden agenda are, "How can I gain status in our group," or "How can I get my side over," or "How can I get someone else down." Or maybe the group has the agenda of "Sure, we'll agree with the leader in words, but we are certainly not going to carry out his policies." And these hidden agenda must be looked at.

THELEN: Or you can also have another example of a group hidden agenda. The leader has sufficiently stifled any ideas. Therefore to avoid a feeling of frustration you get out any idea that is halfway reasonable and looks plausible and it will be voted for, no matter what. But you can interview the people afterwards and find out that nobody really wants that decision.

KNOWLES: Which is one reason the Communists have a reputation for keeping the meeting going until three in the morning.

SHEATS: McBurney, *I am a little worried at this point in terms of whether we shouldn't now begin*   *Sheats recommends moving*

257

to deal rather specifically with some recommendations or suggestions that can be made for improv-
ing group processes. We have tended to pick
rather negative illustrations. Let us look at the
converse of it. *Specifically, what can we suggest
to our listening audience?*

*to a consider-
ation of pos-
sible solutions.*

KNOWLES: I would like to suggest one thing which
has to do with the climate under which the group
works. Typically in our Parent Teacher meetings,
our luncheon clubs, our boards of directors, etc.,
we set up a very formal rigid kind of climate in
which there is formal language. You address the
chair. You follow rules of procedure that are extremely formal, etc. It is my observation that this
inhibits and cuts off creative thinking. The best
kind of thinking is done in groups in which there
is a warm, friendly, informal kind of atmosphere.

McBURNEY: Now, as I follow you, gentlemen, *you
seem not to be speaking in behalf of eloquent ora-
tory.* Am I right in that, Thelen? *(Laughter)*

*McBurney in-
jects humor.
Example of
climate-mak-
ing.*

THELEN: Yes, we are trying to get an effective communication which has to do with the readiness of
the listener to accept the communication as well as
the floweriness of the speaker who is initiating the
communication.

BRADFORD: You asked for some examples, and I
think one is something we have been studying for
five years. How can conferences be made more
effective? Our conferences this week will stress
part of that. We hope to avoid the usual conference where the planners are afraid there will be
poor thinking or nothing thought about at all and
therefore they plan everything and everyone is told
what to say beforehand or speeches are planned.
Instead, you can encourage them to think critically.
They come out with far more than they have ever

258

come out with before and they are highly enthusiastic. One thing perhaps is to start a group meeting with a little problem census: What are the problems that we are facing? So from that we draw a common problem. The group then is able to make a decision: let's explore this, the leader constantly tossing in methods of exploration or suggestions as to how we might possibly work, but the basic content decisions become the group decisions.

SHEATS: As a corollary to that, we also suggest another condition; namely, that a group to work most productively and effectively ought to have some kind of action outlet or action orientation, and that its procedures should be directed not to having talk for talk's sake, but to working on a problem with a view to things with which that group has power to act concerning that problem.

McBURNEY: Let me say a word here. There are all kinds of groups in which you don't have to be concerned at all about having an action outlet. They are constituted for this precise purpose of determining action. They don't have to decide what they are going to talk about. What they are going to talk about is dictated by the problem, the situation in which they find themselves. I am talking about industrial relations groups, all kinds of community conflict groups. You don't have to worry about an agendum there. You don't have to worry about finding some course of action. That's their job, to find action. *Will this cooperative procedure that you men are talking about function in that kind of a hard situation* where real conflict exists?

McBurney stimulates argument by proposing a new angle.

THELEN: I think so. I think the usual charge that discussion processes are inefficient doesn't take the full picture into account. If you think of how much action follows and include the time spent in reaching a decision and also the time in taking action, you will find there is more action for the same amount of time and energy than if somebody comes in and says, "Now look, boys, here is what we have to do!" because although that is making a decision very quickly, you are going to have to set up elaborate machinery to see it through and continually to needle people to make them carry through.

BRADFORD: I would say a fundamental factor of all groups is this: All of them can get together. The problem is to get together better, and to get together better they have to know where they are bad, which means they have to keep on looking at how they are working as well as what they are doing. Now usually this is what the leader is doing, but he keeps the knowledge to himself. The group can learn and be helped to see that they can spend a little time in looking back and asking how did we do, what did we do, observing what they did and then talking about it. These were mistakes we made today. We blocked him off. We created tension on this part. And then tomorrow or the next time we meet, let us keep conscious of those factors so that we can improve. I would say that groups can grow, but they can only grow systematically on the basis of collecting knowledge about where they are at fault or not at fault.

McBURNEY: *What are you going to do in these conflict situations where these cooperative procedures break down* for one reason or another, and heaven knows they are breaking down all around us. *Look at the international scene. Look at the industrial scene.* I take it that strikes and clubs and guns are evidences of failures of these processes.

McBurney does some reality testing by proposing specific instances of problem.

KNOWLES: But, McBurney, aren't they breaking down largely because they haven't been using processes that are designed to help them in the jobs they have to do? They are using borrowed techniques from other situations that don't apply in this.

BRADFORD: There are also — and this I think is a long answer . . . I don't know the answer to those questions . . . I doubt if anybody here does . . . but it means these are areas in which we must put more intensive study. This year, for the first time, I think, a team went to Paris to study how our International Conferences work. Many studies like that will help us to get at all the dynamic forces which affect any group situation, and from that we will ultimately find our answers. I know they are not easy, but this is a path, a method of scientific inquiry which will lead us there.

THELEN: I think you are right, Bradford. I think we have to recognize that we are talking about a kind of tool that will be developed only from experience and from thinking about experience, and any experience is a failure experience if you expect too much from it right at the beginning. So all I say is we should have confidence that there is something here. We should think of everything we do as experimental, as a learning experience, and in the meanwhile be continually alert to where it is right to use groups, where it doesn't work, etc.

McBURNEY: *Do you think you men give enough attention to the role of authority and the role of the expert in this group process?*

McBurney again stimulates discussion by proposing another new consideration.

BRADFORD: It is certainly necessary to be in there. It depends on how you use it. I have watched many an expert ruin a group by insisting on giving the wrong information at the wrong time or the right information at the wrong time. It is a matter of always having authority but using it correctly, and that is a matter of study, too.

THELEN: It is also the problem of deciding what authority to use. So under some conditions the group may be under the authority of a method of solution of a problem, but under other conditions it is under the authority of a wiser person who has some experience; under other conditions it is under the authority of a person who can feel the pulse of the public.

McBurney: In conclusion, I think it is fair to say that the methods we employ in working together probably as much as anything else determine the kind of people we are and the kind of society in which we live.

What Effects Does a College Education Have on a Person's Religious Beliefs?

(Verbatim transcript of an impromptu radio discussion broadcast over station WNUR, Evanston, Illinois, on November 16, 1950.)

HAIMAN: *The other day I was walking through the library and noticed a book* on the shelf with a very interesting cartoon on the cover. It portrayed a typical college classroom with the professor standing behind the desk flailing his arms in the air, his long hair streaming down over his ears; and between bookends on his desk were the following titles: *Freud, The Communist Manifesto,* and *Atheism.* In the wastebasket alongside his desk were these books: *The U.S. Constitution, The Ten Commandments,* and *The Holy Bible.* Now this book was of vintage 1920, and perhaps the present beliefs about what goes on in colleges are not quite as they were at that time. But certainly there are, today, many sincerely religious people who are still suspicious of what goes on behind our ivory towers. In an attempt to throw some light on this subject, we have brought to our microphone four North-western University seniors to discuss the question: "What effects does a college education have on a person's religious beliefs?" Our participants tonight are Rusty Brown of Cleveland, Ohio; Bill Biel of Canton, Ohio; Bill Emmennegger of Monroe, Wisconsin; and Cliff

Haiman initiates discussion with concrete, vivid problem.

Ford of Chicago, Illinois. *Biel, I wonder if you'd start us off by clarifying what is meant by this term "religious beliefs." Are we talking about organized religion, or just what do you have in mind?*

Haiman asks for definition.

BILL BIEL: Well, of course it's a tough concept to put your finger on, and can be identified and defined in many different realms and aspects. About two years ago I was taking an anthropology course and I was quite certain that religion could be defined as a philosophy of living — a set of morals, ethics, and a way we go about things in our relationship of man to man. But the professor wanted to define the thing and confine it even much more strictly; he said that religion can be defined only as a belief in a Divine Power — or some great metaphysical power which lies out of the realm of the finite world in which we live. And that's about as far as the anthropologists would go with us on that.

BILL EMMENNEGGER: Well, one thing on that, Biel, — it seems to me that in our society (*and we're talking primarily about the American education system, as I see it*) we should consider religion primarily in the sense of Christianity and the Christian stems. That's not dealing with any particular sect, but all the sects that are involved in the Christian stems. There's no point in going into the possibility of strengthening the Oriental religions because we

Emmennegger proposes a delimitation.

aren't exposed to enough of that to be strengthened, even if we were originally of Oriental stock.

HAIMAN: *In other words, you would suggest then that we confine* this discussion to the influence of our colleges on the Hebrew-Christian tradition in the United States. Is that the idea?

Haiman clarifies the limitations that are emerging.

EMMENNEGGER: Yeah, that's right. That's the way I would see it.

HAIMAN: *In the formal sense, Bill?* In the church sense? Church-going as a definition of religion?

Haiman seeks further clarification of terms.

EMMENNEGGER: Well, not necessarily. I think probably most of the families I have in mind though are. The people who are sending their children to college — the Christian stem — a lot of them are and a lot of them aren't. In any case there's an exposure to the Christian beliefs — some stronger, some weaker in their youth. Now it is from that point, as they enter college, with that amount of exposure, that amount of strength in Christian beliefs — are those strengths weakened or made stronger in the colleges. You see, as I see it, that's the issue.

RUSTY BROWN: I would certainly go along with you on that, Bill. I remember when I first came up here, coming from a community where the Church League group was quite a pillar in that community, I immediately went over to the Church League group here. What a surprise it really was because there weren't too many other students from the freshman dorm; there weren't too many other campus students. And gradually I fell into the rut that many of us do — just finally losing interest and drifting away from it. It seems as though it's sort of a fad — a period which we all go through in trying to get our basic concepts; and religion at that time doesn't seem to fall in with us. Perhaps we feel more sufficient at this time of our life than at any other time because physically and mentally we are quicker and keener than we probably ever will be. It seems as though we can get along by ourselves, and therefore we don't have to fall back on religion.

HAIMAN: *Before we continue along that line, Rusty,* to find out what the effects of a college educational atmosphere are, *I'd like to clarify a couple of other questions in my mind about definitions.* Where does the agnostic and the atheist come in? Is that a form of religious belief or is it a form of non-religious belief? *Cliff, what do you . . . ?*

Haiman sidetracks consideration of this problem until other troublesome terms have been clarified.

CLIFF FORD: I think it's definitely a form of religious belief, in the sense that we're talking about religion, — considering it from a point of our beliefs before we get to school. I think that there are people who believe that the nature of the origin of the world and the nature of God is pretty inexplicable; and that, in coming to college, their beliefs are strengthened or weakened accordingly. And I think the same holds true with Atheism.

Haiman draws in the only one who has not participated.

BIEL: I think, if I may turn a little verbal

somersault here, that just the term agnostic almost implies a great almighty power. I mean it implies there is something there — we can't put our finger on it and identify it — but yet the supposition and the inference that it is existent is almost inherent within the term itself, "agnostic." And the same with "atheist." Now an atheist, of course we know, is a person who says there is no God at all. But if we want to take a broader definition of religion, and one which we seem to be tending toward in our current society, in which religion is a code of ethics and morals and so on — well then, even an atheist has a certain code, a certain set of standards by which he must live. And therefore his religion must fall along these relationships of man to man — whether or not he believes in a great almighty power — it's irrelevant — his code of living makes him a religious man.

EMMENNEGGER: I think that's a very important point. I think we all know a lot of people personally who, though they don't profess any particular sect, or they don't even go so far as to say that they believe in Christianity as such, live a better Christian life — are better examples of the principles of Christianity — than a lot of open professors of any particular sect. So I think that probably the wise thing to do is consider whether these principles — we'd probably call them a form of goodness — are strengthened or weakened by a college education.

267

FORD: Of course, we're tacitly assuming here that the college education is only having an influence — that it's not changing anybody. *I'd like to put the argument over so far as to actually consider whether or not we're not only being strengthened or weakened but actually whether we're making a tremendous change* in our beliefs too. Whether or not we came in as Christians — in the sense of being devout Presbyterians or something — and we have now changed to an agnostic viewpoint. *I'd like to at least clarify whether or not we're going to include that.*

Ford proposes broadening the limits of the discussion.

Asks for verification of this proposal.

HAIMAN: *Well, as I understand it, we're going to use for the purposes of this discussion a rather broad definition* of religion which makes everyone, even an agnostic or an atheist, have a religion, because he has some kind of set of codes — morals that he lives by. And we're interested, then, in finding out what the effects of a college education are on the person's moral code, ethical code, and so forth. *Is that right, Bill?*

Haiman attempts to sum up definitions and limits thus far agreed upon.

Checks his summary for verification.

EMMENNEGGER: Yeah, that's right. I don't think this is necessarily important but yet I do feel we should bring it in. And that is that we're talking about colleges that do not stand on any particular principle — they're not teaching any specific Christian principle. We're generalizing here. We're saying that it's a non-sectarian college.

HAIMAN: *Non-sectarian, liberal arts colleges like Northwestern.*

Haiman incorporates additional suggestion into summary.

EMMENNEGGER: That's right.

HAIMAN: OK. *Well on that basis then I wonder if we can't move ahead here* and answer the question: "What effects *does* college have?" It seems that most prejudices — popular prejudices — have *some* basis in fact, anyhow. Does this cartoonist who drew the picture of the long-haired professor have any basis in fact? Are the colleges making agnostics and atheists out of the students?

Haiman suggests moving to analysis of the problem.

BROWN: I think there is a definite tendency in colleges nowadays to emphasize the technical aspects of education; and I think it's generally considered quite foolish nowadays to argue Science vs. Religion. And I adhere to that also. However, I do think that that has an effect on our thinking. With so much emphasis on the technical knowledge, we seem to forget that a religious approach to truth is no more assumptive than a scientific approach to truth. In other words they're both searching and beginning on unreasoned presumptions. They each commit themselves to awakenings that will fall into their line of belief and with their pursuits.

BIEL: Well, Rusty, I want to pick up that little circle and go off on almost a tangent from the point you have drawn. And that is, I do happen to believe that man has a direct relationship to God — simply as a being, as a living, human organism — that he has a relationship to God and need not go through the context of a society, or

269

through an organized religion, or even through an educational system. Now this particular belief tempers that man's attitude, while living in that society, and while participating in the learning process. Now the education process, as I see it, as well as any other environmental process in our society — which includes social life, dances, and all phases of that — all affect that human organism and give him certain beliefs. Now if you want to say the total beliefs and the total attitudes and, of course, the resultant of that, the total manifestations of each human organism are his religion, then I'll say that education not only formulates a man's attitude — I mean in regard to religion — but actually it points the thing. But I don't happen to believe that education itself is the predominant thing that affects that person's belief. I believe that there is more in our environment that causes it. I mean, we all know that we learn more after we leave the classroom than we do in it.

EMMENNEGGER: *Well, then you'd say that* the education tempers the religion, or the initial belief, but it doesn't necessarily change it?

Emmennegger seeks clarification of Biel's opinion. Attempts to restate it in less complicated language.

BIEL: Yeah, I'll go with that. It can't change it. I don't believe that education can change a person's belief — if he *believes* it. Now if he is believing things eclectically. . . .

HAIMAN: *What do you mean by that?*

BIEL: Well in this particular case I

Haiman also seeks to bring this man down to earth.

mean by choice — making choices of his belief — in other words trying to support it factually — say, "I believe this because there is so much support for it. I don't believe this because there isn't enough support for it." Then of course, we're following the reflective process and education is the keynote there. Every bit of wisdom and knowledge that we can gather is of great importance. But to me the educational process is merely a minute part of a person's total belief and total set of values; and simply because he does have this direct relationship with God he can always go to this Divine Power for his outlook.

FORD: I, unfortunately, agree, for the most part. *I was interested more in Rusty's idea* that the technical aspect, being stressed as much as it is, seems to lead us away from religious viewpoints; or from thinking in terms of religion rather than in technical things.

Ford directs discussion back to main course by tactfully sidetracking Biel's contribution.

BROWN: Yes, the reason I said that was the fact that I do think the churches have failed. Where science has gone ahead in big strides religion hasn't kept up with it. But I sometimes wonder if the very knowledge of that fact — I mean, why should we look at it negatively and say, "Well, all right, religion doesn't appeal to Joe College anymore." If religion hasn't kept up with the times, isn't it our responsibility to do something about that? — if the church has failed or doesn't have the hold on youth that it might have.

271

FORD: *You seem to be slipping into a different definition of the term "religion"* now. I have the feeling that you're talking about the formalized, institutionalized sort of thing.

Ford attempts to keep thinking channelled to the limits originally staked out.

EMMENNEGGER: *Yeah, we've got to remember, Rusty, that we're talking about* — that whatever belief it was when you came in, how does education, if at all, temper this thing. I'd like to point out, before I say anything else, that, after all, we only have our own experience; and in so far as we do I can only speak for myself. But, as I see it, the college education has been overstressed in its importance — in the sense that teachers are too persuasive, books are too persuasive. I think that the mind of the college student has been undersold to a large degree. Now as far as any beliefs on morals or on how Christian or on how religious or nonreligious you are, I think that probably the social aspects of life in college have as much to do with the forming of these factors as does the teaching. This is not to overlook the power of some certain teachers who are extremely persuasive — I don't deny that — I have been affected greatly by a number of teachers — but I think that it's been overdone; I don't believe that the colleges are the nests of iniquity that a lot of people have claimed that they are — or have implied, anyway, that they are.

Emmennegger supports Ford's leadership effort so as to make it stick.

HAIMAN: *Well, what you're saying then, I believe, Bill,* is that not only might the classroom and the professor

Haiman restates opinion in attempt to clarify it for group.

and the strictly educational experiences affect the person's beliefs and attitudes on religion, but that also his social life — his fraternity activity, the whole atmosphere in which he lives — on the campus —

EMMENNEGGER: Yes, I would see that sort of thing in many ways being more important because — well, I find that my religious beliefs have been strengthened, if anything, since I've been in school. I find that, more and more, the technology and materialism and so forth, though a great advantage to society in many ways — I see its great disadvantages and I see what an arid credo that thing is in itself. I find that there's a lack of purpose in living — that is, I find more and more a need for a creed.

FORD: Regarding the social life idea, I agree very much. I think that a college student who believes very much in some particular religion will manage somehow — I don't know what the trick is or how they do it, but they manage somehow — to think in compartments. If they have a course where they stress atheism — or not stress it, but where they keep presenting it to you with some pretty valid arguments — the same student manages somehow not to be particularly affected by it in any other place than right in that classroom itself.

HAIMAN: *Another way of saying that, Cliff,* might be that in a lot of our science courses and social sciences we're

Haiman restates the previous opinion and in so doing "sneaks" in his own feelings on the subject.

taught to approach problems through
the scientific method. To analyze, to
think through. And people come to college, they learn that, and they accept it,
for scientific problems. But when you
get over into the area of ethics and
morals they abandon that method completely and they use other methods.
Now what I'd like to ask is this: Doesn't
the mere fact that college continually
promotes the idea of approaching all
problems reflectively and scientifically
— I think that's the essence of education — to make people approach things
rationally and intelligently — doesn't
that, in a way, work against at least
some of the more mystical aspects of
religion, anyhow.

EMMENNEGGER: *Well I don't know that
I like the terminology right there,* because, you're implying right now that
by being mystical there is nothing rational about religion. And I wouldn't
agree with that to begin with. I think
that there's a great deal that is rational
about religion. I don't say that I can
draw you a picture of God or that I
can lead you to God and show him, or
prove it in a chemical formula — but
that's been the popular concept, especially in our society of late, that since
you can't prove it, since I can't show
it to you, there is no God. That's what
results in this materialistic type of society we have today.

*Emmennegger objects to
the moderator's terminol-
ogy, which in reality indicates a disagreement with
the leader's views. Free
and permissive atmos-
phere apparently prevails.*

HAIMAN: *Now wait; it's not an "either
— or," "there is or there isn't." You can
also take the middle position* that since

*Moderator is now knee-
deep in the discussion.*

274

you can't draw a picture I just don't know whether there's a God or not.

EMMENNEGGER: Yeah, that's right.

HAIMAN: That'd be the agnostic point of view.

EMMENNEGGER: That's right, but I don't think that — well, I forget your original statement right at the moment.

FORD: I think you're absolutely right; I think that's very possible; that you can get to the point where if your original beliefs (perhaps I'm incorrect in thinking this is what you said) — that is, if you have a feeling beforehand about Christianity or religion which is pretty vague, and you run across all this sort of thing, that you can actually become convinced that the agnostic idea is the best.

EMMENNEGGER: Well but you're saying that you're approving of confusion. You're saying that "I've seen so many possibilities and have no rational reason to go in any direction —

FORD: No, no — you're just feeling suddenly that you've come to some sort of a realization that perhaps isn't religion and perhaps isn't all particularly formalized religion just sort of an arbitrary thing that somebody just decided, "Let's have it this way."

BIEL: Look, you've been sitting here watching me seethe for a while — perhaps I'm getting a little bit nervous — it's not a frustration so much as it is a

275

strong belief that's beginning to bother me here. Now we've interpreted religion as a code of morals and ethics and so on. But nevertheless we've got to infer that this code of morals and ethics is tempered by a belief in a greater power than ourselves. Otherwise why have codes of morals and ethics? Why go from "birth unto death"? — these are all questions we can never answer. We have to —

EMMENNEGGER: *We haven't denied that! We simply have it delimited to that.*

Emmennegger attempts to confine discussion to the immediate issue at hand.

BIEL: *Well, now let me go on here.* Now look. If, without the realm of our finite existence (and by finite existence I mean everything that we can identify scientifically and everything that we shall ever know as scientists — inferring that each man is a scientist) — outside of that realm of the finite must lie this power of almighty being or divine goodness, or whatever you will, that tempers our very living within that finite scope. Now —

Biel rejects this attempt at leadership.

HAIMAN: *Why?* Why MUST there be, Bill?

Haiman probes the argument further in an attempt to find a basis for resolving the conflict.

BIEL: Well simply because it has a realm of being within man's mind — if only within my mind then it has a realm of being which tempers my very attitudes and very living. I can't support it by reflective thinking — as a matter of fact I don't think the Messiah will ever show up because reflective thinking will prove that he can't exist anyhow! (*Laughter*)

BROWN: Maybe I can help out there a little, Bill, when you were trying to say why you believed in that. In a course I took, "Man and the Physical World," — probably you've taken it too —

BIEL: Yeah.

BROWN: The fact there was so very apparent to me — that confirmed me in a belief in an almighty power — was the fact that one week we were reading of the finite — as you were speaking of — the next week we were studying the infinite. And in both the finite and the infinite there seemed to be such an extreme (as Einstein has used the term) "orderliness" in the universe. And — if I can use a quotation that he used at the end of one of his articles — it was "One law, and one element, and one far off divine creation toward which the whole world seems to move."

FORD: I don't feel any of that. That's all I want to say.

EMMENNEGGER: *Well, are we going to pursue this idea* of a specific belief — I mean, that you're going to try to prove something here. *Or are we going to talk about the effect that college education has upon you* — whether you believed or didn't believe when you went in?

Emmennegger tries to bring discussion back to central issue.

BROWN: Well, that was what I was saying there. Because I was doubting when I went into the course. But when I came out I believed much more strongly.

BIEL: You mean to say that we want to use a college education to prove there's a God?

EMMENNEGGER: No, on the contrary, I don't think that a college education proves or disproves anything. All it does is give you — it develops a certain rational ability; and in that rational ability, if you try to round God up, so to speak, within the folds of that rational insight, you're going to get into, as I see it, very hot water. And yet you can go toward an understanding of God with rationality.

HAIMAN: I'd like to inject one idea along that line, Bill. A little earlier you said that we may leave things in confusion as a result of trying to approach the question of whether or not there is an Almighty through rational efforts.

EMMENNEGGER: No, I simply said, when Cliff said something about resulting in an agnostic because you came in without any specific belief in anything particular concerning the spiritual and the abstract, and that eventually you become an agnostic, because you got a little bit of this and a little bit of that you weren't sure where you stood and therefore you believe that none of it had any great force.

FORD: Or better yet, that none of it seemed a very rational explanation. Nothing about the creation and the origin and so forth seems satisfying enough that I'm going to blindly — *I'm sorry* — feel enough to believe.

Ford attempts to soothe ruffled feelings that he observes.

278

HAIMAN: *It seems to me that what Bill, and Biel, and Rusty are perhaps saying is* that rationality is not enough and that you need more than that; *whereas Cliff is perfectly satisfied* to answer as many questions as he can rationally, and those that he can't he'll just say, "I won't answer those." It doesn't disturb him; it doesn't make him confused; he's perfectly satisfied not to have answers.

FORD: Well, you see, I have been brought up pretty much under a formalized system and it's taken me a long time to shake off the bonds of that. And so, I'm in sort of a transitional phase now, I imagine, and perhaps I'll never get any farther than this, where it took me a long time to realize that I was going to church every Sunday actually just to sit in the choir and smile at the people and show off. And it took me a long time to realize that. Now that I've gotten that far, I haven't quite made this other step yet, I don't think.

EMMENNEGGER: Well, I'd like to point out, as far as the rationale is concerned in leading to religion — I'm not saying that it closes the door. I think a lot of examples could be given of where intellectuals little by little inch away from it till they go to the extreme of denying everything and then many of them come back, and, they claim, through a rational process. I'm just saying, don't close the door to rationally approaching religion. You implied that. I know that you didn't really

Haiman summarizes and points up the present state of the conflict.

279

mean it when you said "blindly" — but you *did* say blind; and there is that popular concept that if you believe something you can't prove, it's a blind faith. And that's a hard word.

BROWN: And, after all, the scientist starts out too with an hypothesis — which is just a stab in the dark.

BIEL: Well, look. A correlation of true belief, emotionalism and rationalism, is the thing that makes man the intellectual being that he supposedly is — the Reasoning Animal. But the scientific method and the rational way of approaching things is merely a way of organizing those things that we can deal with, such as matter, energy, and the things that we know within our material universe — the things which dogmatic religious men say are the creation of the Father — these things are the things that we deal with scientifically. Now science does nothing more than give us an organized way of going about dealing with them. Science makes no intention at all of explaining what a God is, or what an Almighty power is. Now an almighty power must lie beyond the rational, must lie beyond the scientific method simply because the scientific method is devised only to explain that which is finite. And if God, and the terms like "Eternal" are used — why the terms so finite as "rational" and "science" couldn't possibly cover it.

EMMENNEGGER: *Well, I think that's the point Dr. Haiman made a little while*

Emmennegger attempts to relate and pull together

ago when he implied that it goes beyond the rational. In other words, you can think about it just so far and then — well, as Thomas Aquinas said, "I believe that I may know." He began from that principle. You have to believe beyond the point that you can see. And many people say, "Why do you *have* to?" — and of course, there you're lost, if you say you *have* to. But as we feel about it, you have to. As some one else feels about it — well, that's a highly individualistic thing. *As is the issue tonight.* I believe that the effect that the college education has on the *original belief that the person carries to college is a matter of the individual you're talking about.* You don't make any generalizations and say this is the way it happens to a whole strata or a whole group or a stereotype of people.

HAIMAN: *I think that's obvious from our discussion here tonight.* We have four college students with four rather different views of what effects a college education has. *I wonder if, recognizing that it has different effects on different people, we might not push one step farther and ask the next question — whether or not these effects are desirable.* Are colleges inciting undesirable things with regard to religion? Are colleges doing desirable things? Or are colleges neutral on the subject?

BIEL: Well, this is one of my favorites, to tell you the truth. I happen to believe that if two men who are sitting side by side in a pew for ten years of their lives

loose threads in the discussion.

Emmennegger attempts to resolve the basic conflict in the discussion.

Haiman gives support to Emmennegger's proposal for settling the difference.

Suggests moving the discussion forward to the evaluation phase.

281

in a church walk out on Monday morning, and even though they have been reading the same book, listening to the same preacher, minister, rabbi, or whatever the case may be, that on Monday morning they will believe different things. Now to me that is a simple, logical (excuse the expression) way of showing that each man individually and personally has a direct relationship with God. He doesn't have to go through an organized religion. Collective religion to me is a contradiction in itself. Each man has this relationship. He can learn the code and the way through this collective religion, perhaps, but his relationship is still direct and personal.

EMMENNEGGER: Well, I think that some professors in a college, who themselves have inherent beliefs of righteousness — whether it be because they believe in a specific Christian sect or religion — will teach their subjects accordingly. I believe that it does, as you say, to a good extent neutralize itself. Some, who are atheists, will bend over backwards to try to destroy the little belief a student might have and others will do their best to reinforce it. I remember one college professor who began his lecture with, "I make no apologies for my belief in God" and carried on from there. In fact he was very proud of his belief in God, and I was proud of him.

HAIMAN; *How would you summarize this thing, Rusty?*

Haiman requests a summary.

RUSTY BROWN: *I'd summarize it in this way.* We *do* get out of the home situa-

Brown provides a summary.

282

tion, which perhaps has been tempered by a formal religious aspect, and for the first time we get a chance to think things out for ourselves at college. And it's when we think it out for ourselves and come to our own decisions, and when we accept some beliefs and discard others, and then when they become our own, then we have arrived at the conclusion which we want to follow for life.

HAIMAN: *Cliff?*

Haiman draws in the one participant who has not yet had a final say.

FORD: I just feel approximately the same thing. I think that as long as the colleges continue — or this particular college, let's say, continues — to present the facts as objectively as they can, with a minimum of the personality factor entering in, then the effect of the colleges on religion will be a good thing.

HAIMAN: We've heard these opinions from four Northwestern students. What do you think?

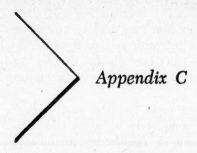

Appendix C

SAMPLE LEADERSHIP PROBLEMS: CASE STUDIES

The three case studies presented in this appendix are true accounts of leadership problems. They have been written by students in our course in Group Leadership. Fictitious names have been substituted in the first and third cases for the protection of the authors.

We present these stories and the problems they pose in the hope that our readers will be stimulated to comb their own experiences and write up similar case studies for class discussion.

Case I
(Author's name withheld by request)

Ted served one term as president of Fraternity X, skipped a term, and now has been re-elected for another. Of his record as president during the first term the following can be said: he ran the meetings in what seemed to be a fairly democratic manner. However, the informed people in the house knew that Ted had organized pressure groups before every meeting in which he wanted to push something through.

Ted has a good politico's voice and doesn't believe in coddling people. He believes mostly that people will want what will do *them* the most good, and consequently he presents all his arguments in those terms. He doesn't care if people are clubbed or have their toes stamped on in the process. The funny part of his manner is that he knows what tact is and uses it bluntly (if you can imagine such a technique).

Ted has some personal characteristics that interfere with his being a democratic leader. His strength, power and persistence in the face of opposition earn him the label of "autocrat" in a short time, even by those who don't know him very well. He is never able to take as he can give; is quite inflexible and short on credit-giving qualities. Consequently one can't honestly say that he has either a well-adjusted personality or a healthy respect for human beings.

When it comes to knowledge of the topic Ted is at his strongest. He always has a subject covered completely by plans which he comprehends so well that he cannot be thrown by attempts to detour him mentally. His mind is quick and clear, and I think that now we are staring at the real reason for his success — he is always one jump ahead of everyone else. His ability to verbalize is not quite on a par with the calibre of mind he has, but he still manages to get a final force into his phrases which no one feels much like challenging.

During his first term Ted was never remote from any situation, never desisted from expressing his own desires, and consequently seemed to give the group the feeling that they had to hurry and make a decision for Ted — even if they might not be quite satisfied with it. This reveals that Ted has vitality — of an extreme type. He is calm, but the calm is not real. Rather it is an "I'll be calm in spite of the situation" attitude.

As I see it, Ted does not feel as though interpersonal relation-ships have much effect on the action of the group he is leading. He is sensitive only to the feelings of individuals toward him, not to-ward each other. He feels that the issue at hand, not the people in the group, is the important thing; and he is sure he can guide that issue to its proper culmination — no matter how the people in the group feel toward each other. Consequently he overlooks all handling of personality problems within the group.

Ted has been re-elected, however, and chiefly on the premise that he doesn't fool around and can get things done. The group seems to prefer being relieved of some of the burden of governing themselves, even if they are slightly irritated by some of his actions. The philosophy seems to be: "As long as he doesn't go too far, he's all right."

PROBLEM: Should I, as a member of Fraternity X who believes in democratic procedures, attempt to do something in order to help build a more democratic group? If so, what can I do?

Case II
(Written by Rosemary Hoefle)

Two years ago, I needed a summer job. The City of Toledo Recreation Department was desperately in need of park supervisors and playground leaders, so I applied. Plus the fact that the work paid well, I eagerly anticipated three months of relaxing in the sun. My friends told me that Wilson Park was in a poor section of town, that the children in the neighborhood were hoodlums and vandals, and that their parents had an instinctive antipathy for city workers, including cops. I refused to be pessimistic. Wasn't I protected by the large orange and black seal of the City of Toledo Recreation Department which was sewed on my uniform as a sign of authority?

The first day as playground leader at the park, two eighteen-year-old Polish boys tried to push me into the swimming pool. A playful little girl ripped off the "seal of authority" and nearly traded it for a stolen bicycle tire before I got it back. A hungry urchin purloined my lunch; an irate parent demanded to know why I wasn't teaching handicraft; and Joe, the neighborhood moron, a man of forty whose mental growth had stopped when he was ten, insisted on using the slides and swings. I was a leader in name only, and the kids knew it.

At home that night I thought the whole thing over and planned a course of action. The heterogeneous group obviously didn't want a leader. They only wanted to use the park equipment (baseballs, croquet sets, basketballs, etc.) and have as much fun as possible. Annoying me was a prime source of their enjoyment. The desires of the group were evident; all I had to do was try to lead. I began by:

a) First becoming friends with the lad who regularly mowed the park area. Lennie, a university student, was highly respected by all the younger neighborhood boys because of his athletic prowess. Adults in the Wilson Park area knew him and liked him also. Needless to say, his help was invaluable when fights had to be broken up or arguments had to be settled. First he handled these problems; gradually I took his place.

b) In attempting to identify myself with the group I thought of telling them that I was Polish. (Wilson Park is located in the heart of Toledo's Polish and Negro section.) However, my name doesn't sound anything like Cousino, Novak, or Suski, and I doubted if they would believe me. Instead I truthfully told them I was a Catholic. Long hours of discussing the relative merits of their respective parochial schools ensued. They may have been trouble-makers, but the kids loved their religion and they were glad I could appreciate it too.

c) Most of the children came from underprivileged homes; they were not used to much attention from their families. Many would spend the entire day at the Park while their parents worked at one of the nearby factories. I appointed ten "guards" from the most antagonistic and hostile group of boys and told them they would be responsible for enforcing the Park's rules (only one person per swing, no diving, etc.). They accepted the responsibility.

d) I tried to find time during the day to satisfy as many little play groups as possible. With the younger girls I told stories, jumped rope, and taught art and knitting. They, in turn, taught me how to crochet. With the boys I played baseball, volleyball, croquet, and "territories" (a jolly little game played with jack knives). In all of these activities I tried to be merely a passive participant or observer.

e) The large concrete swimming pool was used by hundreds of dirty little kids every day. Guards were appointed to watch the younger children while I gave swimming lessons. This was another responsibility — one for which they received the privilege of having a special hour in the pool all to themselves.

Every Friday we cleaned the pool. Rather than assigning boys to do it the first time, I started to scrub it myself. Soon a crowd gathered. Out of the corner of my eye I saw a Negro minister from a church several blocks away. Shortly after I had started, a six-year-old boy hollered, "Hey, I wanna do it too." I told him I was sorry but the job required boys who were strong enough to handle buckets and brushes. Immediately ten or twelve older lads volunteered. We made the work fun; it always drew an audience from the playground, and soon my waiting list for helpers far surpassed the number of scrub brushes.

The summer ended successfully. Wilson Park swimmers won several cups in an all-city swim meet. Our handicraft classes made bird-houses which were exhibited at the Recreation Center. And Moron Joe taught us all how to play pinochle.

PROBLEM: Analyze the techniques of leadership described in this story in terms of the theories and principles set forth in the textbook.

Case III
(Written by Jeri Jensen)

The discussion I am about to describe was held in the offices of one of America's largest corporations. The purpose of this planning board meeting was to determine employee policies in a new plant.

Each of the members to be involved in the discussion entered the chrome and leather room individually. Smith, Jones and Wilson (senior members of the committee) collected at one end of the room, reviewing golf games and exchanging cigars; while Green and Brown (junior members of the committee) involved Younger (organizer of the new plant) in a conversation that showed they still had the dust of the college campus on their shoes. Thomas and Swanson were entangled in a discussion of the world situation. It was evident that there was going to be a rift in the relations between the generations in addition to the differences in age, experience, and education.

Chairman Elder, who has about as much personal magnetism as an angry hornet, bustled in twenty minutes late, slammed down his brief case on the long polished table and said, "Well, gentlemen, let's get going." The older members sat on one side of the table and the junior representatives set up camp on the other side. There was no attempt at climate-making; the atmosphere was quite frigid as Elder asked Younger, "All right, Younger, just what is it that is holding up that show at the new plant?"

Younger reviewed the progress made on the factory. He explained that work was being held up because of the lack of employee policies, and set forth the policies he had considered for the situation, all of which were quite liberal and followed a generally "modern" attitude in dealing with employees.

Smith, Jones, and Wilson could hardly wait until Younger was through before they began attacking the liberal suggestions. Elder gave no one a chance to say anything as he delivered a twenty-five minute oration on the fallacies in Younger's planning. Green and Brown immediately rallied to Younger's cause, while Thomas tossed in his beliefs on the world situation. On one occasion, when Younger tried to defend his own position, he was met with, "Shut up, youngster!" from Elder.

The discussion — I hesitate to call it that — fell apart into an argument over the ethics of employer-employee relations in general, the world crisis, and the comparative merits of Princeton, Dartmouth, and Harvard. All of this led to Jones throwing his pen against the wall, and Green's answering him with the smashing of an ash tray into the table. This wrangling continued for roughly two hours. About the time that men began lunging at each other, Younger asked for a break in order that the atmosphere might clear. To this Elder answered, "You aren't afraid are you, young man? Let's get this settled here and now." Swanson (a vice president of the company), who had not been making many contributions, pointed out the advisability of following Younger's suggestion, and Elder adjourned the meeting for thirty minutes. The two factions retired to separate quarters.

When the discussion resumed, Elder announced that the older members of the committee had decided that employee policies in the new plant should conform with regular company systems. Younger thereupon presented, in a calm and rational way, the best case for mature discussion methods that I have ever heard.[1] The room was quiet until Swanson said something to the effect that the committee was supposed to be made up of rational men, capable of settling problems by democratic means. There were a few nods of assent, and Younger unofficially slipped into the role of group leader.

The discussion continued for well over five more hours, during which time Younger guided the group through a rational, effective process in determining policies for his new plant. Of course there were moments when certain members tried to get into another all-out fracas, but each of these attempts was handled with compromise and gentle social pressure from the rest of the group. I was interested to see how the feeling of cooperation was quick to

[1] Miss Jensen observed this discussion from behind the secret confines of a closet door.

spread, even to the most reticent of the group. I was particularly interested in watching the reaction of Mr. Elder. During the first part of the "new regime" he was very quiet and appeared to be sulking in his tent. As the group progressed, however, he was carefully drawn in by Younger. There was an awareness within the group of the urgency of "getting along" with each other. By the conclusion of the discussion all ill feeling was reconciled, the task was accomplished, and Younger was hailed as hero of the day.

PROBLEM: How can groups whose meetings are typically plagued with difficulties such as those encountered in this discussion be enabled to achieve similar "happy endings"?

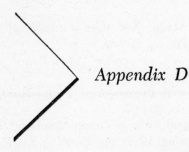

Appendix D

BIBLIOGRAPHY

ADORNO, T. W., E. FRENKEL-BRUNSWIK, D. J. LEVINSON, and R. N. SANFORD. *The Authoritarian Personality.* New York: Harper, 1950.

ALLPORT, FLOYD H. *Social Psychology.* Boston: Houghton Mifflin, 1924.

———. *Institutional Behavior.* Chapel Hill: University of North Carolina Press, 1933.

ARISTOTLE. *The Rhetoric.* Trans. Lane Cooper. New York: Appleton-Century-Crofts, Inc., 1932.

AUER, J. J., and HENRY L. EWBANK. *Handbook for Discussion Leaders.* New York: Harper, 1947.

BALES, ROBERT F. *Interaction Process Analysis.* Cambridge, Mass.: Addison-Wesley Press, 1949.

BARNARD, CHESTER. *Dilemmas of Leadership in the Democratic Process.* Princeton, N.J.: Princeton University Press, 1939.

———. *The Functions of the Executive.* Cambridge, Mass.: Harvard University Press, 1948.

BARRON, MARGARET, and ASSOCIATES. "The Vermont School for Training in Group Leadership," *Adult Education Bulletin,* XII (June, 1948), pp. 140–48.

BARZUN, JACQUES. *Teacher in America.* Boston: Little Brown, 1944.

BAXTER, BERNICE, and ROSALIND CASSIDY. *Group Experience — The Democratic Way.* New York: Harper, 1943.

BAVELAS, ALEX, and KURT LEWIN. "Training in Democratic Leadership," *Journal of Abnormal and Social Psychology,* XXXVII (January, 1942), pp. 115–19.

BELLIN, SEYMOUR, and FRANK RIESSMAN. "Education, Culture, and the Anarchic Worker," *Journal of Social Issues*, V (1949), pp. 24–32.

BENNE, KENNETH. "Leaders are Made, Not Born," *Childhood Education*, XXIV (January, 1948), pp. 203–08.

———. "The Future of Work-Survey Conferences," *Adult Education Bulletin*, XII (February, 1948), pp. 93–96.

———. "Democratic Ethics in Social Engineering," *Progressive Education*, XXVI (May, 1949), pp. 204–07.

———, and PAUL SHEATS. "Functional Roles of Group Members," *Journal of Social Issues*, IV (Spring, 1948), pp. 45–46.

———, and BOZIDAR MUNTYAN. *Human Relations in Curriculum Change*. Illinois Secondary School Curriculum Program Bulletin No. 7, June, 1949.

BION, W. R. "Experiences in Groups," *Human Relations*, I (1948), II (1949), and III (1950).

BIRD, CHARLES. *Social Psychology*. New York: Appleton-Century-Crofts, Inc., 1940.

BISCH, LOUIS E. *Be Glad You're Neurotic*. New York: McGraw-Hill, 1946.

BOGARDUS, EMORY S. *Leaders and Leadership*. New York: Appleton-Century-Crofts, Inc., 1934.

BRADFORD, LELAND P., and JOHN R. P. FRENCH, JR., Issue Editors. "The Dynamics of the Discussion Group," *Journal of Social Issues*, IV (Spring, 1948).

BUSCH, HENRY M. *Leadership in Group Work*. New York: Association Press, 1934.

———. *Conference Methods in Industry*. New York: Harper, 1949.

"California Leadership Training," *Adult Education Bulletin*, XI (June, 1947), p. 147.

CAMERON, NORMAN. *The Psychology of Behavior Disorders*. Boston: Houghton Mifflin, 1947.

CANTOR, NATHANIEL. *The Dynamics of Learning*. Buffalo: Foster and Stewart, 1946.

CARLYLE, THOMAS. *On Heroes, Hero-Worship and the Heroic in History*. New York: Crowell, 1840.

CARROLL, LEWIS. "Through the Looking Glass and What Alice

Found There," *The Complete Works of Lewis Carroll.* Garden City, N.Y.: Garden City Publishing Co., 1942.

CASSON, HERBERT N. *Tips on Leadership.* New York: B. C. Forbes, 1927.

CHAPIN, F. STUART. "Socialized Leadership," *Journal of Social Forces,* III (November, 1924), pp. 57–60.

CHASE, STUART. *The Tyranny of Words.* New York: Harcourt, 1938.

COCKING, WALTER D. "Satisfactions from Democratic Leadership," *School Executive,* October, 1948.

COLUMBIA ASSOCIATES IN PHILOSOPHY. *An Introduction to Reflective Thinking.* Boston: Houghton Mifflin, 1923.

Constitution of the United States of America.

COOPER, ALFRED M. *How to Conduct Conferences.* New York: McGraw-Hill, 1942.

COUSINS, NORMAN, and THOMAS K. FINLETTER. "A Beginning for Sanity," *Saturday Review of Literature,* XXIX (June 15, 1946).

COWLEY, W. H. "Traits of Face-to-Face Leaders," *Journal of Abnormal and Social Psychology,* XXVI (October–December, 1931).

COYLE, GRACE. *Group Experience and Democratic Values.* New York: Woman's Press, 1947.

CUNNINGHAM, RUTH, and ASSOCIATES. "Leadership and the Group," *National Education Association Journal,* November, 1948.

CURTIS, GEORGE WILLIAM. *Orations and Addresses.* Ed. Charles Norton. New York: Harper, 1894.

DASHIELL, J. F. "Experimental Studies of the Influence of Social Situations on the Behavior of Individual Human Adults," *A Handbook of Social Psychology.* Ed. Carl Murchison. Worcester, Mass.: Clark University Press, 1935, pp. 1097–1158.

Declaration of Independence.

DEUTSCH, MORTON. "A Theory of Cooperation and Competition," *Human Relations,* II (1949), pp. 129–152.

DEWEY, JOHN. *The Public and its Problems.* New York: Holt, 1927.

———. *How We Think.* Revised ed. Boston: Heath, 1933.

EICHLER, GEORGE A., and ROBERT R. MERRILL. "Can Social Leadership be Improved by Instruction in its Technique?" *Journal of Educational Sociology,* VII (December, 1933), pp. 233–36.

ELLIOTT, HARRISON. *The Process of Group Thinking.* New York: Association Press, 1932.

FINAN, JAMES. "Inside the Prison," *Readers Digest,* May, 1950, pp. 61–72.

FRANK, LAWRENCE K. "Dilemma of Leadership," *Psychiatry,* II (August, 1939), pp. 343–61.

FRENCH, JOHN R. P., JR. "Retraining an Autocratic Leader," *Journal of Abnormal and Social Psychology,* XXXIX (April, 1944), pp. 224–37.

FOLLETT, MARY P. *Creative Experience.* New York: Longmans, 1924.

GRAY, THOMAS. "Elegy Written in a Country Churchyard," *Works,* Vol. I. Ed. Edmund Gosse. London: Macmillan, 1884, pp. 71–80.

GREGG, J. M. *Handbook of Parliamentary Law.* Boston: Ginn, 1910.

HAIMAN, FRANKLYN S. "An Experimental Study of the Effects of Ethos in Public Speaking," *Speech Monographs,* XVI (September, 1949), pp. 190–202.

HALSEY, GEORGE D. *How to be a Leader.* New York: Harper, 1938.

HANNAFORD, EARLE S. *Conference Leadership in Business and Industry.* New York: McGraw-Hill, 1945.

HEIDER, FRITZ. "Social Perception and Phenomenal Causality," *Psychological Review,* LI (1944), pp. 358–74.

———. "Attitudes and Cognitive Organization," *Journal of Psychology,* XXI (1946), pp. 107–12.

HEMPHILL, JOHN K. *Situational Factors in Leadership.* Ohio State University Studies No. 32, 1949.

HENDRY, CHARLES E., Issue Editor. "Leadership in a Democracy," *Journal of Educational Sociology,* XVII (March, 1944).

HEYNS, ROGER W. *Effects of Variation in Leadership on Participant Behavior in Group Discussions.* Dittoed Publication of Conference Research. Ann Arbor, Michigan. December 6, 1948.

HOLLINGWORTH, H. L. *The Psychology of the Audience.* New York: American Book Co., 1935.

HOMANS, GEORGE C. *The Human Group.* New York: Harcourt, 1950.

HORWITZ, MILTON W., JOSEPH LYONS and HOWARD V. PERLMUTTER. "Induction of Forces in Discussion Groups" (to appear in *Human Relations*).

HOWARD, PALMER, and RONALD LIPPITT. "Training Community Leadership Toward More Effective Group Living," *Adult Education Bulletin*, X (August, 1946), pp. 168–74.

JACQUES, ELLIOTT. "Interpretive Group Discussion as a Method of Facilitating Social Change," *Human Relations*, I (1948), pp. 433–39.

JEFFERSON, THOMAS. "First Inaugural Address," *The Writings of Thomas Jefferson*, Vol. 3. Ed. A. A. Lipscomb. Washington, D.C.: Thomas Jefferson Memorial Association, 1905.

JENKINS, WILLIAM O. "A Review of Leadership Studies with Particular Reference to Military Problems," *Psychological Bulletin*, XLIV (January, 1947), pp. 54–79.

JENNINGS, HELEN HALL. "Leadership — a Dynamic Redefinition," *Journal of Educational Sociology*, XVII (March, 1944).

———. *Leadership and Isolation*. New York: Longmans, 1943.

JOHNSON, A. B. *The Meaning of Words*. Milwaukee: John Windsor Chamberlin, 1948.

JOHNSON, WENDELL. *People in Quandaries*. New York: Harper, 1946.

KELTNER, JOHN. "Committee Dynamics: Leadership Aspects," *The Gavel*, XXXII (March, 1950), pp. 59–63.

KLINEFELTER, C. F. *Report of a Training Conference for Foreman Conference Leaders*. U.S. Office of Education Vocational Division Bulletin No. 164 (June, 1932). Washington, D.C.: U.S. Government Printing Office, 1932.

———. *The Training of Foreman Conference Leaders*. U.S. Office of Education Vocational Division Bulletin No. 125 (1927). Washington, D.C.: U.S. Government Printing Office, 1927.

———. *Social Leadership*. U.S. Office of Education Vocational Division Bulletins No. 231. Washington, D.C.: U.S. Government Printing Office, 1945.

KNICKERBOCKER, IRVING. "Leadership: A Conception and Some Implications," *Journal of Social Issues*, IV (Summer, 1948), pp. 23–40.

KRECH, DAVID, and RICHARD S. CRUTCHFIELD. *Theory and Problems of Social Psychology*. New York: McGraw-Hill, 1948.

LARRABEE, HAROLD A. *Reliable Knowledge*. Boston: Houghton Mifflin, 1945.

LEE, IRVING J. *Language Habits in Human Affairs*. New York: Harper, 1941.

LEIGH, ROBERT D. *Modern Rules of Parliamentary Procedure.* New York: Norton, 1937.

———. *Group Leadership.* New York: Norton, 1936.

LEIGHTON, ALEXANDER H. *The Governing of Men.* Princeton, N.J.: Princeton University Press, 1945.

LEVINE, SOL. "An Approach to Constructive Leadership," *Journal of Social Issues,* V (Winter, 1949), pp. 46–53.

LEWIN, KURT. "The Dynamics of Group Action," *Educational Leadership,* I (January, 1944), pp. 195–200.

———. "Experiments in Social Space," *Resolving Social Conflict.* New York: Harper, 1948.

———. "Forces Behind Food Habits and Methods of Change," *National Research Council Bulletin No. 108,* October, 1943.

LINDEMAN, EDUARD C. "Leadership: A Function of Democratic Experience," *Journal of Educational Sociology,* March, 1944.

———. "The Ethical Foundations of Democracy." Sermon delivered on May 8, 1949, at the Unitarian Church, Evanston, Ill.

LINK, HENRY C. "Definition of Social Effectiveness and Leadership Through Measurement," *Educational and Psychological Measurement,* IV (Spring, 1944), pp. 57–67.

LIPPITT, RONALD. "The Psychodrama in Leadership Training," *Sociometry,* VI (August, 1943), p. 291.

———. *Training in Community Relations.* New York: Harper, 1949.

LOCKE, JOHN. "An Essay Concerning the True Original Extent and End of Civil Government," *in Civil Government,* Book II. Ed. Ernest Rhys. New York: Dutton, 1924.

MACHIAVELLI, NICOLO. *The Prince.* Ed. Ernest Rhys. Trans. W. K. Marriott. New York: Dutton, 1908.

MAIER, NORMAN R. F. "The Quality of Group Decisions as Influenced by the Discussion Leader," *Human Relations,* III (1950), pp. 155–74.

MANDER, A. E. *Logic for the Millions.* New York: Philosophical Library, 1947.

McBURNEY, JAMES H., and KENNETH G. HANCE. *Discussion in Human Affairs.* New York: Harper, 1950.

McGREGOR, DOUGLAS. "Conditions of Effective Leadership in the Industrial Organization," *Journal of Consulting Psychology,* VIII (1944), pp. 55–63.

MELBY, ERNEST. "Leadership is Release of Creativity," *School Executive*, November, 1948.

MEREI, FERENC. "Group Leadership and Institutionalization," *Human Relations*, II (1949), pp. 23–40.

MERRIAM, CHARLES E. *Four American Party Leaders.* New York: Macmillan, 1926.

MILL, JOHN STUART. *On Liberty and Other Essays.* New York: Book League of America, 1929.

MISHLER, ELLIOT G. *Ascendant and Submissive Members and Leaders: Their Interaction in Group Discussion.* Dittoed publication of Conference Research. Ann Arbor, Michigan. Spring, 1949.

Naval Leadership. U.S. Naval Institute, Annapolis, Md., 1949.

NEWCOMB, THEODORE M. "Autistic Hostility and Social Reality," *Human Relations*, I (1947), pp. 69–86.

———, EUGENE HARTLEY, and OTHERS. *Readings in Social Psychology.* New York: Holt, 1947.

New Yorker, August 17, 1946, pp. 49–60. "Seven Men on a Problem."

OVERSTREET, HARRY A., and BONARO W. OVERSTREET. *Leaders for Adult Education.* New York: American Association for Adult Education, 1941.

PETERMAN, JACK. *Verbal Participation: Its Relation to Decision-Satisfaction and the Leader Function in Groups.* Paper presented at Midwestern Psychological Association meeting, Chicago, Illinois, April, 1949.

PHILLIPS, ARTHUR E. *Effective Speaking.* Chicago: Newton Co., 1908.

PIGORS, PAUL. *Leadership or Domination.* Boston: Houghton Mifflin, 1935.

PLATO. *The Republic.* Trans. B. Jowett. 3rd ed. Oxford: Clarendon Press, 1888.

PLUTARCH. *The Lives of the Noble Grecians and Romans.* Trans. John Dryden. Rev. A. H. Clough. New York: Modern Library, 1932.

PRESTON, M. G., and R. K. HEINTZ. "Effects of Participatory vs. Supervisory Leadership on Group Judgment," *Journal of Abnormal and Social Psychology*, XLIV (1949), pp. 345–55.

Report on the International Control of Atomic Energy. Washington, D.C.: U.S. Government Printing Office, 1946.

RICKARD, PAUL. "An Experimental Study of the Effectiveness of Group Discussion in the Teaching of Factual Content." Ph.D. Dissertation, Northwestern University, 1946.

ROBERT, HENRY M. *Robert's Rules of Order, Revised.* Chicago: Scott, Foresman, 1943.

ROGERS, CARL R. *Counselling and Psychotherapy.* Boston: Houghton Mifflin, 1942.

ROSENBERG, MORRIS. "The Social Roots of Formalism," *Journal of Social Issues,* V (1949), pp. 14–23.

ROUSSEAU, JEAN JACQUES. "From the Social Contract," *The World's Great Thinkers.* New York: Random House, 1947.

RUSSELL, BERTRAND. *Authority and the Individual.* New York: Simon and Schuster, 1949.

———. *Power.* New York: Norton, 1938.

SAADI, MITCHELL, and PAUL FARNSWORTH. "The Degrees of Acceptability of Dogmatic Statements and Preferences for their Supposed Makers," *Journal of Abnormal and Social Psychology,* XXIX (July–September, 1934), pp. 143–50.

SARETT, LEW, and W. T. FOSTER. *Basic Principles of Speech.* Boston: Houghton Mifflin, 1946.

SCHENCK v. U.S. *Official Reports of the Supreme Court,* 249 US 47. Washington, D.C.: U.S. Government Printing Office, 1919.

SCHREIBER, JULIUS. *It Pays to Talk it Over.* Washington, D.C.: National Institute of Social Relations, 1947.

SHAFFER, LAURANCE. *Psychology of Adjustment.* Boston: Houghton Mifflin, 1936.

SHEFFIELD, ALFRED D. *Creative Discussion.* New York: Association Press, 1927.

SHELLEY, PERCY BYSSHE. "Ozymandias of Egypt," *The Poems of Percy Bysshe Shelley,* Vol. II. Ed. C. D. Locock. London: Methuen, 1911.

SHERIF, MUZAFER, and HADLEY CANTRIL. *The Psychology of Ego-Involvement.* New York: Wiley, 1947.

SHERWOOD, ROBERT. *Roosevelt and Hopkins.* New York: Harper, 1948.

SIMPSON, RAY H. *A Study of those who Influence and those who are Influenced in Discussion.* New York: Columbia University Teachers College, 1938.

SMITH, HENRY L., and L. M. KRUEGER. *A Brief Summary of the Literature on Leadership.* Bulletin of the School of Education, Indiana University, IX (September, 1933).

SMITH, T. V. *The Democratic Way of Life.* Chicago: University of Chicago Press, 1926.

STOGDILL, RALPH M. "Personal Factors Associated with Leadership: A Survey of the Literature," *Journal of Psychology,* XXV (January, 1948).

————. "Leadership, Membership and Organization," *Psychological Bulletin,* 1950.

————, and CARROLL SHARTLE. "Methods for Determining Patterns of Leadership Behavior in Relation to Organization Structure and Objectives," *Journal of Applied Psychology,* June, 1948, pp. 286–91.

SWARD, KEITH. *An Experimental Study of Leadership.* Ph.D. Dissertation, University of Minnesota, 1929.

TEAD, ORDWAY. *The Art of Leadership.* New York: McGraw-Hill — Whittlesey House, 1935.

TERMINIELLO v. CHICAGO. *Official Reports of the Supreme Court,* 337 US 272. Washington, D.C.: U.S. Government Printing Office, 1949.

THELEN, HERBERT. "Educational Dynamics: Theory and Research," *Journal of Social Issues,* VI (1950). Entire Issue.

THOREAU, HENRY D. "Civil Disobedience," in *The Writings of Henry D. Thoreau,* Vol. 10, Riverside Edition, pp. 131–70. Boston: Houghton Mifflin, 1898.

THRASHER, FREDERICK M. "Leadership in the Gang," *The Gang, A Study of 1313 Gangs in Chicago,* Chapter 18. University of Chicago Press, 1927.

To Secure These Rights. Washington, D.C.: U.S. Government Printing Office, 1947.

Town Meeting. Bulletin of America's Town Meeting of the Air. Vol. 15, No. 32 (December 6, 1949).

TRALLE, HENRY E. *The Psychology of Leadership.* New York: The Century Co., 1925.

UTTERBACK, WILLIAM E. *Group Thinking and Conference Leadership.* New York: Rinehart, 1950.

WAGNER, RUSSELL, and CARROLL ARNOLD. *Handbook of Group Discussion.* Boston: Houghton Mifflin, 1950.

WERKMEISTER, W. H. *An Introduction to Critical Thinking.* Lincoln, Nebraska: Johnsen Publishing Co., 1948.

WHATELY, RICHARD. *Elements of Rhetoric.* London: B. Fellowes, 1841.

WHERRY, ROBERT J., and DOUGLAS H. FRYER. "Buddy Ratings: Popularity Contest or Leadership Criteria?" *Sociometry,* XII (February–August, 1949), pp. 179–90.

WHITEHEAD, T. N. *Leadership in a Free Society.* Cambridge, Mass.: Harvard University Press, 1936.

WILSON, GERTRUDE, and GLADYS RYLAND. *Social Group Work Practice.* Boston: Houghton Mifflin, 1949.

YOUNG, KIMBALL. *Social Psychology.* New York: Appleton-Century-Crofts, Inc., 1944.

ZELENY, L. D. "Experiments in Leadership Training," *Journal of Educational Sociology,* XIV (January, 1941), pp. 310–13.

———. "Characteristics of Group Leaders," *Sociology and Social Research,* XXIV (November–December, 1939), pp. 140–49.

Index

Abstract nature of social policies, 60–61

Accessory needs, 81–82

Accident, as a source of leadership, 16–17

Acheson, Dean, 155

Action groups, 79–80

Adaptability
in use of parliamentary procedures, 202
in use of reflective thinking pattern, 163–164

Adenauer, Konrad, 23

Administrative leadership, 66–67

Advocate leadership, 62, 68–69, 113, 154, 201

Agenda
hidden vs. regular, 89–91

Aggressive behavior
causes of, 86, 149
techniques for checking, 149–150

Agreeing to disagree, 179

Allport, Floyd, 75, 78

Ambivalence toward leaders, 20–21

Analyzing a problem, 159–160

Anarchy, 43–44, 148

Anthony, Susan B., 162

Appeals from the decisions of the chair, 205, 212–214

Arapesh, 19

Arbitration, 180–181, 199–200

Aristocracy, 30–31

Aristotle, 69

Atomic Energy Committee, 155–156, 157

Attitude, as determinant of effective leadership, 116–118, 229

Authoritarianism
and Carlyle, 28
as a type of leadership, 29–30, 58–71
definition of, 29–30
history of, 30–32
philosophy of, 30–32

Authority, ultimate, 33, 34

Autocratic leadership
definition of, 29–30, 33–34
on a continuum, 44

Bales, Robert F., 75, 77, 89

Barkley, Alben, 204

Barnard, Chester, 49, 64–65, 67, 73

Barnlund, Dean, 224–227

Barnlund-Haiman Leader Rating Scale, 225, 226, 237–239
instructions for use of, 239–243

Barron, Margaret, 228

Baruch, Bernard, 156

Barzun, Jacques, 71

Bavelas, Alex, 17, 220, 221

Baxter, Bernice, 115

Bell, Alexander Graham, 162

Bellin, Seymour, 93

Benne, Kenneth, 38, 74, 75, 85, 223, 229

Bethel, Maine, 38, 219, 229

Biel, William, 245, 263 ff.

Bird, Charles, 12

Bisch, Louis E., 57

Blind-spot in discussion, 133

Bogardus, Emory, 18, 122

Boys' gangs in Chicago, 12

Bradford, Leland, 38, 245 ff.

Bridges, Senator Styles, 142

Brown, Doris, 245, 263 ff.

Bryan, William Jennings, 118, 121

Bunche, Ralph, 182

Busch, Henry M., 37

Caesar, 56

Cameron, Norman, 84, 90

Cannon, Joseph, 214

Cantor, Nathaniel, 138

Cantril, Hadley, 76

Carlyle, Thomas, 15, 16, 28, 31–32, 48, 231, 233

Carroll, Lewis, 183

Case study method

as a stimulus to discussion, 140–141
in industrial relations, 141
in teaching of law, 141
Cassidy, Rosalind, 115
Casson, Herbert, 11
Catharsis, emotional, 55
Chairman of debate, 33, 200–202
Chapin, F. Stuart, 36–37
Charismatic leaders, 68–69
Chase, Stuart, 93
Chicago, boys' gangs, 12
Ching, Cyrus, 182
Churchill, Winston, 68, 119, 121
Clarifying concepts, 157–158
Clear and present danger doctrine, 205
Climate-making, 41, 132–135, 242
Clock-watching, 170
Closing debate, 210–211
Cohesiveness, 99, 103
Collaborative decisions, 33, 51–53
Columbia Associates in Philosophy, 187
Columbus, Christopher, 162
Commanding, as a method of leadership, 5
Committee chairmen, 46
Communication, 92–93
Compensation
and overcompensation, 84–86
as a source of leadership, 18
Competition, 91–92, 103, 200
Concluding discussion, 174
Conditioning
as an explanation of social behavior, 83–84
as a source of leadership, 18–21
in the formation of values, 186
Conflict (see also Resolving conflict)
extrinsic and intrinsic, 94–95, 136–137, 181, 182–196
in evidence, 183–184
in reasoning, 184–185
in values, 185–188
semantic, 182–183
Conformity, 55–57, 62–65, 148
Content-orientation, 89, 103
Continuum
from anarchy to totalitarianism, 43
from democracy to autocracy, 44

from learning group to action group, 80
Cooper, Alfred, 69, 144, 154
Cooperation, 91–92, 103, 200
Cousins, Norman, 156
Cowley, W. H., 9
Coyle, Grace, 118, 122, 123
Creativity, release of, 37, 41
Crutchfield, Richard, 21, 76
Culture, as an influence on leadership, 19
as an influence on morale, 54
as an influence on social behavior, 83–84
as an influence on values, 186
Cultural determinism, 15
Curtis, George W., 30

Dean, 72, 126
Debate, 180–181, 200–201
Decentralization, 66
De gustibus non est disputandum, 185
Delaying controversial issues, 193–194
Democratic leadership
definition of, 32–34, 45–46
history of, 34–36
limitations of, 57–66
philosophy of, 29, 34–42, 230–233
values of, 51–57
Demosthenes, 121
Dependence, 19–21, 143–144
Determinants of leadership behavior, 22–24
job to be done, 23
leader's personality, 23–24
personality of the followers, 24
sanctions of the leader, 24
Determining group objectives, 158–159
Devil's advocate, 136
Dewey, John, 37, 154
Difference of opinion, 55–57, 135
Diffusion of leadership, 37, 38–39, 111–112, 245–283
Diplomacy, need for, 131–132, 147
Directiveness, degree of, 6, 22, 42
Director, 72
Discipline, of discussion, 148
Discovering and describing solutions, 161–163

Discussion
  groups, 12, 37–38
  moderator of, 6, 33, 121–122
Discussion leader, 70–71, 112, 113–
  128, 224–227
Diversion, 194
  to leader, 194
  to other matters, 194
  to other participants, 194
Divine right of kings, 14, 31
Domination, 6, 7–9, 18–19, 85, 113–
  114, 149
Douglas, William O., 205–206
Dramatizing a problem
  case study method, 140
  films, 141
  role-playing, 139–140
  vivid description, 140
Dynamics
  of leadership, 3–27
  of a group, 38, 75–105

Ego-orientation, 89
Ego-satisfaction, in leadership train-
  ing, 231
Eichler, George, 16
Elaborating contributions, 171
Elliott, Harrison, 38
Emerson, Ralph Waldo, 51, 57
Emmennegger, William, 245, 263 ff.
Emotional involvement, 192
  confusion of disagreement with
    personal hostility, 93–95
  techniques for obtaining, 136–141
E pluribus unum, 55–56
Estes, Charles, 193
Executive, 61–62, 63, 66–67, 113, 154
Expert, 57, 59–60, 70–71, 261–262
Exploitation
  by a member of a discussion group,
    148
  by an advocate, 154–155
Extrinsic conflict, 94–95, 136–137,
  181, 189–196
Extroversion, 116
Evaluating solutions, 163
Evidence, 183–184

Face-saving
  needs for, 189

techniques of, 189–191
Fairbank, John K., 142
Faith, 188
Farnsworth, Paul, 17
Father figure,
  leader as, 20
Feed-back, 228
Filibuster, 203–204
Finletter, Thomas K., 156
Flexibility, 91–92, 200
Follett, Mary P., 38
Followership, 5
Food-saving habits, 52–53, 252
Force, 179–180
Ford, Cliff, 245, 263 ff.
Foster, William T., 70
Freedom
  and leadership, 6–7
  and social control, 34–35
  as a relative matter, 7
  continuum of, 43
  definition of, 7
  of speech, 205–206
Free will, need for appearance of,
  191–192
French, John R. P., 221
Freud, Sigmund, 39
Frustration-aggression formula, 86

Ghandi, Mohandas, 68
Gray, Thomas, 232
Great Books, 227
Great Man doctrine of Carlyle, 15–16,
  31–32, 231
Group
  definition of, 76–77
  growth, 80, 102–104, 249
  learning and action, 79–80
  maturity, 102–104, 112
  socio- and psyche-, 90–91
  standards, 99–102, 131–132
  structure, 95–97, 99–102
  voluntary and involuntary, 78
Group builder, 37
Group compellor, 67
Group dynamics, 38, 54, 75–105
Group mind, 78–79
Guidance, 5, 6

Haiman, Franklyn, 9, 17, 245, 263 ff.

Halsey, George D., 48
Hamilton, Alexander, 30
Hance, Kenneth, 38, 86, 94, 154
Hannaford, Earle S., 66, 133, 227
Harbord, Major General, 49
Hartley, Eugene, 76
Harvard University, 67, 142, 219
Heider, Fritz, 94
Heredity
  and environment, 83–84
  as source of leadership, 14
Hidden agenda, 89–90, 95, 134, 254, 257
Hitler, Adolph, 3, 53, 56, 233
Hoefle, Rosemary, 287
Hollingworth, H. L., 70
Holmes, Oliver Wendell, 205
Homogeneity, 99
Hopkins, Harry, 119
Horwitz, M. W., 94
Howard, Palmer, 228
Humor, 127, 194
Huxley, Thomas, 153

Ideas, as interaction level, 89
Identification, 82–83, 93–95
Indirect leadership, 4
Individualism, 62–65, 148
Inequality, the fact of, 58–60
Information-giver, 70–71
Inhibition
  as quality of leadership, 121–126
  of emotional responses in group, 95
Initiating discussion, 167–168, 242
Institutionalization, 8, 131
Instructor, 70–71, 120, 154
Integration, 181–182
Intelligence, 12, 53, 59
Intelligent partiality, doctrine of, 125
Interaction, 88–102
  leadership as, 5
  on the idea level, 91–95
  on the social-emotional level, 95–102
  psychological, 76–77
Interpersonal relations
  handling of, 130–150
  workings of, 95–102
Intimacy, 99
Intrinsic conflict, 94, 181, 182–188
Involvement, 82–83

emotional, 136–137
Iowa Child Welfare Research Station, 54, 100
Irreconcilable conflict, 180–181, 186, 199–201

Jackson, Robert, 205–206
Jacques, Elliott, 40
Jefferson, Thomas, 29, 35, 39, 52
Jennings, Helen Hall, 90, 115
Jensen, Jeri, 289
Jesus Christ, 34, 68, 232
Johnson, A. B., 183
Johnson, Wendell, 93
Judicial leaders, 61, 63, 67–68

Kansas, University of, 94
Knowledge, 119–120
Knowles, Malcolm, 245 ff.
Krech, David, 21, 76
Krueger, L. M., 13, 127

Labor-management relations, 40, 64, 92, 141, 160, 180, 183–184, 193
Laissez-faire, 73
Larrabee, Harold, 184
Leadership
  acts of, 5
  attempts at, 5
  conscious, 5
  creative, 4
  definitions of, 4–6
  direct, 4
  face-to-face, 4
  indirect, 4, 116
  intellectual, 4, 116
  as interaction, 5
  planned, 5
  self-constituted, 8
  as a series of functions, 38, 111–112, 253–256
  socialized, 37
  sources of, 9–22
  spontaneous, 5
  types of, 66–71, 125–126
  unconscious, 5
Leader-worship, 20
Learning groups, 79–80, 139
Lee, Irving J., 93
Lenin, Nikolai, 68
Lewin, Kurt, 17, 38, 53, 54, 100, 101, 220, 252

Lewis, John L., 68, 192
Lilienthal, David, 155
Limiting the problem, 156–157
Lincoln, Abraham, 68, 118, 233
Lippitt, Ronald, 100, 223, 228
Locke, John, 34, 51
Logic, 93
Luther, Martin, 15, 68
Lyons, J., 94

Machiavelli, 31, 123, 129
Magical powers, 15–16
Maier, Norman R. F., 154
Majority rule, 202–204
Mander, A. E., 184
Manipulation, 60, 69, 148, 154–155
Maturity of a group, 102–104, 112, 114
Maxwell School of Public Administration, 67
Means and ends, 57, 73, 104, 186–187
Mehlig, Lee, 133
Melby, Ernest, 37
Mellowness, 127
Menotti, Gian Carlo, 130
Merei, Ferenc, 131
Merriam, Charles E., 9, 118, 127
Merrill, Robert R., 16
Methodological agent, 33
Michigan, University of, 38, 219
Mill, John Stuart, 33, 34–35, 44
Minority rights, 204–206
Moderator of discussion, 6
Mohammed, 68
Morale, 54–55, 220–221
Moreno, J. L., 40, 96
Moses, 68
Motions
making, 206–208
seconding, 208
Muntyan, Bozidar, 76
Mussolini, 18

McBurney, James H., 38, 86, 94, 154, 245 ff.

Napoleon, 18
National Training Laboratory in Group Development, 38, 40, 219, 228–229
Naval Leadership, 19

Needs, as motivation for joining groups, 77–80, 81–82
Negative involvement, 137–139
Newcomb, Theodore, 76, 94
Nondirective counselling, 42
Nonparticipation
causes of, 145–146
techniques for handling, 146–147
Non-sequiturs, 93
Northwestern University, 224

Objectifying antagonistic contributions, 192–193
Objectivity by the leader, 121–126
Observers, 97, 224–226, 227–229, 239–243
Obstacle of numbers, 65–66
Ohio State University, 219
Oligarchy, 44, 60
On-the-job training, 220–221
Open-mindedness, 57, 91–92, 155–156
Oppenheimer, J. Robert, 157
Order of precedence of motions, 208–211
Orientation, as part of training, 220
Overdependence, 54, 143–144
Overstreet, Bonaro, 71, 116, 129, 153
Overstreet, Harry A., 71, 116, 129, 153
Ozymandias, 232

Parliamentary law, 124, 201–215, 258
Partizan, 68–69
Pecking order, 8
Perlmutter, H. V., 94
Permeability, 99
Permissive atmosphere, 41–42, 130–131, 133–134, 223
Personal factors associated with leadership, 9–10, 12–14
Persuasion, 68–69, 191–192
Peterman, Jack, 13
Phillips, Arthur E., 70
Philosopher-kings, 30
Physical prowess, 8–9, 12
Pigors, Paul, 6
Plato, 3, 4, 30, 118, 229
Playboy, 85
Plutarch, 9, 229
Pointing out differences, 174
Pointing out similarities, 173

Polarization and saturation, 18
Pope, Roman Catholic, 46
Post meeting reaction sheets, 97, 146
Prestige, as source of leadership, 17–18
Prince, The (Machiavelli), 31
Problem-orientation, 89
Process-orientation, 89, 103
Productivity, 80, 103
Progressive education, 37, 51, 59–60
Propagandist, 68–69
Providence, as source of leadership, 16
Psyche-group activities, 90–91, 98, 103, 134
Psychoanalytic
   explanation of dependence, 20
   explanation of submission, 20
Psychodrama, 223
Psychotherapy, 39–42, 126

Quakers, 147
Questioning techniques, 167

Rationalization, 87
Reality testing, 173
Reasoning
   analogies, 184
   conflict in, 184–185
   generalizations, 184
   syllogisms, 184
Recesses, 194–195
Recognition by leader, 133, 143, 207
   formal and informal, 207
   obtaining the floor, 207
Recognition-seeker, 85
Recording discussion, 169–170
Reed, Thomas B., 214
Reflective thinking pattern, 154–164, 185
Representative system, 65–66
Republic (Plato), 3, 4, 30
Research Center for Group Dynamics, 38, 219
Resistance to change
   sources of, 230–232
   methods of overcoming, 230–233
Resolving conflict, 174, 178–215
   by agreeing to disagree, 179
   by arbitration, 180–181, 199–200
   by force, 179–180
   by integration, 181–196
   by majority vote, 199–215

   in evidence, 183–184
   in meaning, 182–183
   in reasoning, 184–185
   in values, 185–188
Respect for others, as quality of leadership, 114–118
Restraint, 121–126
Reuther, Walter, 68
Rickard, Paul, 51
Riessman, Frank, 93
Robert's Rules of Order, 206–207, 211, 213
Rogers, Carl, 41, 42, 126
Role-playing
   as hidden agenda, 89–90, 150
   to stimulate emotional involvement, 139–140
   for training leaders, 197–198, 221–224, 226
Roosevelt, Franklin D., 15, 52, 68, 119, 121
Roosevelt, Theodore, 24, 118
Rosenberg, Morris, 95
Rousseau, Jean Jacques, 36, 39
Russell, Bertrand, 56, 64, 79
Ryland, Gladys, 76

Saadi, Mitchell, 17
Sanctions, 24
Sarett, Lew, 70
Schenck vs. U.S., 205
Schreiber, Julius, 40
Scientific method, 152–164
Seeking further information, 172
Seeking further opinions, 171–172
Self-analysis, 228
Self-constituted leadership, 8
Semantic difficulties, 60, 93, 182–183
Seniority
   in age, 14
   in service, 14
Setting standards, 173
Shaffer, Laurance, 84
Sheats, Paul, 85, 245 ff.
Sheffield, Alfred D., 38
Shelley, Percy Bysshe, 232
Sherif, Muzafer, 76
Sherwood, Robert, 119
Sidetracking irrelevancies, 170–171
Simpson, Ray A., 12, 120
Situational differences, 10–12

Smith, Henry L., 13, 127
Smith, T. V., 37, 53
Social behavior, 83–87
Social control, 7, 34–35, 43, 214
Social-emotional level of interaction, 89–91, 95–102
Social pressure, 56–57, 100–102, 132, 143
Social sensitivity, 115
Social workers, 70, 126
Socialized leaders, 37
Sociodrama, 223
Sociograms, 96–98
Socio-group activities, 90–91, 103
Sociometry, 96
Specific skills of leadership, 21–22
Speech, as medium of leadership, 4
Spokesman-leader, 65–66
Standards of a group, 99–102
Status
in role structure, 99–102
of instructor vs. discussion leader, 125–126
Stimulating argument, techniques for, 135–136
Stogdill, Ralph M., 10, 11, 12, 13, 127
Strong man concept of leadership, 6, 231–232, 254–255
Submission, 7–9, 19–21
Summarizing, 168–169
Supervisor, 72
Sward, Keith, 9

Taft, Robert, 68
Talkativeness, 13
Task-area, 89
Tavistock Clinic, 40
Tead, Ordway, 6, 21
Terminiello case, 205–206
Testing validity of contributions, 172–173
Thelen, Herbert, 76, 90, 245 ff.
Thomas, Norman, 68
Thoreau, Henry D., 55, 63, 74
Thrasher, Frederick, 12
To Secure These Rights, 161

Totalitarianism, 43–44, 148
Tradition, 14
Training leaders, 16, 58, 219–234
in business and adult education, 227–229
in colleges, 224–227
on-the-job, 220–221
role-playing, 221–224
Transition-making, 168–169
Truman, Harry, 15, 155
Two-thirds requirement, 202–203, 204, 212
Types of leadership, 66–71, 125–126
Tyranny
of indecision, 61–62
of the majority, 33, 44–45

Undebatable motions, 211–212
United Nations, 141, 155–156, 203, 204
Unity, 55–56, 135
Utterback, William, 122

Values
conflicts of, 92, 185–188
of group members, 87–88
Verbal facility, 13, 121
Vitality, 127

Waelder, Robert, 42
We-feeling, 77, 83, 98
Werkmeister, W. H., 184
Wesley, John, 68
Western Reserve University, 224
Whately, Richard, 69
Whitehead, T. N., 66
Wilson, A. T. M., 40
Wilson, Gertrude, 76
Wilson, Woodrow, 52, 118
Withdrawing behavior, 86–87
Wright Brothers, 162

Young, Kimball, 7, 8, 54

Zeleny, L. D., 16
Zuni, 19